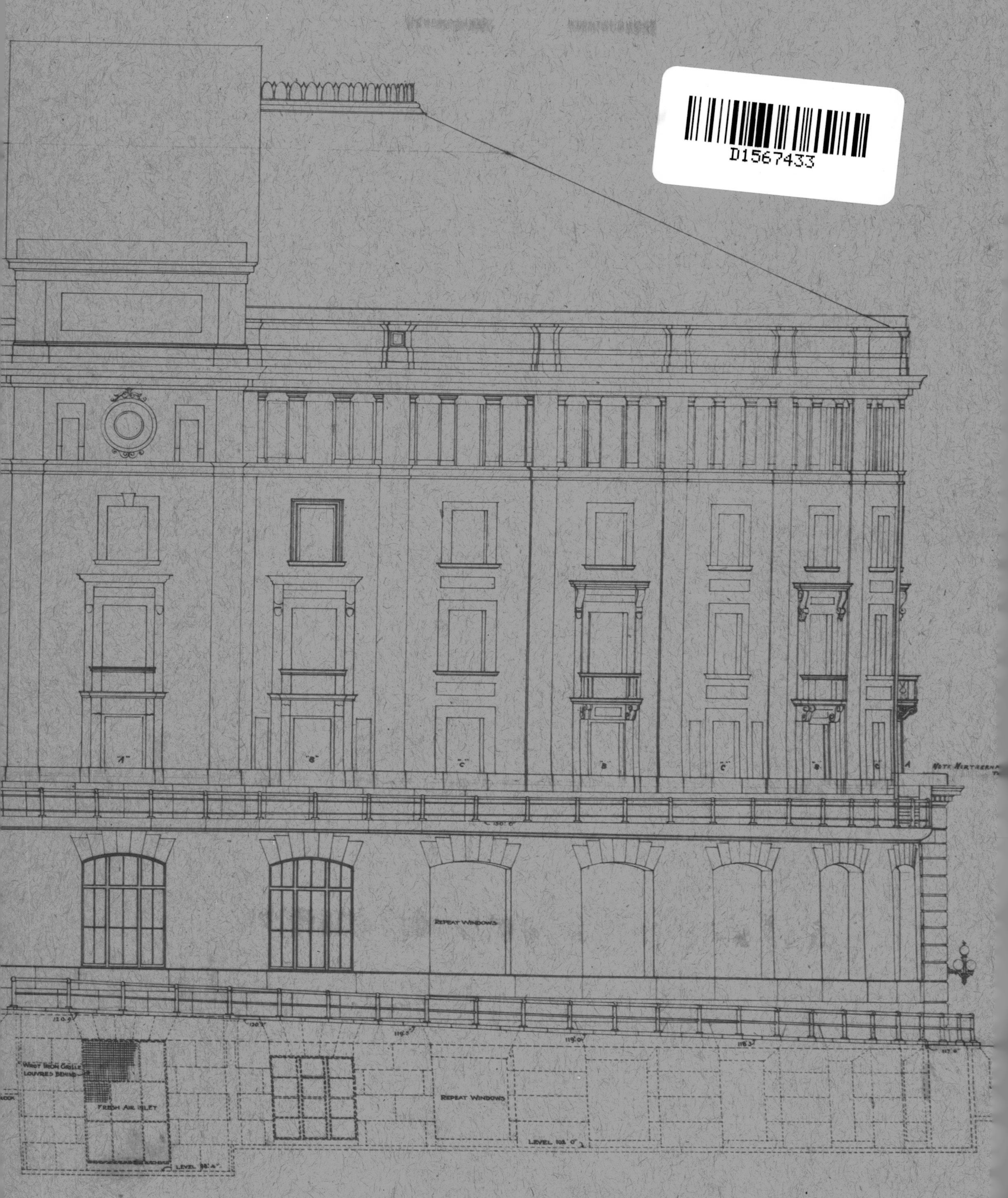

HTS
RK. CITY

MASTERING McKIM'S PLAN

COLUMBIA'S FIRST CENTURY ON MORNINGSIDE HEIGHTS

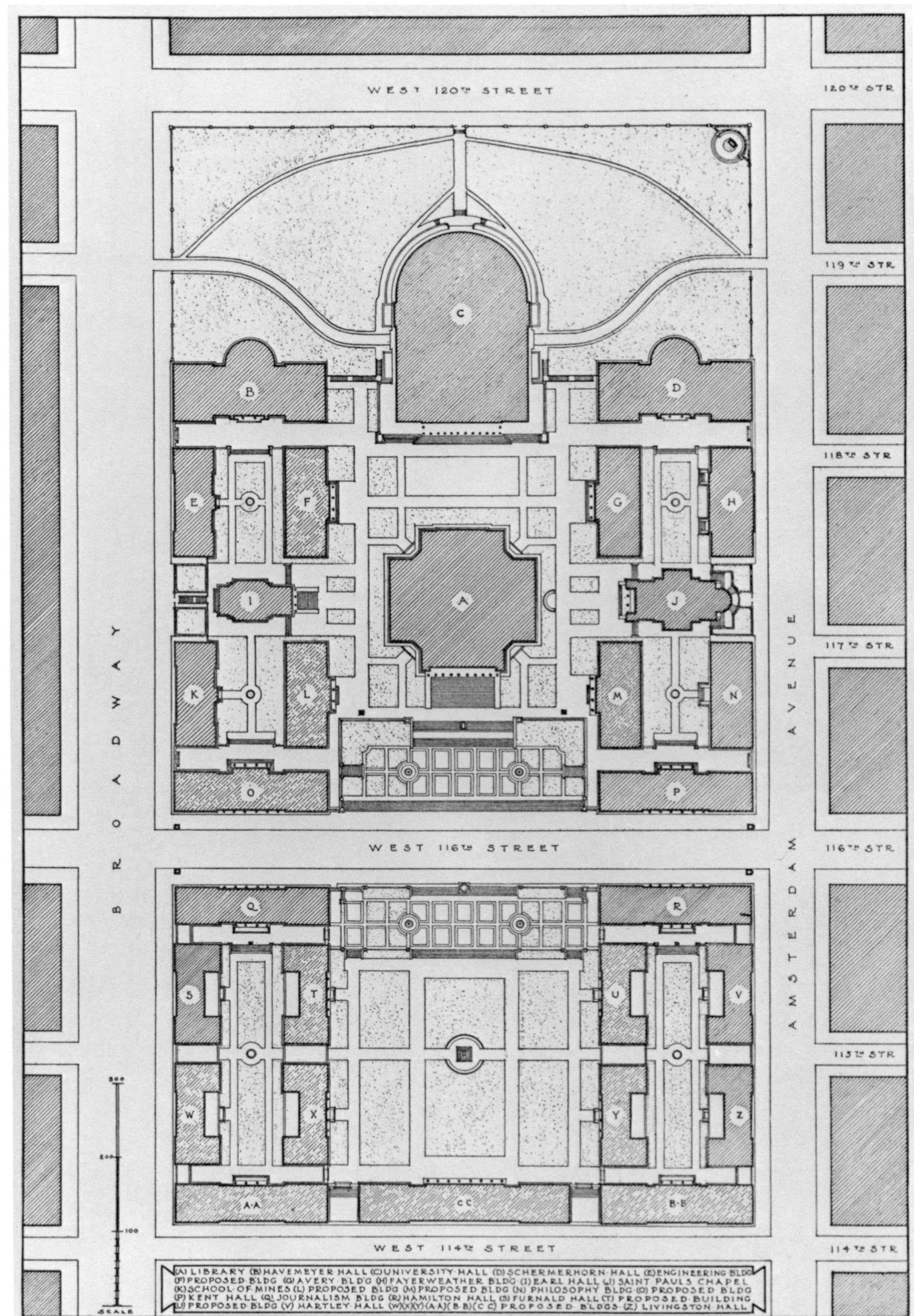
WEST 120TH STREET
120TH STR
119TH STR
118TH STR
117TH STR
116TH STR
113TH STR
114TH STR
WEST 116TH STREET
WEST 114TH STREET
BROADWAY
AMSTERDAM AVENUE
SCALE
(A) LIBRARY (B) HAVEMEYER HALL (C) UNIVERSITY HALL (D) SCHERMERHORN HALL (E) ENGINEERING BLDG
(F) PROPOSED BLDG (G) AVERY BLD'G (H) FAYERWEATHER BLD'G (I) EARL HALL (J) SAINT PAULS CHAPEL
(K) SCHOOL OF MINES (L) PROPOSED BLD'G (M) PROPOSED BLDG (N) PHILOSOPHY BLDG (O) PROPOSED BLDG
(P) KENT HALL (Q) JOURNALISM BLDG (R) HAMILTON HALL (S) FURNALD HALL (T) PROPOSED BUILDING
(U) PROPOSED BLDG (V) HARTLEY HALL (W)(X)(Y)(A A)(B B)(C C) PROPOSED BLDGS (Z) LIVINGSTON HALL

MASTERING McKIM'S PLAN

COLUMBIA'S FIRST CENTURY ON MORNINGSIDE HEIGHTS

By Barry Bergdoll

with a photographic essay by Hollee Haswell

and catalogue by Janet Parks *and* Barry Bergdoll

Miriam and Ira D. Wallach Art Gallery

Columbia University in the City of New York

1997

This publication is issued in conjunction with two exhibitions held at Columbia University, 8 October 1997 through 17 January 1998:

Mastering McKim's Plan: Columbia's First Century on Morningside Heights at the Miriam and Ira D. Wallach Art Gallery
and
Constructing Low Memorial Library: A Chronicle of a Monumental Enterprise in the Rotunda of Low Memorial Library

The exhibitions and publication have been made possible through the generosity of the Office of the Executive Vice President for Administration and The Central–National Gottesman Foundation.

COVER: McKim, Mead & White, Projected campus built to full density, 1903 (cat. 45)

ENDLEAVES:
(front) McKim, Mead & White, University Hall: east elevation, 1900 (cat. 65); (back) McKim, Mead & White, University Hall: longitudinal section, 1900 (cat. 66)

FRONTISPIECE: McKim, Mead & White, Comprehensive plan for Columbia University's expanded site, 1903 (reproduced from *Monograph of the Work of McKim, Mead & White* [1915])

Published by the Miriam and Ira D. Wallach Art Gallery, Columbia University in the City of New York

Library of Congress Catalog Card Number 97-74871
ISBN 1-884919-05-7
ISBN 1-884919-04-9 pbk.
Distributed by
the Columbia University Press

CONTENTS

FOREWORD

As we celebrate the centennial of the Morningside Heights campus, I am tremendously proud to reflect on Columbia's growth and achievements spanning the past 100 years. Following 143 years in Lower Manhattan and then in Midtown, Columbia, under the direction of its president, Seth Low, moved to its permanent home on Morningside Heights. President Seth Low's visionary leadership not only brought us to this site but also ensured that planning and architecture would play an integral role in shaping our reputation as one of America's leading universities.

The brilliant master plan, which he commissioned from Charles Follen McKim, integrated his keen sense of the monumental importance of a great university with the civic responsibility inherent in such an institution. Low Memorial Library, a gift from Seth Low in honor of his father, was the first of McKim's buildings to be constructed on the Morningside Heights campus. A dominant and defining architectural presence, it continues today to stand as a signature for Columbia and as a tribute to the cultural and educational values on which this university is built.

This catalogue and the exhibitions that it accompanies constitute an important survey of the architectural milestones in Columbia University's commitment to creating spaces for learning and research, to forming partnerships with neighboring institutions and communities, and to strengthening our reputation as America's premier international university. To Barry Bergdoll, Hollee Haswell, and Janet Parks, I extend my sincere thanks and congratulations. Their comprehensive record of the development of our campus offers a history with resonance for each of us who study or work here, for alumni/ae who have lived in its midst, and for our neighbors.

Columbia is indeed fortunate to have the enthusiasm and generous support of Miriam and Ira D. Wallach. It gives me tremendous pleasure, on behalf of the university, to express our deepest gratitude to them for their gifts to endow the Wallach Art Gallery, which ensures the continuing vitality of the cultural life on campus. Without their support neither the excellent programming for which the gallery has earned an international reputation nor its award-winning publications would be possible. On the occasion of this centennial celebration, I am delighted to be able to acknowledge their generosity yet again.

George Rupp
President

PREFACE

In 1754, when King's College was founded, George Washington was an obscure twenty-two-year-old who was unknown outside his little corner of Virginia. The colonies were distant outposts of the British Empire, and there was no such place as the United States of America. To be sure, New York City was already 130 years old, but it was not impressive by European standards, and it had been surpassed in size and importance by both Boston and Philadelphia. It had fewer than 20,000 inhabitants and did not stretch even to Chambers Street. Greenwich Village was well to the north and separated by almost two miles of marsh from the Battery. In 1754, New York had no public transportation system, no garbage pickup, no municipal water supply, and no professional police or fire departments, not to mention any building more than three stories in height.

The past 243 years have seen enormous changes both in the institution and in the city that has always surrounded it. From a schoolhouse that accommodated eight students and a single instructor next to Trinity Church, Columbia has evolved into one of the world's most distinguished centers of learning, with several campuses, dozens of specialized institutes and professional schools, 20,000 students, and 2,500 faculty members. Its 180,000 alumni/ae have gone on to become leaders on every continent and in every field of human endeavor.

New York has also gone on to fame and prosperity. It surpassed Philadelphia in 1810 to become the largest city in the United States, and Mexico City by 1830 to become the largest in the western hemisphere. By 1900, New York was the second largest city in the world (after London), and by 1930 the largest. It remains the only American municipality ever to exceed four million inhabitants. And in 1990, each of its five boroughs was large enough to have been an important city in its own right, with Queens having more inhabitants than Philadelphia, Brooklyn several times as many as Boston or San Francisco, the Bronx far more than Detroit, and Staten Island more than St. Louis.

Clearly, the university and the metropolis have grown and prospered together over the centuries. Columbia has long mirrored many unusual qualities of New York: its creativity and energy, its heterogeneity and diversity, its competitiveness and toughness, its openness to new ideas and movements, its disregard for convention and conformity. Indeed, Gotham has become so intertwined with both the image and the reality of the institution that this closeness has been recognized in its official name: Columbia University in the City of New York. No other college so recognizes and celebrates its relation to a municipality.

Because Manhattan Island is so small and crowded, first-time visitors to the Columbia campus are often amazed to discover a beautiful and spacious oasis in the midst of New York's bustling commercial streets and dense apartment buildings. The fact that the campus has worked so well and remained so attractive and pleasant for so long is not an accident. It is instead the result of an excellent master plan and of the determined efforts of a few people to adapt that plan to changing circumstances. Not every decision has been a happy one, and not every building has been successful. But, on balance, the campus of Columbia University is a treasure and has been recognized as such by generations of scholars and planners.

This book celebrates the centennial of the great Charles Follen McKim master plan, and it evaluates the many ways in which the campus has evolved–and in some instances failed to evolve–over the past century. It also represents the first tangible product of Columbia's 250th Anniversary celebration, which will run from 1997, with the opening of these exhibitions, through 2004. Along the way a whole series of publications, events, and convocations will remind us of all that has been achieved since King George II granted a charter to a little college in 1754, and of the challenges and opportunities that lie before Columbia as it begins new centuries of service to the nation and the world.

I share President George Rupp's gratitude for the many hours of hard work that Barry Bergdoll, Hollee Haswell, and Janet Parks put into this book and the accompanying exhibitions. What a wonderful way to begin the 250th Anniversary of Columbia University.

Kenneth T. Jackson
Barzun Professor of History and Social Sciences and *Co-Chair, 250th Anniversary Committee*

INTRODUCTION

Mastering McKim's Plan and its catalogue grew out of a desire to examine and celebrate Columbia University's first hundred years on Morningside Heights. The exhibition might have been scheduled to mark the anniversary of any number of benchmarks in the complex chain of events between 1891 and 1897 that led to Columbia College's bold decision to move uptown, reorganize itself as a university, and design a new campus, just years after a handsome series of buildings had been erected at Forty-ninth Street. We have chosen to celebrate the last threshold, the first day of classes held on Morningside Heights, on 4 October 1897, not because it was the end of a grand design but because it was the beginning of a process in which the image and identity of the university and the elaboration of the campus master plan would evolve in tandem. The centennial, it seemed to us, should, in the tradition of the research university, be as much a moment of self-examination and discovery as of commemoration.

The groundwork for the show was laid in an undergraduate seminar on American campus design conducted by Barry Bergdoll of the Department of Art History and Archaeology in the autumn of 1994, one hundred years after the adoption of Charles Follen McKim's master plan for the new campus. Working closely with Janet Parks in the Department of Drawings and Archives of Avery Architectural and Fine Arts Library, the students undertook research on aspects of Columbia's architectural history, learned to work with the rich collection of primary sources and archival materials on campus, and discussed the possible form for an exhibition, to be entitled "Unbuilt Columbia," in the department's Wallach Art Gallery. Other universities have produced fascinating histories both of themselves as institutions and of the place of their own buildings and open spaces within the history of architecture from the oblique angle of what didn't happen. It seemed that the centennial of the Morningside campus, given the abundance of materials in the Avery Architectural and Fine Arts Library which had never been examined as a group, provided an ideal occasion to look at larger issues in the social and political history of American architecture through the lens of Columbia's daily environment.

Although the members of that art history seminar, now alumni and alumnae of Columbia and Barnard Colleges, will recognize aspects of our work and discussions, the concept of the analysis and the exhibition have evolved considerably during the last three years. It soon became clear to the curators, Barry Bergdoll and Janet Parks, that both the fascination and the continued relevance of Columbia's architectural history were located less in the majestic composition of Low Library or in the preservation of its harmonious and spatially subtle red-brick frame conceived by McKim, Mead & White more than a century ago, or even in the collection of realized and unrealized additions, changes, and extensions to that original conception which are preserved in the archives. Rather, what commands our attention is the very phenomenon—rare in American campus design—of a master plan that has governed an institution's form and growth and helped to shape its identity for a full century. Colleges and universities in rural and suburban settings—which provide the most immediate embodiments of campus life in the American collective imagination—have tended to grow empirically and loosely in their verdant landscapes. If Thomas Jefferson's Rotunda and lawn at the University of Virginia have remained the symbol of that university, anyone visiting Charlottesville today will find that the pattern of life on the UVA campus has been dispersed over a much larger landscape; the lawn, far from being the focal point of daily activity, has become something of a preserved oasis. Columbia, however, held in check by the New York City grid plan, by the rapid rise in value of adjacent real estate on Morningside Heights, and sometimes by neighborhood and even student protest, has had, for better or worse, to direct its attention over and over again to its original campus. McKim's Low Library and the monumental composition of stairs, terraces, and green spaces it dominates continue to be the focus of daily life at Columbia, hosting a student and neighborhood population that President Seth Low and architect Charles Follen McKim could scarcely have imagined in 1897. The campus and the neighborhood have grown together to produce one of the most compelling and perennially appreciated spaces in New York City. Master plan and grid plan have been in dialogue for more than a hundred years, ever since work began on transforming four (later six) square blocks of the Manhattan grid into an ideally planned metropolitan campus. *Mastering McKim's Plan* and this catalogue are a first attempt to trace something of that dialogue. As with many dialogues there are moments of discordance and meandering, and always the chance to return to the ground rules for a fresh look.

As work on the exhibition progressed it attracted the interest of many others at the university involved with the history and future of the campus. In 1995, to mark the centenary of the laying of the cornerstone of Low Memorial Library, and thus of the new campus, Michael Stoller, the editor of *Columbia Library Columns*, invited Hollee Haswell and Barry Bergdoll to contribute to a special issue of the magazine dedicated to the history of Columbia's libraries. Hollee Haswell's article, much expanded here, grew out of plans that she had been developing since 1993 for an exhibition in the Rotunda of Low. That article confirmed the exceptional nature of a very fine collection of construction photographs of

Columbia's first building on Morningside Heights, not only a precious historical record for the university but also an ensemble that deserves to be brought to the attention of historians of photography.

In the spring of 1996 Bernard Tschumi, dean of the Graduate School of Architecture, Planning and Preservation, and himself involved in reflecting on McKim's master plan while designing the new student center, Alfred Lerner Hall, enthusiastically embraced the suggestion of an exhibition of student design work related to issues of the Columbia master plan and its interface with the Morningside Heights neighborhood. In the autumn term of 1996 the design studios in the school's various divisions–architecture, planning, urban design, and historic preservation–all looked at campus or neighborhood sites and issues. A selection of that work, reflecting current architectural concerns, attitudes, and formal interests, is being exhibited in the Arthur Ross Gallery in Buell Hall and published separately by the school.

Acknowledgements

Both as authors of the texts in this catalogue and as curators of the two exhibitions–*Mastering McKim's Plan: Columbia's First Century on Morningside Heights* and *Constructing Low Memorial Library: A Chronicle of a Monumental Enterprise*–we have accumulated numerous debts of gratitude, large and small, on and off campus, since planning began more than three years ago on this ambitious project. We owe the greatest thanks to Emily Lloyd, the executive vice president for administration, for her early and continuing support and enthusiasm. Not only has she ensured the publication of this catalogue but her office funded the conservation of key architectural drawings from the early planning history of Columbia on Morningside Heights, a service to the collective memory of the university that will far outlive this exhibition.

Research on the exhibition and selection of the objects was facilitated by the helpfulness, generosity, and expertise of the staffs of the Avery Architectural and Fine Arts Library and its Department of Drawings and Archives, Columbia University Archives, the Columbiana Collection, and the New-York Historical Society, all of whom have been patient and extended special courtesies during long sessions working in their collections. Angela Giral, the director of Avery Library, has been an enthusiastic supporter of this endeavor. In Avery's Department of Drawings and Archives Dan Kany, assistant to the curator, and student assistants Laura Tatum and Alexandra Klein helped out on numerous occasions. Julie Roth, a graduate student in art history, provided invaulable assistance with many aspects of the early preparation and research. We are likewise indebted to Lilly Hollander for her skillful and timely conservation of many important drawings. Heartfelt thanks are especially due to Rhea Pliakas and Linnea Anderson for their unflagging generosity with time, information, and advice; and it is our sincere hope that these exhibitions and the catalogue are a tribute to the zeal and intelligence that they have devoted to organizing the Columbia University Archives and facilitating access to that extraordinary but largely untapped resource. Thanks also to DiAnn Pierce of the Office of the Secretary for help with the minutes of the trustees and also to David Hill. Dwight Primiano's contribution to the project is evident throughout the catalogue in the high quality of photographic reproductions of work from the Avery collections. With extraordinary care Marty Messik made photographic reproductions from the original proof prints depicting the construction of Low Memorial Library and also took photographs of other works in the Columbiana Collection. Throughout the preparation of the catalogue and the exhibitions, we have relied on the dedicated staff of the Miriam and Ira D. Wallach Art Gallery: to Sarah Elliston Weiner, who has shepherded this project from beginning to end and devoted many long hours to upholding the highest standards; to Jeanette Silverthorne and Melissa Radford for their help in coordination of catalogue and exhibition; and to Larry Soucy for his work on the installation.

We have benefited enormously from the assistance of Mary Beth Betts, the curator of drawings at the New-York Historical Society, who helped us to navigate the rich collection of McKim, Mead & White materials there and brought to our attention many of the finest images in the exhibition. The staff of Avery Library has worked with colleagues at the Historical Society on their projects and greatly appreciate their reciprocal cooperation. Wendy Haynes and her successor, John Kuss, helped in providing photographs from the New-York Historical Society.

Sincere appreciation is extended to Ted Goodman for his timely and expert preparation of the index.

Barry Bergdoll would particularly like to thank a number of individuals, both on and off campus, who unstintingly gave their time and insights. At the Schomburg Center for Black Culture of the New York Public Library research was greatly assisted by Janice Quinter, who has prepared an exemplary finding aid to the Collins collection of materials concerning Columbia's expansion projects in the 1960s and the Morningside Park gymnasium. At the office of I. M. Pei & Partners, Chris Sawyer was particularly helpful. For their help with the drawings and master plan documents still held in active use by the Columbia University Department of Planning Design and Construction, Bernhard Haeckel, Irwin Lefkowitz, Andrew Nelson, and Richard Harris merit special thanks as does Wendy Feuer, the director, Planning Framework Studies, Morningside Heights and the Columbia campus. Welcome advice came from friends and colleagues involved in Columbia's architectural and institutional history, many of whom also participated in the University Seminar on the Morningside Centennial held during 1996 and 1997. In addition to Andrew Scott Dolkart, whose knowledge of Morningside Heights is boundless, these include Aaron Warner of the University Seminars, Robert McCaughey of Barnard College, Bette Weneck of Teachers College, Paul Bentel of the preservation program in the School of Architecture, Michael Stoller of the Columbia

University Libraries, Mary Woods of Cornell University, Deborah Gardner, Travis B. Jacobs of Middlebury College, Michael Gotkin, Michael Susi, Michael Rosenthal, Kenneth Jackson, Stephen Murray, Allen Staley, and David Rosand. The earlier research of Francesco Passanti and the permission to reproduce his reconstruction of the original topography of the new campus site is gratefully acknowledged. The research of three former students—Zack Levy, Hideki Yamamoto, and C. Drew Armstrong—was extremely useful. For their advice and for insight into more recent planning history on campus, thanks to Bernard Tschumi, James Stewart Polshek, Robert A. M. Stern, Peter Gluck, Robert Kliment, and Frances Halsband.

Hollee Haswell extends deepest thanks to Mary Monroe, William O'Malley, and Carol Pardo for bibliographical assistance; to Marcelle Moran for information regarding Vermont granite; to Schuyler Warmflash for information regarding nineteenth-century building technology; and to Sarah Wilson for her technological assistance.

Barry Bergdoll
Associate Professor of Art History

Janet Parks
Curator of Drawings, Avery Architectural and Fine Arts Library

Hollee Haswell
Curator, Columbiana Collection

COLOR PLATES

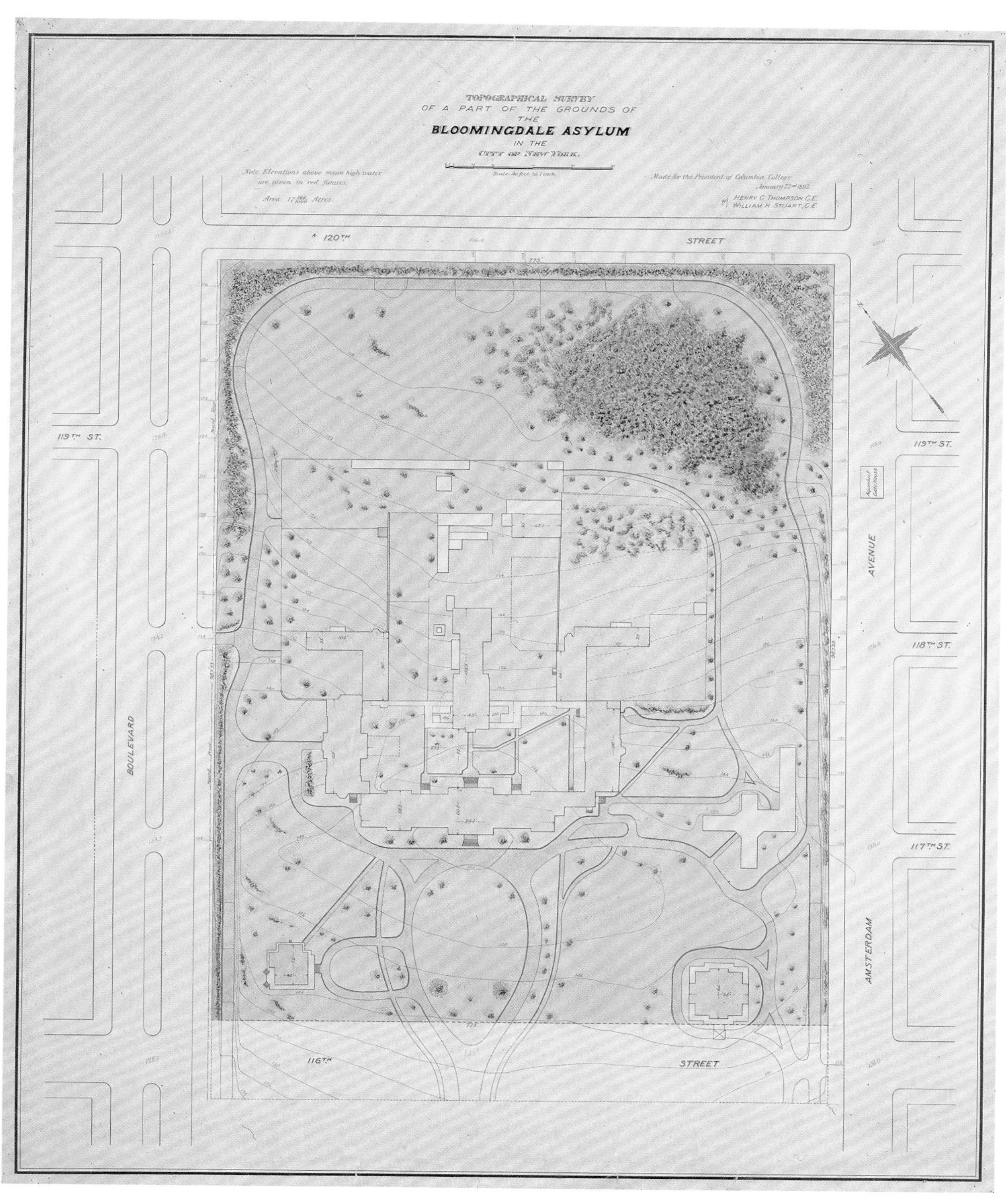

PLATE I Henry C. Thompson and William H. Stuart, Topographical survey of the grounds of the Bloomingdale Asylum, 1892 (cat. 2)

PLATE 2 Ware and Olmsted, Composite scheme, 1893 (cat. 11)

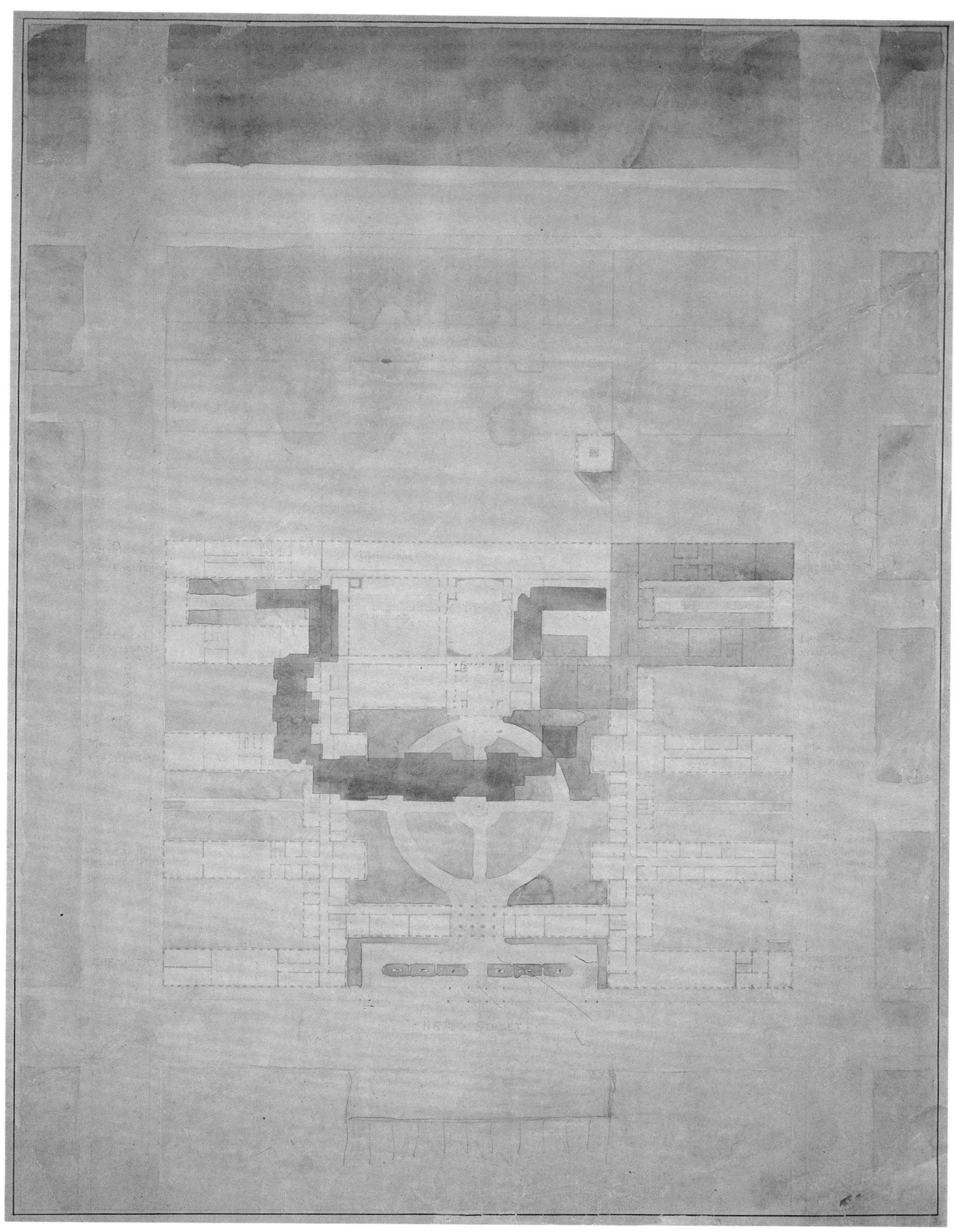

PLATE 3 Ware and Olmsted, Composite scheme, 1893 (cat. 12)

PLATE 4 McKim, Mead & White, Proposal for University Hall, ca. 1896 (cat. 61)

PLATE 5 McKim, Mead & White, Dormitory proposal for the Grove, 1899; Hughson Hawley, renderer (cat. 62)

PLATE 6 McKim, Mead & White, Bird's-eye view of projected campus built to full density, 1903; Jules Crow, delineator (cat. 45)

PLATE 7 McKim, Mead & White, Campus from library platform, grade 150, looking south, 1903; Jules Crow, delineator (cat. 46)

PLATE 8 McKim, Mead & White, Pierce Hall: perspective, ca. 1927–28; Fritz Steffens, delineator (cat. 27)

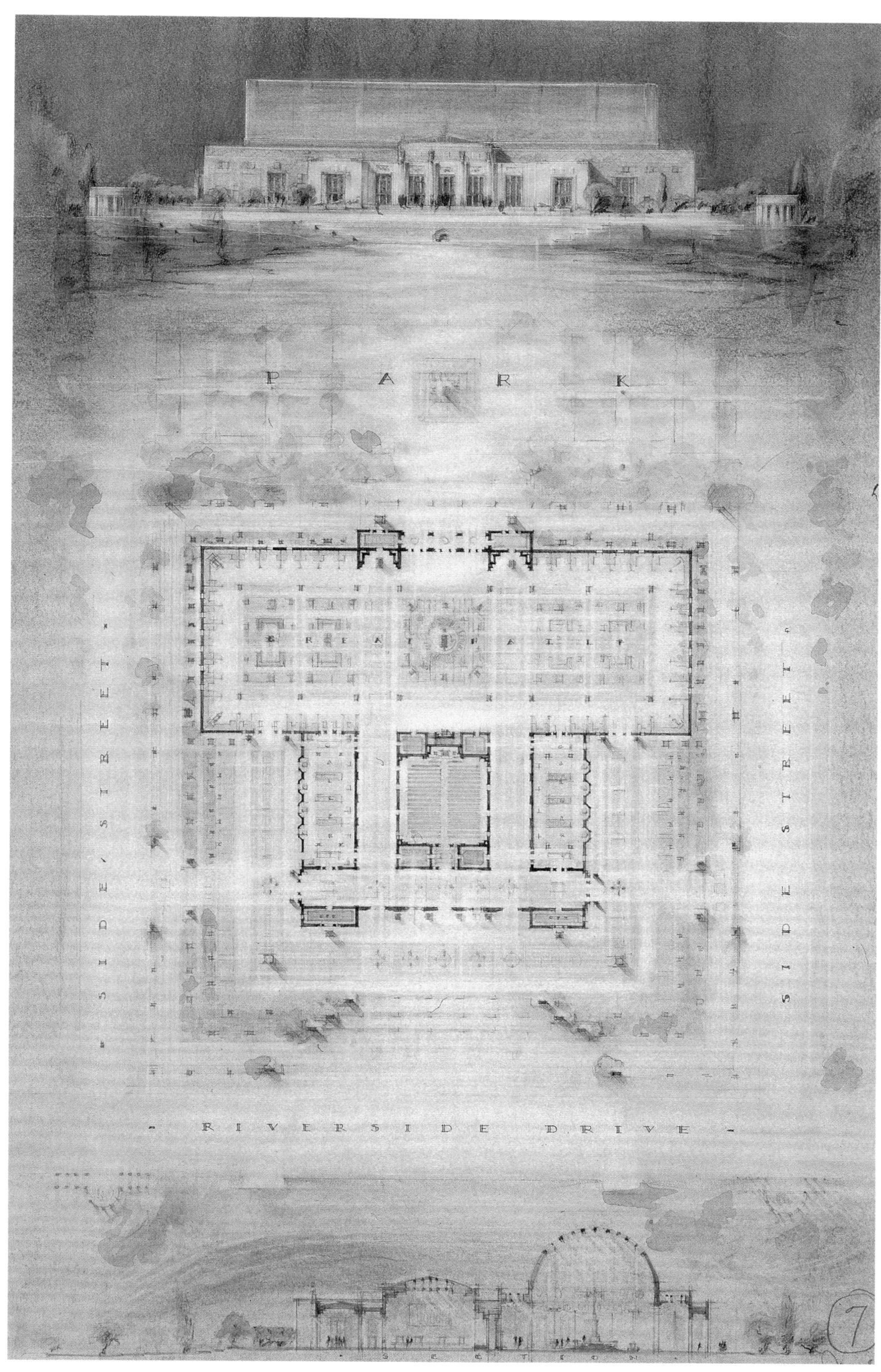

PLATE 9 Max Abramovitz, Design for stadium in Riverside Park, 1931 (cat. 89)

PLATE 10 McKim, Mead & White, 120th Street elevation, Scheme B, 1926 (cat. 72)

PLATE 11 Harrison & Abramovitz, Dormitories for East Campus, ca. 1965; Robert Schwartz, delineator (cat. 87)

PLATE 12 Adams and Woodbridge, Elevation on 120th Street, 1957 (cat. 77)

PLATE 13 Harrison & Abramovitz, Law School, ca. 1961 (cat. 86)

PLATE 14 I. M. Pei & Partners, South Field project, 1970; Robert Schwartz, renderer (cat. 99)

PLATE 15 Alexander Kouzmanoff, Avery Library extension, ca. 1974 (cat. 104)

PLATE 16 James Stirling, Michael Wilford & Associates, Chandler North project: perspective view from campus, 1982 (cat. 108)

PLATE 17 Bernard Tschumi, Alfred Lerner Hall, 1996 (cat. 114)

MASTERING McKIM'S PLAN

COLUMBIA'S FIRST CENTURY ON MORNINGSIDE HEIGHTS

FIGURE 1 *Morningside Park looking west toward the Bloomingdale Asylum, ca. 1890 (cat. 1)*

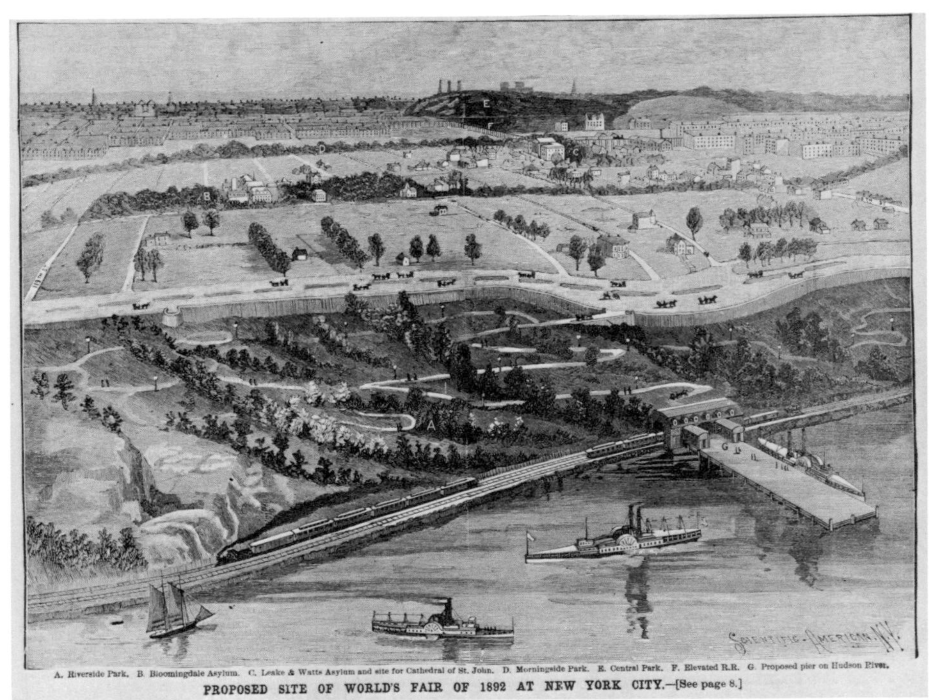

FIGURE 2 *Morningside Heights viewed from the Hudson River, 1892, engraving (reproduced from* Scientific American, *4 January 1890)*

BARRY BERGDOLL

THE GENESIS AND LEGACY OF McKIM, MEAD & WHITE'S MASTER PLAN FOR COLUMBIA UNIVERSITY

Columbia's move uptown had been the talk of New York since the idea was first broached by the college's trustees in the early 1890s, but the World's Columbian Exposition in Chicago in the summer of 1893 was the stage for the announcement to the nation. "It is a site worthy of a great university in a metropolitan city, situated upon the summit of an acropolis with the Hudson River to the West and a precipice on the east,"[1] explained the promotional brochure accompanying the college's display in the educational section of the New York State Pavilion at the fair. How many remembered that several years earlier some of Gotham's boosters had proposed this very plateau on the Upper West Side—later baptized Morningside Heights largely through Columbia's efforts—as the site of the celebrations of the 400th anniversary of Columbus's voyage during New York's failed attempt to outbid Chicago (figs. 1 & 2)?[2]

Chicago's "White City" was recognized almost overnight as a vision of the future American city, one in which classical harmony and artistically crafted and ornamented open spaces could establish a new hierarchy of public or civic over private and commercial values, thus reversing the forces that had given rise to the phenomenal growth of America's cities in recent decades (fig. 3). But even as the exposition's plaster-over-lathe pavilions slid from imperial splendor to romantic ruin in record time, more permanent visions were being planned. By the end of the decade college campuses and civic centers around the country had taken their cue from the fair's classical imagery and assertion of timeless values to celebrate America's delayed cultural independence.

Columbia's trustees and president were among the very first to respond to the World's Columbian Exposition. Even as crowds (including Columbia students on special travel grants) flocked each day to the fairgrounds on the shores of Lake Michigan in the summer of 1893, back in New York Columbia's trustees were at work crafting a plan for a new campus with the counsel of architects. Two of them—Charles Follen McKim and Richard Morris Hunt—had been instrumental in laying out the fair. The local college was seeking to become a "great university" worthy of national attention just as its site, happily anomalous in its verdant openness, was, as Columbia's brochure explained, at the very heart of a quarter "destined to be notable."[3] This seminal moment in Columbia's history was

FIGURE 3 *Court of Honor, World's Columbian Exposition, Chicago, 1893, photograph by Charles Dudley Arnold (Avery Library)*

orchestrated by the college's first nonacademic president, Seth Low, who was deeply involved in the 1890s both with consolidating the various parts of Columbia into a university and with preparing the city charter for the consolidation of Greater New York. New York's new charter was approved in late 1897, only weeks after Columbia began new classes at its spacious new campus. In a New York that now embraced the lower part of Westchester County and the western end of Long Island, Columbia's position atop the "Morningside Acropolis"[4] would not be a retreat to the country, as some trustees and alumni had advocated, but an assertion of prominence in the expanding metropolis, already the second largest city in the world.

From the first, architecture was both a vital tool in Columbia's reinvention of itself as an urban research university and a reflection of the trustees' new determination to abandon years of ad hoc problem solving. "The first building will condition, by its location and its architecture everything that is to follow, and no pains are to be spared to secure thoroughly digested and acceptable plans," the world's fair pamphlet announced,[5] paraphrasing decisions hammered out in tense debate behind the closed doors of the trustees' meetings during Seth Low's first three years at the helm. The plan was indeed everything, and it has to some extent conditioned much of what Columbia has done in the century since its move to Morningside Heights.

All were keenly aware, in 1893, that the new site's major advantage was its sharp contrast with the grid plan of the city itself, which remained for this part of upper Manhattan to some extent a paper project rather than a reality (fig. 4). Jealously protecting the integrity of the 17½-acre site on the Heights "an unbroken rectangle, 775 feet by 947⅓ feet, on the crown of the island," Columbia set about to offer a vision of planning and civic responsibility in marked contrast to the unbridled and self-interested real estate speculation that was

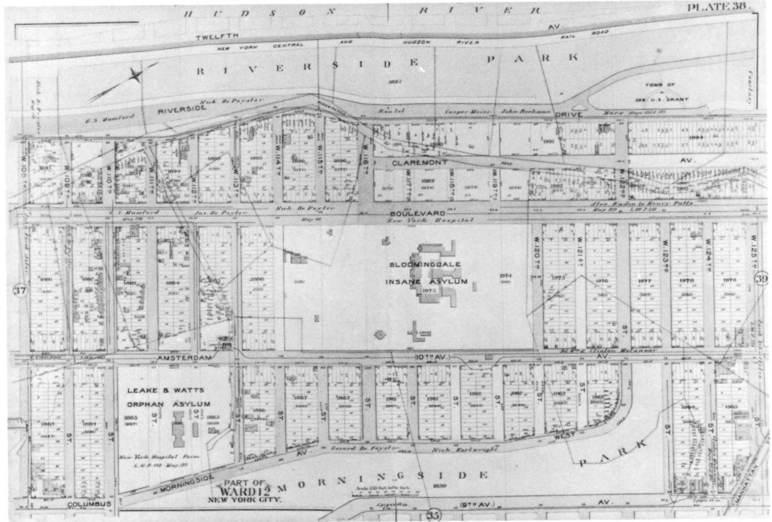

FIGURE 4 *Real estate survey of Morningside Heights neighborhood in 1891 (reproduced from George W. and Walter S. Bromley,* Atlas of the City of New York, *Philadelphia, 1891)*

FIGURE 5 *South Court looking west, ca. 1897 (Columbiana Collection)*

quickly filling every last square inch of Manhattan's 1811 grid plan with its repetitive rectangular blocks. The trustees used their influence to fight attempts to open city streets through their new site, which surfaced as they negotiated the purchase of the land from the New York Hospital, and over the years they lobbied the state legislature to protect the integrity of the site. Between 1892 and 1894 they were successful in having a role in the grading of both 116th and 120th Streets, even in having 120th Street widened, thus creating a permanent frame of broad avenues around the original four-block campus. And in 1896, as the college prepared to leave behind its overcrowded Midtown site at 49th and Madison, a single city block besieged by trains and street cars, noise and dust, the trustees declared their commitment to New York and to the ideal of an urban university, adopting the name "Columbia University in the City of New York."

The Morningside site, attractive for its verdant openness, was surveyed and prepared to receive an institution many times larger than the college unpacking its crates of books and scientific equipment over the course of the summer of 1897. Only one building, the new library, faced McKim's grand composition of South Court—as McKim called the landscaped plaza and monumental stairs facing 116th Street—when the new Columbia opened its doors on October fourth that year, but it was plainly visible to everyone that a monumental, symmetrical framework had been laid over the site (fig. 5). Even if it took generations to fulfill, the tone, scale, and pattern of development had been established, as had the fact that development would be complexly intertwined with the growth of the city itself. Not only would the grid plan of the city and the master plan of the campus remain in a state of continual negotiation, but Columbia's trustees themselves would move back and forth between generating wealth from the city, often in real estate, and providing stewardship for the campus, set apart as a monument to their cultural and educational values. Nor has the process set in motion in the 1890s come to an end. Still today not all the sites designated on the plan accepted in late 1894 are filled, nor is it likely that some of them ever will be. The latest reflection on the master plan, commissioned from Beyer, Blinder Belle in 1996,[6] proposes the possibility of selectively building on some of McKim's sites and preserving the unintended openness of others.

The master plan presented by Charles Follen McKim in 1894, after an intense year of discussions among architects, trustees, and faculty, remains a subject of debate, negotiation, and institutional image as Columbia once again is abuzz with an ambitious capital campaign of new construction. And the inherent tensions between that plan and the New York City grid continue to challenge Columbia's designers. This three-part essay is the story of the master plan and its vicissitudes over the course of a century when the vision of the City Beautiful in both architecture and urban design has seen a remarkable fall from grace and return to critical reappraisal. It was equally a century in which Columbia University created itself anew, not without frequent tension with Columbia College, and eventually with its neighbors on Morningside Heights.

I. COLUMBIA AND PLANNING AND ARCHITECTURE BEFORE McKIM, MEAD & WHITE

FIGURE 6 *King's College in the skyline of colonial New York City (Palm Tree Print), etching by Pierre Canot (Art Properties)*

The college's downtown and midtown sites and the limits of the Manhattan grid

Even before seeking out Morningside Heights, Columbia had moved uptown twice along with the city's push northward on Manhattan Island. In 1760 the college outgrew the site adjacent to Trinity Church, where it was chartered in 1754 as King's College, and moved north to a three-acre site near Park Place, renamed College Place. There it occupied an impressive four-story building crowned by a cupola that took its place as a landmark amid the church spires that still dominated the skyline in the late eighteenth century and figured prominently in engravings of the city (fig. 6). In 1773 Myles Cooper, the college's second president, described the grounds in terms remarkably similar to those used 120 years later to underscore the benefits of Morningside Heights:

> The College is situated on dry gravelly soil, about 150 yards from the banks of the Hudson River, which it overlooks; commanding from the eminence on which it stands, a most extensive and beautiful prospect of the opposite shore and country of New Jersey, the City and Island of New York, Long Island, Staten Island, New York Bay with its islands, the Narrows, forming the mouth of the Harbour . . . and being totally unencumbered by any adjacent buildings and admitting the purest circulation of air from the river, and every other quarter has the benefit of as agreeable and healthy a situation as can possibly be conceived.[7]

As late as 1810 Columbia College, as King's College was renamed after the Revolution, was averaging but seventeen graduates a year. Nonetheless, the idea of moving farther north had already been put forth, more to escape surrounding city conditions than to respond to internal pressures for change or expansion. In November 1802 a committee considered whether the college should expand on its existing site or

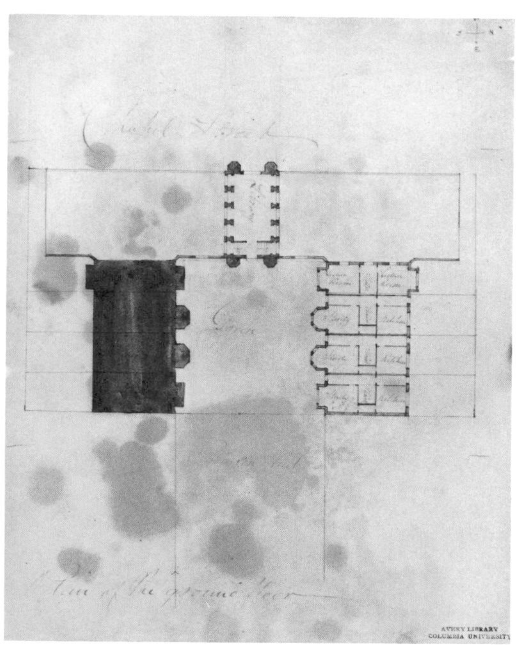

FIGURE 7 *James Renwick Sr., Project for Columbia College: plan, 1813 (Avery Library)*

FIGURE 8 *James Renwick Sr., Project for Columbia College: front and side elevations of the hall and library, with details of Gothic window designs, 1813 (Avery Library)*

consider the "propriety of removing the College to some more convenient situation,"[8] a discussion that would recur for more than a century. The city had begun to close in on the openness and greenery of the college's site, and along with rapid urbanization and the great expansion of New York's port came new worries for the tutors of the college's mostly resident, all-male student body. In addition to the noise of the district, a stone's throw from the bustling docks of the Hudson, the college was next to an area gaining notoriety for prostitution.

A pattern for the rest of the century was announced in 1813 and 1814 when, within a few months, the college's trustees both reviewed architectural plans to rebuild the existing site with an impressive complex of new buildings and petitioned the New York State legislature for a grant of land far above the northern limit of the city's growth. James Renwick Sr.'s scheme for the Park Place site (figs. 7 & 8) was centered on a neo-Gothic library to which symmetrical extensions for classrooms could be added as needed. Had it been built, Columbia's new buildings would not only have anticipated the Gothic Revival movement in American campus design by nearly a decade, but the college also would have shared with its frequent rival Union College–which was in Schenectady and the only other college in New York State–the distinction of drawing up the first great formal composition for expansion of an American college. In 1813 Union College commissioned a great neoclassical crescent design, centered on a circular building, designed by the French émigré architect Joseph Ramée. Possibly in response Columbia sought to assert its associations with ancient British universities by proposing a neo-Gothic design.[9] Professor Renwick's plan was quickly shelved, however, in favor of repairs and additions to Columbia's existing, classical style building.

The appeal to the state legislature for the site of the Elgin Botanical Garden–a failed project of the college's botany professor David Hosack–would, on the other hand, play a decisive role in Columbia's future. These twenty acres, approximately four city blocks lying north of Forty-seventh Street and fronting on the west side of Fifth Avenue (the streets had been traced just a few years earlier on the commissioner's plan), were to become, with the northward march of development, extremely valuable property. Although the state legislature made the grant in 1814 on the express condition that the college move there within twelve years, the college seemed divided on the project from the beginning. In 1816 the trustees appointed a new commission to consider a move, but they stipulated that no sites north of Astor Place be considered. Three years later the trustees were able to have the state suspend the deadline for occupying the Botanical Garden site. But the college seems to have mustered neither the resolve among its trustees, administration, and faculty nor the resources to create a campus on this multiblock site. By the end of the century this landholding had become one of the college's most profitable investments and would remain so, leased after 1929 to Rockefeller Center, until it was sold in 1985. The trustees' joint stewardship of an educational institution and of an important portfolio of investment properties was also established as a dynamic, even sometimes a tension, with profound implications for Columbia's future.

Throughout the early nineteenth century Columbia remained a conservative institution, bound fairly closely to New York's Episcopalian elites and drawing largely on local sons for its classical curriculum. Although shaken from time to time by challenges of competition, most notably when the University of the City of New York (later New York University) was founded in 1830, the curriculum and teaching staff of the relatively small college remained little changed for more than three decades. Within a year of taking up his post in 1849, Charles King, the college's first nonclerical president, began to agitate for relocation to the Fifth Avenue site. In 1851 Richard Upjohn, the leading Episcopalian architect and tastemaker of the day, and a pioneer and ardent defender of the American Gothic Revival, began to work on a comprehensive plan for developing the property; his designs unfortunately have never resurfaced. Although the financial incentives for putting the lower Manhattan site on the market were enormous, the college lacked resources for new buildings.

In 1857, after several years of debate, the trustees decided to apply proceeds from the sale of the College Place property towards acquiring the grounds of the Deaf and Dumb Asylum located at Forty-ninth Street between Madison and Fourth (Park) Avenues, just a block away from the Botanical Garden site, since its existing buildings could be occupied as a temporary campus. Upjohn's scheme was put on ice for better times. The asylum buildings were adapted as classrooms and, with the expansion of the scientific curriculum, as laboratories. When the outbreak of the Civil War made it clear that building on the larger site west of Fifth Avenue would need to wait at least a few more years, a simple president's house (1862) was built on the corner of the asylum grounds. The post–Civil War years witnessed a volatile economy that confirmed the trustees' caution, and in the end Columbia College remained for forty years, almost to the day, on its temporary site. Although the *Evening Post* of 11 May 1857 had described the new site as "a delightful one, and undesirable only on account of its distance uptown,"[10] it was not long before the phenomenal growth of Manhattan above Forty-second Street, especially after the arrival of the railroad into Grand Central and the northern push of speculative residences and commerce, made conditions at Forty-ninth Street increasingly untenable.

While the trustees maintained vigorously in the 1890s that the Forty-ninth Street site had never been considered anything but temporary, there is considerable evidence that over the years the college had vacillated. From the first, President Frederick A. P. Barnard insisted that the "obvious and manifest destiny of the College" required a new site. For Barnard this destiny was the forging of a university of diverse departments and even professional schools, dedicated to research rather than to classical humanistic pedagogy, a position he shared with Harvard's Charles Eliot and with William Gilman of the newly founded Johns Hopkins. All were admirers of the German research university. "When schools shall here grow up of Civil Engineering, of Astronomy, and of the many applications of the sciences to the useful arts, of Architecture, of Commerce, of the Fine Arts, of Natural History, of Linguistics, of Political History, and of Philosophy, it needs no argument to prove that the present site, ample as it may seem for the College as it is, can never suffice for the College as it will be," Barnard wrote in his 1866 annual report.[11] In the 1870s the college again confronted the issue on two fronts. In 1871 a commission was appointed to look into new sites, even outside the city, leading to the purchase of the Wheelock property at 162nd Street. At the same time the college looked into acquiring sites adjacent to its Forty-ninth Street block, with the hope that the city might authorize the closure of a street to create a larger campus uninterrupted by traffic.

Columbia's efforts were indirectly supported by the great landscape architect Frederick Law Olmsted, who had brilliantly exploited the single exception to the iron-clad rule of the grid with Central Park, which he designed in 1857, the year Columbia moved to Forty-ninth Street. Throughout his long professional career, in which he would advise not only on city parks but also on numerous campus designs and overall city plans, Olmsted remained an outspoken critic of the Manhattan block plan. This undifferentiated framework not only ignored the very topography that Olmsted set out to enhance, but it also made the development of a monumental cityscape all but impossible. In the grid, he complained, the only value was the sheer quantity of salable square feet. The grid would defeat any attempt to create a hierarchy of exceptional and background buildings, public and private, institutional and commercial. While Americans increasingly admired the axial boulevards of Haussmann's Paris, with its grand directional avenues spotlighting palaces, museums, the opera house, and new churches, Olmsted complained that the grid plan adopted in New York made it all but impossible to develop any institution of large size, and prevented dramatic perspectival views of buildings or appreciation of them from a distance:

> If a proposed cathedral, military depot, great manufacturing enterprise, house of religious seclusion or seat of learning needs a space of more than sixty-six yards in extent from north to south, the system forbids that it shall be built in New York. . . . There are numerous structures, both public and private, in London and Paris, and most other large towns of Europe, which could not be built in New York, for want of a site of suitable extent and proportions. . . . There is no place under the system in New York where a stately building can be looked up to from base to turret, none where it can even be seen full in the face and all at once taken in by the eye; none where it can be viewed in advantageous perspective. . . . Such a distinctive advantage of position as Rome gives St. Peter's, Paris the Madeleine, London St. Paul's, New York under her system gives to nothing.[12]

Olmsted offered but one concrete example of the frustrations of the grid plan: "The Trustees of Columbia College sought for years to obtain the privilege of consolidating two of the uniform blocks of the system . . . in order to erect sufficient buildings for their purpose, in one unbroken group, but it was denied

FIGURE 9 *Columbia College at 49th Street, Reading room of C. C. Haight's library (Columbiana Collection)*

FIGURE 10 *Columbia College at 49th Street, View of Hamilton Hall: Madison Avenue elevation (Columbiana Collection)*

FIGURE 11 *Columbia College at 49th Street, Library: campus elevation (Columbiana Collection)*

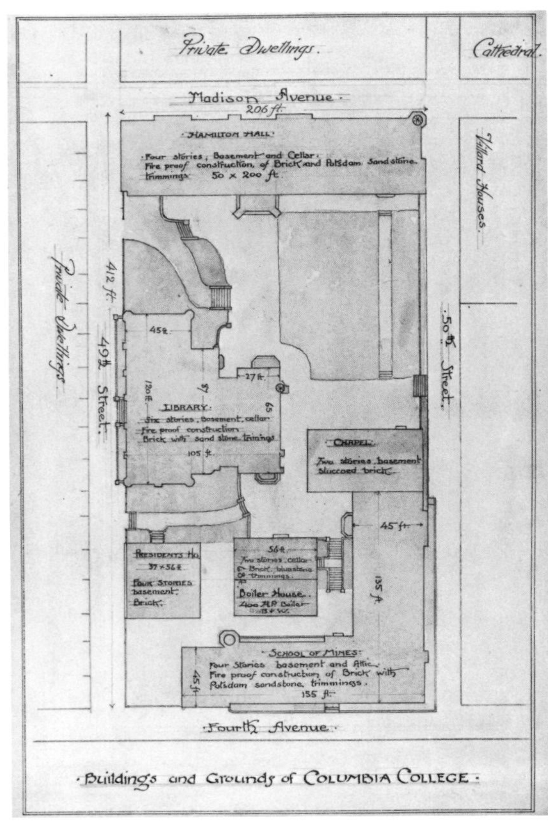

FIGURE 12 *Columbia College at 49th Street, Site plan drawn for sale of property after the removal of the college to Morningside Heights, ca. 1897 (Avery Library)*

them."[13] Along with the increasing value for revenue of the Elgin Botanical Garden property, this was the major impediment to the trustees in developing a new campus on the other side of Fifth Avenue.

From his arrival in the president's office in 1864, Barnard encouraged relocating the college to a more ample site where his vision of a university could develop, but his plans were soon overwhelmed by the day-to-day demands of both a growing institution and city. One by one he consented to constructing new buildings at Forty-ninth Street. A commentator looking over the group of buildings that rose in the 1870s and 1880s to form Columbia's neo-Gothic campus noted that "the die was cast by the erection of a solid and permanent building for the School of Mines on the old grounds" in 1873, replacing a temporary structure that the trustees had authorized in 1865. "Columbia had found her permanent home," the writer lamented in 1884, "and her architect has had to meet the difficult problem of housing a great and growing university within the contracted limits of a city block."[14] By then Charles Coolidge Haight had designed three new buildings for the college, beginning with a new structure for the School of Mines facing Fourth (Park) Avenue (built in three phases: 1874, 1880, 1884), Hamilton Hall for undergraduate lecture rooms and faculty and trustee rooms along Madison Avenue (1879–1880) and a soaring library building (1881–1883) at mid-block facing Forty-ninth Street (figs. 9–12).

Many colleges were expanding in the early 1870s, including Columbia's chief rivals in the increasingly competitive quest for students and tuition.[15] In the 1870s the trustees noted that Harvard in particular, with its growing facilities and reputation for student life, was drawing away the best students, including local boys who might have gone to Columbia. Many regretted that at its midtown site Columbia had not provided for students to live on the campus. "Were it in our power to offer the same variety of attractions which Harvard offers, it would be impossible for such a phenomenon to present itself,"[16] Barnard concluded in an appeal before the trustees in May 1874 for a building campaign at Forty-ninth Street. Expansion would create up-to-date laboratory space, permit the revised and more liberal curriculum Barnard advocated, and foster a range of extracurricular activities that would keep students for longer hours on this commuters' campus. All of this could be achieved only with new buildings.

As early as 1847 an article in the *American Literary Magazine* describing the new Gothic library at Yale had declared that "a college must have buildings . . . because there must be something to give the public a pledge of the permanence of the institution—and something that will be a center of attachment for its members."[17] Having made do for fifteen years in a former asylum, Columbia was eager to establish its reputation. By the early 1870s plans for impressive ranges of Gothic buildings in that most vigorous and earnest style known as High Victorian had already been announced at Harvard, Yale, and Princeton. In 1874, while Columbia trustees debated whether or not to go forward with Barnard's building campaign, Trinity College in Hartford, another prominent Episcopalian college, published stunning plans for its new campus by the English High Victorian master William Burges. Barnard laid before the trustees his strategy for advancing Columbia without abandoning hopes of a future move:

> We shall build here, if we build at all, not on the theory of merely temporary occupation, but upon that of occupation which is practically permanent; permanent in such a sense that the buildings whatever they may cost, shall have paid for themselves over and over again in the largely increased usefulness of the institution. We shall build also in such a manner that when they are abandoned they shall not be lost, but shall be valuable and useful to those who may succeed us on these premises.[18]

What is remarkable in Columbia's history in the last quarter of the nineteenth century is not that the institution built an entirely new campus with a magnificent library, but that it built *two* such campuses. Indeed, the buildings erected in the decade from 1874 to 1884, culminating in Haight's magnificent Gothic reading room (fig. 9), would serve Columbia for just ten to fifteen years before they were abandoned for Morningside Heights.

Haight's appointment, which effectively launched his architectural career, reflects something of the close-knit Episcopalian world of the board of trustees of Columbia College in the mid-nineteenth century. A graduate of the class of 1861, Haight, all but untried as an architect, was given his first commission for the School of Mines while his father, Benjamin I. Haight, a minister in Trinity Parish and a Columbia trustee, was serving as acting president of the board in 1874.[19] Haight's architectural designs adeptly juggled the college's potentially contradictory desires and appeased for the time being tensions in the faculty between the growing "University Party" and the defenders of the status quo. With these designs Columbia would both mark its presence in the city as a cultural institution and craft a protected space for its students that evoked a collegiate ambiance, which for most Americans in the nineteenth century was already associated with verdant settings and ivy-covered buildings. The first two architectural moves on the site were to raise blocks along the short street fronts of Madison and Fourth Avenues that would both capture what vistas the gridded streets of Midtown had to offer and create protective barriers converting the interior of the site into a tranquil academic precinct. The School of Mines was architecturally restrained, not only because of its utilitarian program of scientific laboratory space but also because it provided a wall between the campus block and the New York Central tracks—owned by the family of college trustee Cornelius Vanderbilt—which still ran in an open cut down the center of Fourth (Park) Avenue. Along Madison Avenue, Hamilton Hall formed an asymmetrical composition punctuated by gables, dormers, a vast chimney for the advanced ventilation that Haight introduced in the classrooms, and a great open turret at the corner of Fiftieth Street (fig. 10). Hamilton Hall declared the college's ambitions in the emerging institutional and cultural landscape, which included St. Patrick's Cathedral (1858–1879) diagonally opposite and St. Luke's Hospital a few blocks north.

The Greek portico of the original asylum building was now largely hidden from view, and the streetscape bristled with a modern Gothic imagery redolent of Columbia's origins in Trinity Parish–since the 1840s housed in a Gothic Revival design by one of Haight's mentors, Richard M. Upjohn–and evocative of prestigious English colleges. Even that sharp-penned father of American architectural journalism, Montgomery Schuyler, admired both the urban composition and the originality with which Haight both accommodated and found architectural expression for the complex program of the new campus buildings. Haight's Gothic was no "mere reproduction of old work . . . it would take its place in the High Street of Oxford, or among 'the backs' of Cambridge, without a jar, with much less incongruity, indeed, than almost any of the modern additions to those ancient seats of learning."[20] With the completion of the library building on Forty-ninth Street in 1884 (fig. 11) Haight turned Columbia's city block into an urban academic cloister, a double quadrangle separated by the stacks of the library. It divided the block almost exactly in the center and nearly touched the corner of the old asylum building, which by 1884 he was planning to replace with another range along Fiftieth Street.[21] Within the block the site was terraced to accommodate a crest in the topography of Manhattan at this point, which added to the picturesque oblique views. Haight seems to have been a master at creating such views, judging from the handful of surviving images depicting the interior of the Midtown campus. Most building entrances were located on the interior of the block rather than on the street, which resulted in a continuous, if highly active, wall to the city. Piece by piece Haight had defined a cloistered block approach for Columbia, which he would continue to refine in his plans for the General Theological Seminary, along Twentieth Street in Chelsea in the 1880s, and which would be emulated by both Teachers College and the Union Theological Seminary once they moved to Morningside Heights, in 1894 and 1905 respectively.

The distinctly collegiate associations of Haight's Gothic were thrown into high relief in the early 1880s as the Madison Avenue frontage of the block immediately north of the college came to host the Villard Houses, a scholarly and refined composition in which the rising architectural firm of McKim, Mead & White transformed both the model of the Italian Renaissance palazzo and the handling of the New York City row house. In 1880 the trustees had looked into purchasing all or part of that block north of Fiftieth Street between Madison and Park, but they were unable to have the price lowered from the $500,000 demanded. Nor were they willing to meet that price a year later when Villard gave them another chance before starting construction on his new property.[22] The style of the Villard Houses and the evidence of the escalating property values were indications of great changes afoot in New York architecture and real estate.

Despite considerable acclaim in the period's guidebooks for Columbia's "handsome and commodious brick buildings in collegiate Gothic style,"[23] many in the faculty realized that the number of students and the burgeoning library collection would soon outpace Columbia's recent spate of physical growth. "Columbia is confined in the scant block at Madison Avenue and 49th street and the trains from Grand Central Station make the intellectual life not worth living there,"[24] noted the recently hired faculty member Brander Matthews in 1892. His complaints found numerous echoes among Columbia's scientists in its prospering School of Mines whose experiments were severely compromised by the vibrations of the trains running beside the campus. Just weeks before Matthews's remarks, the trustees had taken a huge financial gamble and had authorized the acquisition of a new site far to the north, at 116th Street.

Seth Low and the forging of a metropolitan university

"The College has taken on the functions and assumed the aspect of a University," Barnard noted proudly in 1882, two years after John W. Burgess had organized the Faculty of Political Science, the first of the graduate divisions of the college.[25] For Barnard and Burgess it was only a matter of time before Columbia changed its name to reflect the new reality, and they were eager to move Columbia into the national spotlight. But throughout the 1880s this minority enthusiasm for emulating the Germanic research university model met with considerable resistance within the faculty and even among the trustees. The outside world, in particular a number of outspoken journalists, were increasingly outspoken in their criticism of Columbia's perceived failure to engage with the culture of the city. As Thomas Bender demonstrates in a penetrating analysis of these tormented years in Columbia's evolution from college to metropolitan university, "Columbia was a closed corporation, more of a real estate investment trust watching the city increase its assets, rather than an educational body."[26] Bender cites in particular the public debate instigated by E. L. Godkin, editor of the *Nation*:

> In 1883 . . . Hamilton Fish, as president of the Trustees, blamed the city, not Columbia for its invisibility and ineffectiveness. Columbia, he suggested is "lost sight of" because New York is such a "center of business, fashion, and pleasure." Harvard, Yale, and Princeton seem to be important because there is nothing else worthy of attention in their respective towns. While granting something of Fish's point, Godkin insisted that in fact the problem was that Columbia was too "secluded, conservative, mediocre." If it is to be a "city college," Godkin asserted, it must "endeavor to increase in every way possible the number of points at which it can come in contact with the life of the city. . . . The more difficult it is to form an intellectual center in New York, the greater the responsibility which rests on its old and rich university."[27]

By the late 1880s tensions between the "university" and "college" factions reached a new pitch in response to Barnard's suggestion in February 1887 that Columbia consider abandoning altogether undergraduate education and recast itself as a university of graduate and professional training. The majority of the faculty was opposed, but the University Party, led by Burgess, had other numbers on their side, for enrollments were on the rise in the graduate Faculty of Political Science and in the School of Mines, as well as in the law and medical schools, while the School of the Arts, as the college was then known, had entered a slump.

Barnard's death in 1889, however, was a temporary blow to the University Party. Seth Low's election by the margin of a single vote in 1889 as Columbia's first nonacademic president is a clear indication that a vocal group within the trustees, dominated by such successful New York business leaders and professionals as Cornelius Vanderbilt and William C. Schermerhorn, was determined to calm the internal strife and to assure Columbia pride of place among the city's cultural and educational institutions also under their stewardship. Immensely wealthy and imbued with extraordinary energy for civic reform and betterment, Low was the model of a new type of president who could guide Columbia toward a different future, furthering the goals of the University Party while appeasing the college faction.

Low had been elected as a trustee on 7 November 1881, just a day before Brooklyn voters elected this former businessman as their reform mayor. For the rest of his life Low's efforts to reform both New York and his alma mater (valedictorian, class of 1870) marched in tandem. Anticipating the great epoch of urban reform, Low devoted much of his energies as mayor to reforming Brooklyn's public school system, removing it from political patronage, instituting free textbooks for all children, and touring regularly the city's schools.[28] As a Columbia trustee he had made it his mission to nudge the college into greater engagement with the city. He organized public lectures by the faculty in a variety of fields, including the sciences and political economy which had only recently become arenas for the college's curriculum. In addition, lectures on the fine arts were given by Columbia professors at the recently formed Metropolitan Museum on Art and on science at the American Museum of Natural History. He was a strong advocate of the emerging field of sociology—even endowing a professorship in this discipline—which most completely embodied his notion of the mutual involvement of the university and the increasingly diverse populations of the city. The signal sent by the trustees in electing him president was received immediately. The *Kansas City Times* wrote on 13 October 1889: "It is one of the most pronounced steps yet made by one of the larger educational institutions in a movement which has been slowly taking shape for years. American education is going to be closer to the life of the nation. Educators are going to be men of experience in the world, of knowledge of affairs, of sympathy with the best practical purposes and aspirations of the people."[29]

Low's first two years at the helm saw a complete reorganization of university administration that remarkably paralleled the theory of applying principles of scientific business organization to municipal government that he had pioneered in Brooklyn, and with which he would attack Tammany Hall after his election as New York City mayor in 1901.[30] The University Council, created in 1890, organized Columbia's loosely affiliated faculties into a collaborative framework and established a forum for the involvement of the faculty in administration. Students would be able for the first time to take classes in any of

Columbia's schools without paying separate fees.

At the same time Low set out to respond to criticism of Columbia's insularity. "New York knows nothing of Columbia and Columbia knows nothing of New York," complained New York Central magnate Chauncey Depew in October 1889.[31] This sentiment was echoed on the eve of Low's official inauguration by the *New York Times*: "Columbia College is very old as American colleges go . . . [but] the feeling is common that Columbia has not done for American education what might fairly have been expected of its age, its wealth, and its metropolitan position."[32] Low's inaugural address stated a mandate for the university that would find its most visible response in the radical decision to build an entirely new campus. In the words of James Martin Keating, a biographer, "Low spoke for a Columbia that would become a great metropolitan university, serving a supporting city and earning its esteem."[33] "The city," Low declared, "surrounds us all with a large and bracing atmosphere. Something of the breadth of view and feeling that travel gives, the cosmopolitan city may bestow upon those who study in it." At the same time the "chief and permanent value to the city" of the college resides in upholding a model of intellectual life "in the great city where finance and commerce alike show their good and their bad sides."[34] A year later in his annual report he revealed the other side of the formula: "I hope it will not escape the notice of any in the city who are working to associate their names with some conspicuous gift to the cause of education, that right here in New York there is a need for a great building to enlarge the faculties of Columbia in the great career which is certainly opening before her."[35]

A master plan for a metropolitan university

Haight's plans for a major building to replace the old asylum building ("Old College Hall") and thereby complete Columbia's Gothic cloister city block had been ready since 1885. And for some time the trustees had been on the lookout for land to develop a gymnasium and playing fields for the college. They were confident that, presented with an attractive project, the Alumni Association—which Seth Low had already reanimated and put on a solid footing back in the 1870s—would help fund any improvement to student life at the college. The Columbia alumni might thus belatedly join the growing movement at other colleges where alumni were funding the expansion and beautification of alma mater. But by "great career" Low was referring not to these individual projects but to his vision of a metropolitan university. To the frustrated endeavors of Barnard, Burgess, and Samuel Bulkley Ruggles, Seth Low would now add his own conviction that the urban university could both serve and benefit from a diverse urban population, eroding boundaries between academic pursuits and public life and service.

In May 1891 a special trustees' Committee on Site was appointed, including, in addition to Low, W. C. Schermerhorn, George L. Rives, Cornelius Vanderbilt, and the Reverend Morgan Dix. The committee considered three options: moving the college to a country site and leaving the Forty-ninth Street site for "the university work"; developing the individual schools on different sites throughout the city; or finding a new site large enough to "permit the university to retain its essential character as a university in the heart of the city of New York."[36] The language alone left little doubt as to which option corresponded to the trustees' vision of Columbia, but they carefully outlined the drawbacks of the first two possibilities. The first had already been rejected years earlier, around 1857, when a thousand-acre site in Westchester was briefly pursued but dropped in favor of remaining in the city. Once again Columbia would pledge allegiance to the "clear advantage to the country of having some of its college-bred men trained under city conditions," as the trustees observed, noting that in founding yet another rural college "Columbia would be entering upon a competition in a new field, already crowded." While the second option–the dispersed model–had certain metropolitan advantages in that the medical school could be located near a major hospital and the architecture school near the Metropolitan Museum of Art, it obviously ran counter to the university ideal Low and others were working so hard to realize.

The issue was essentially decided by the time the committee had its report printed in December 1891. For in August of that year John B. Pine, a prominent Wall Street lawyer and clerk of the trustees, had called the board's attention to the pending sale of the grounds of the Bloomingdale Asylum of the New York Hospital at 116th Street and the Boulevard (as Broadway was then called), and in November Seth Low wrote a confidential letter to Herman H. Camman, chairman of the hospital's real estate committee, inquiring whether the hospital would give the college an option on the property and name a price compatible with the public character and purpose of the college. Within a month, the hospital offered the northern two-thirds of the tract for $2 million. Speculative development in this area, little accessible by public transportation, had failed several times to take off, although the blocks of lower-lying Harlem to the east and north were rapidly being covered by row houses and apartment buildings.[37] By the summer of 1891 both St. Luke's Hospital and the Cathedral of St. John the Divine were studying plans to relocate to this promontory; some of the members of Columbia's site committee also sat on the boards of these two Episcopalian institutions. The trustees had no illusions that the virtually rural environment of the Heights would remain long intact, but they were eager to seize the opportunity to acquire what was by nearly anyone's calculations the last large plot on Manhattan Island undivided by streets.[38] Columbia might then become a major player in crafting a landscape on the cusp of development. In this "portion of the city likely to be well built up," as Pine noted, the university could be a major force in channeling the course of development rather than a passive witness to the growth of the city, as many felt Columbia had been at Forty-ninth Street. "There is no other site upon this island where a great building will be so conspicuous and so impressive. . . . there is no other that can be expected to be kept so secure from the invasion of ordinary uses," the *New York Times* stated.[39]

While some of the trustees balked at the $2-millon price tag for the four-square-block site, a small group was convinced that the acquisition of the site would inaugurate a new era in the college's financial affairs. Since the mid-1880s there had been considerable discussion of Columbia's failure to tap into the rising tides of philanthropy, both that of alumni and of the city's wealthy industrialists and investors, all of whom should be eager to memorialize themselves in public cultural and educational institutions. "The fine situation and great advantage which the property offers as a building site," Pine pointed out, "would afford a strong inducement to the generosity of those interested in the College.... A policy that shall place the College more conspicuously before the eyes of the public... will ensure for it support which will be no less generous than that accorded to other like institutions."[40]

Even as they calculated how much the sale of the current campus and its buildings could supplement funds recently willed to the college by Daniel Fayerweather, Pine and Low continuously tutored the more conservative trustees in what might be called the politics of philanthropic speculation: "The reestablishment of the College upon a scale commensurate with the size and importance of the city, will unfailingly command the confidence and support of the alumni and of the public."

Negotiations with the hospital and debates over whether the college should acquire more than the four blocks north of 116th Street (the hospital also owned the two blocks to the south as well as considerable land on the west side of the Boulevard) continued into late spring 1892, by which time the first subscription, $5,000 from Abram S. Hewitt, had been received.[41] The press chimed in with articles and editorials endorsing Columbia's appeal. "The College will have the rare chance of treating its ground as a whole from the very start. The Cathedral and the College nobly housed on the plateau would give New York an architectural crown such as no other American city is ever likely to wear," noted the *Christian Union*, adding that the $2 million "ought to be raised as a matter of local duty."[42] While the *Evening Post*, pointing out that Harvard had received more than $4 million recently from its alumni, concluded an editorial with: "Columbia College may now be said to be making its first serious appeal to the bounty, not only of its own alumni, but to that of all persons blessed with wealth, who feel an interest in the growth of this great city into something higher and better than a place where money may be made quickly and spent frivolously."[43] A liberalization in New York's laws on bequests and charitable trusts in 1893, which also gave greater protection to the intentions of donors, was passed just in time to confirm Low and Pine's optimism.[44]

Planning the new Columbia

"Make no little plans, they have no magic to stir men's blood. . . . Make big plans . . . remembering that a noble, logical diagram once recorded will never die but long after we are gone will be a living thing asserting itself with ever growing insistence," were the lessons for the future that Daniel Burnham proposed after the World's Columbian Exposition closed in 1894.[45] Shortly after the exposition had opened its doors in June 1893, McKim proposed Burnham for an honorary degree at Columbia's next commencement, pointing out that it was Burnham who had both raised architectural design to the level of urban design and created a model for professional collaboration among a group of architects within a strong planning framework.[46] Columbia had by then already embraced Burnham's techniques and was applying them to its search for a new identity for an institution only recently racked by faculty disagreements. The trustees hoped that both the scale and the imagery of the Chicago exposition might boost them in their new determination to build a private institution as a recipient of civic philanthropy.

Even before the college sought professional architectural advice the trustees had been quite explicit about the possibilities and requirements for the new site. They were impressed with the tenfold increase in size of the college grounds: "Compared with the grounds occupied by other colleges, it is about the size of Harvard Yard and nearly twice the size of the Yale campus. Within its limits could be placed all the quadrangles of the three largest colleges of Oxford or Cambridge."[47] Yet they realized that planning must look toward the future density of both the city and the university: "If a carefully considered system of construction is adopted, the space available for buildings of all kinds will be much greater than that enjoyed by either Harvard or Yale, where economy of space has not been studied."[48] The master plan would be a contract with the future and would forge Columbia's identity in terms of the metropolitan ideals for which Low was fighting and consolidate the vision of a great research university, further advanced by the creation of the Faculty of Pure Science in 1892:

> It may be one hundred years or longer before the block will be developed to its utmost capacity. On the other hand the first building which is placed there will condition everything that is to follow. . . . It seems . . . therefore essential that the trustees should cause such a preliminary study to be made of the possibilities of the block and its best method of development as will command public interest and support and lead to a willingness on the part of our successors to follow in the steps taken by us. A problem like this seems . . . beyond the wisdom of any one man no matter how capable or wise he may be. [49]

A decade earlier, in 1881, Columbia had opened America's second school of architecture, attracting the architect and pedagogue William Robert Ware from M.I.T. where he had established the first professional architectural school in the country. Ware, along with Professor William Petit Trowbridge, an engineer in the School of Mines, was asked to study the problem of planning the new site, but the trustees also thought it wise to turn to a group of prominent practicing architects in the city for advice. Haight, the college's architect since the 1870s, would of course be invited, but the trustees also hoped to include the principals of the two New York firms who had played key roles in Burnham's collaborative team for the World's Columbian Exposition: Richard Morris Hunt and Charles Follen McKim. Hunt, the first American to have attended the Ecole des Beaux-Arts in Paris and now the veritable doyen of American public architecture, was also the family architect of the Vanderbilts, including board member Cornelius Vanderbilt. In 1893 Hunt's great domed Administration Building was the centerpiece of the Chicago fairgrounds (fig. 3).

McKim, whose office McKim, Mead & White had already emerged as the largest American architectural firm, was well known at Columbia, where he had been active in the School of Architecture, even donating considerable money to establish traveling fellowships. Low had even cited him in his inaugural address of 1890 as one of those whose philanthropy would "help make Columbia what she ought to be, beyond all controversy the university of the land."[50] Since 1891 McKim had been Burnham's right-hand man for the large-scale planning issues at the Chicago exposition, where he designed the low-domed Agriculture Building as well as the New York State Pavilion, which housed Columbia's own exhibit. In January of 1892 McKim's partner Stanford White had begun consulting with New York University's President James McCracken on plans either to expand at Washington Square or to relocate uptown, even as NYU's trustees discussed a possible merger with Columbia's board (fig. 13). No firm was so deeply involved in shaping the new image of the American metropolitan university.

Low set out to obtain maximum documentation for the architect's committee, soliciting reports from the faculty on the requirements of each of the college's divisions and sending Ware and Trowbridge uptown to obtain accurate surveys of both the complex topography and the existing buildings (plate 1), which no doubt would need to serve for a number of years before new construction could house Columbia's growing schools. Pine suggested that the "commission" consist of only the three outside architects, with Ware and Trowbridge acting as advisors, since in this way "Messrs. Haight, McKim and Hunt . . . will be likely to feel greater responsibility and take more interest in the matter."[51] Almost immediately the three agreed to disagree and set about preparing separate designs, turning what the college hoped would be a consultation into a de facto architectural competition. In April 1893 each architect submitted a set of plans along with a written analysis of the problem.

The new site proved a tremendous challenge to large-scale formal planning because of its irregular topography (plate 1 and fig. 14). A high point near the center of the southern part of the site—about midway between the Boulevard (Broadway) and Amsterdam at 117th Street—was already occupied by the asylum buildings. From there the land fell away rather rapidly to the north, reaching its lowest level

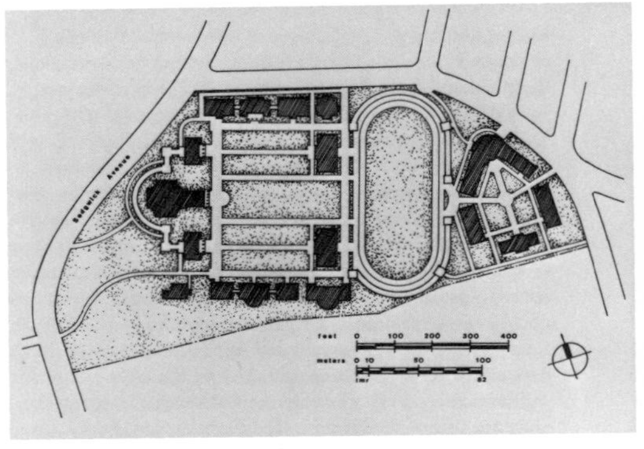

FIGURE 13 *McKim, Mead & White, Master plan for New York University at University Heights, Bronx, 1896 (reproduced from Leland Roth,* McKim, Mead & White, Architects, *New York, 1983)*

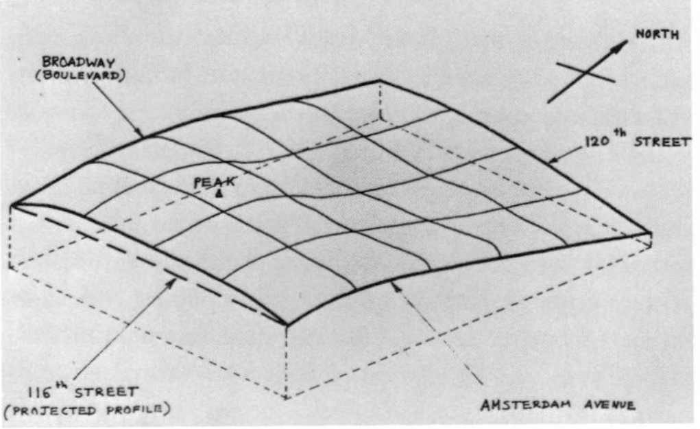

FIGURE 14 *Francesco Passanti, Topographical reconstruction of Columbia's new site on Morningside Heights before construction (courtesy F. Passanti)*

at the northeast corner of the property, at 120th Street and Amsterdam Avenue. Any large formal scheme would certainly require terracing, although it would also be possible to use the variations in elevation on the site to create a series of distinct spaces to foster more intimate settings and to zone the grounds for the different components of the growing university.

This was the approach taken by Haight, who proposed a cloistered design, dividing the site into a series of differently shaped courts, alternatively closed and protected or open to diagonal views into adjacent spaces (fig. 15). The main entrance would be situated on Amsterdam Avenue at about 118th Street, where a library and administration building would rise behind a forecourt and take advantage of tramway traffic there. This orientation would provide a shield from the westerly winds "sweeping from the Palisades across the Hudson." A secondary entrance on Broadway at 118th Street would lead to a large building housing a refectory and a theater, a combination already essayed in Ware and Van Brunt's Memorial Hall at Harvard. Between these two buildings the heart of the new site would be treated as a great open quadrangle, bounded on the north by a gymnasium and on the south by a chapel, part of a T-shaped building for the School of the Arts (as the college was to be known within the university). From this great central quadrangle modest flights of stairs tucked in between the ranges of buildings running east-west would lead to secondary quadrangles on a higher level to the south and a lower level to the north. The north end of the site would be given over to the School of Mines, to which Haight attributed the lion's share of the square footage of faculty buildings, while the south would host the School of the Arts and the law school, as well as extensive dormitories and a free-standing house for the president.

Not only did Haight retain many of the features of the campus he had recently designed for Columbia in Midtown, with its intimacy of bounded interior spaces and its inward focus, but he also seemed to have been aware of the great neo-medieval master plan drawn up in 1893 by Henry Ives Cobb for the University of Chicago (fig. 16). Stylistically the complex would be in "the best type of the Collegiate Architecture of Oxford and Cambridge," complementing the Romanesque imagery of the design selected for the nearby Episcopal Cathedral of St. John the Divine as well as the buildings under construction north of 120th Street for Teachers College by William A. Potter. Haight argued that Gothic was the style that could accommodate the diverse programmatic needs of a university as well as "the irregular levels of the new site," showing his commitment to the doctrine that his spiritual mentor the great English gothic revivalist architect and theorist A.W. N. Pugin called "picturesque utility."

Hunt's proposals (fig. 17) were more schematic than Haight's, although in his most developed variants he suggested a mirror image of Haight's east-west organization with a main entrance in front leading directly to the administration building at the center of the Broadway frontage and a secondary entrance off Amsterdam behind the theater. Along the north-south cross axis he organized chapel, library, and gymnasium. Hunt seems to have taken all the trustees' talk of utility before splendor to heart, for he proposed to organize the entire complex as a vast building surrounding a grandly scaled central courtyard that drew clearly on the tradition of pavilion hospital planning pioneered in France in the early nineteenth century. Like the French hospital plan, Hunt's campus would combine maximum ventilation and sunlight for all the buildings of the university, easy classification of the domains of the curriculum, and a spine of covered circulation connecting all the various parts. His plans were too diagrammatic to imagine just how he proposed to accommodate the irregular terrain of the new site, but he assured the trustees that his scheme "would require the least amount of grading and thus save a considerable expenditure." He even offered a very modest version of his proposal which would concentrate all the initial buildings at the northern edge of the site, facing 120th Street, where the land was relatively level. As for style Hunt recommended "facades, preferably of stone, as being more monumental, say in the Italian Renaissance style."[52]

The three alternatives submitted by McKim, Mead & White are unfortunately lost, yet we know from McKim's memorandum and several letters that he too proposed a formal arrangement, but with a vital difference: His complex faced south toward the city and was intended from the first to form "the crowning feature of the island ... with a commanding view at once of the Palisades to the Narrows

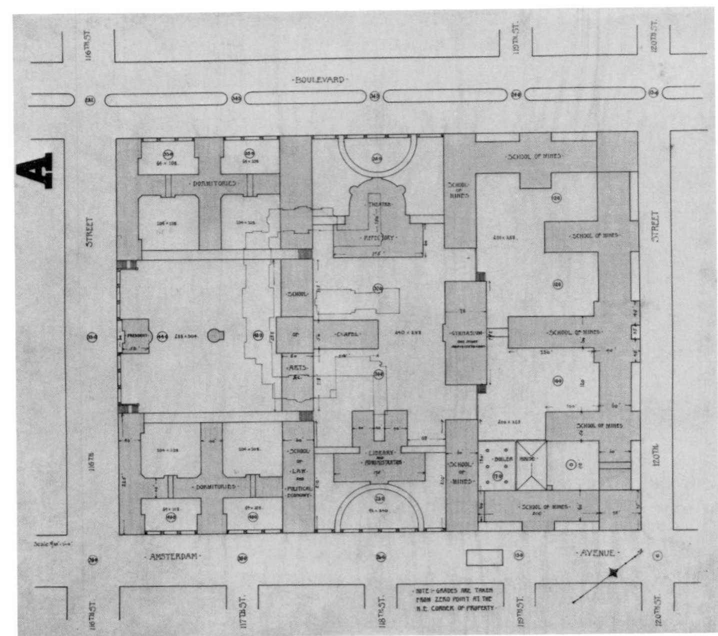

FIGURE 15 *Charles Coolidge Haight, Master plan for Columbia University, 1893 (cat. 10)*

and over both rivers," as he explained in a letter to Olmsted. "No problem could be more admirably suited to monumental treatment,"[53] he stated in justifying his efforts to exploit the terrain for maximum effect. Without his plan it is impossible to know if McKim proposed a great complex of connected structures forming courtyards—indeed he referred specifically to the recently designed Sorbonne in Paris as an appropriate urban prototype[54]—or freestanding buildings forming a subtle series of framed outdoor spaces and axes, as in the plan finally adopted. In his April 1893 memorandum he refers not to courtyards per se but rather to "two separate planes or platforms, a southern and a northern, the southern platform occupying about two thirds of the whole area, the northern about one third ... 15 feet or so below the other." These planes were to create a strict hierarchy of

FIGURE 16 *Henry Ives Cobb, Master plan for the University of Chicago, 1893*

buildings designed with "pure classical forms, as expressing in the simplest and most monumental way the purposes to which the buildings are devoted," and with strict attention to the "wholly municipal character of the problem."[55] From the first meeting with the trustees McKim advocated hiring Olmsted to collaborate on the project, and his own scheme drew considerable inspiration from both their recent collaboration in Chicago and Olmsted's terraced approach to the United States capitol in Washington.

Indeed, when the trustees turned over the three plans to Ware and Olmsted for review, McKim quickly wrote to Olmsted anticipating Ware's objections to the potential expense of preparing the grounds implied by McKim's proposed excavations and terraces "on a plot requiring both." He invited Olmsted to view a plaster topographical model of the site at the McKim, Mead & White office when he arrived in New York from Chicago (where Olmsted was finishing up directing the landscaping of the fairgrounds) and reminded him that Ware's "method of getting at the merits of each composition by *arithmetic* is just a little ludicrous, as when you built the great terrace of the Capitol, in order to accomplish a distinct purpose, you would have immediately rejected any plan which might have been presented at less cost as unwisely economical if it failed to accomplish this."[56]

In late April the trustees gave Ware and Olmsted the choice of submitting either a composite plan or "an alternative plan if they saw fit." On 26 May 1893, they submitted a range of possible new plans (plates 2 & 3), all of which responded to the trustees' admiration for "the large accommodation and open external courts of Mr. Hunt's scheme, and the practical convenience and ample provision for lecture rooms shown in Mr. Haight's, with the symmetry and monumental disposition of Mr. McKim's." While these varied in practical details, Ware and Olmsted's plans essentially sought to correct Hunt's arrangement with some of the essential features and character of McKim's scheme, most notably the entrance from the south, which would provide maximum air and light. This they proposed to handle by building a colonnaded propylaeum entrance to a great square

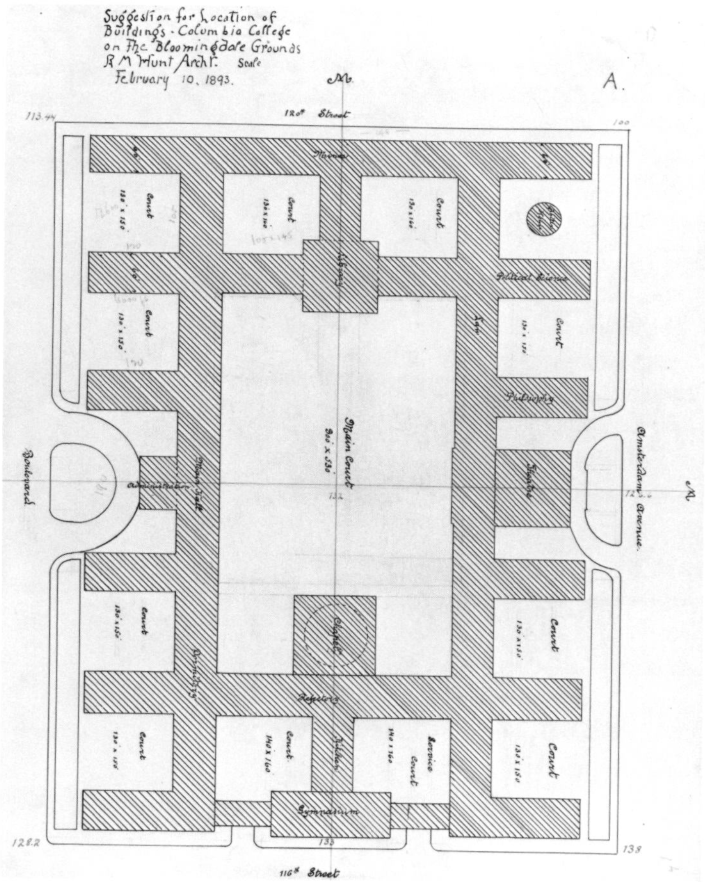

FIGURE 17 *Richard Morris Hunt, Master plan for Columbia University (Scheme A), 1893 (cat. 9)*

courtyard opening in the middle of 116th Street, even suggesting in one design that the university acquire land facing the site on the south side of 116th Street to create a forecourt locked into the city's grid plan. While much of the great civic forum that McKim adopted was already suggested in these plans, as was the apsidal shape and position of McKim's future University Hall, Ware and Olmsted retained in all their variants Hunt's pavilion system with its verdant courtyards along the avenues. Most significantly they proposed, in one scheme, that the trustees only build for the time being on the southern two-thirds of the site, leaving the lower lying northern third undeveloped with the exception of either a small building for the observatory in one variant and the powerhouse in another. "This reduces the present problem," as they explained, "to the determination of the best arrangements to be obtained on the southern half," which "seems to ensure for any plan that may now be adopted a greater likelihood of successful completion, not only because it is a smaller undertaking, but also because the men who are to follow us in the administration of the College are likely to have almost one-half of the space at their command free from all embarrassment to be dealt with by them in the light of their own time."[57] This was a new attitude toward the ethos of master planning and would have enormous consequences for Columbia's future interpretation of its original plan.

The trustees turned the problem back to their committee of three consulting architects, asking them to offer a critique of Ware's plan and to take up now the issue of style. They were to provide "a series of sketches affording a graphic expression of their ideas as to the proper artistic treatment," the whole to be presented after the summer recess. Once again the group was not inclined to work as a committee, in particular McKim and Hunt were no more eager to collaborate with Haight than they had been in the spring. McKim admitted in a letter to Hunt in early September that as far as he was concerned "'Uncle William' Ware's block plan, based . . . upon the plums offered in yours, Haight's, and ours" was nothing more than "a pudding–and a very indigestible one indeed. . . . We have done nothing yet, thinking it best to await your return," he admitted. "What Haight has done I don't know. I hear of large and important drawings containing domes, minarets, towers and steeples (in keeping with his plan)!!!"[58] Clearly for McKim the Beaux-Arts classicism that he and Hunt shared was in stark contrast with the eclecticism of Haight's Gothic.

Over the summer Low had visited the World's Columbian Exposition and returned an enthusiastic advocate–if he had not been already–of monumental classical architecture enhanced by landscaping and a full complement of "civic art." In an article for the *Columbia Literary Monthly* he took the exposition as proof positive of America's cultural and political coming of age and noted the modernity of the classical: "The architectural forms that delight the eye had their birth in the classic days of Greece. On the other hand, the most modern knowledge and experience have entered into the adaptation of these forms for their special uses."[59] Clearly even the modern research university with its rapidly growing scientific laboratories and engaged curriculum could be combined with a campus architecture that returned to the aesthetically uplifting forms of the ancient world. To underscore his determination that Columbia's campus be the most accomplished architectural expression of the modern university, Seth Low negotiated to purchase a series of great folio volumes on recent German university architecture from the German educational display for the benefit of Columbia's architects and architectural students.[60]

By October the three architects were refusing to collaborate, labeling Ware's plans "radically defective" and advocating "as strongly as possible the importance of having the entire work designed by one architect" so that "the mistakes committed by the Universities of Harvard, Yale, and Princeton be avoided on your magnificent site." The Committee on Site met in a long session to review the situation. After drawing up a list of fifteen points about the program and handling of the site, they turned to a lively discussion of "the question of style." This ultimately would decide the matter. "In attempting the Gothic we shall at once appear to be imitating the English universities, and shall thereby suggest a comparison which can scarcely fail to be unfavorable to us." As for the classical, the trustees noted that "the present tendency in architecture in this country seems to be to develop in this direction," which had two significant advantages. It was "the style by which the greatest number of architects can express themselves with fluency and to advantage," given as the future campus would no doubt require the talents of numerous architects as individual philanthropists were found. In addition they noted that the classical architecture of Greece and Rome "is the style which will appeal most strongly to educated popular taste, and will be most likely to secure an imposing architectural effect."[61] This last consideration seemed to resonate with Low's continued insistence that Columbia seek to define itself as a university not only in the public eye but also in the public service, a sentiment that found its expression both in the text he penned for the attic of McKim's Low Memorial Library—"Maintained and Cherished from Generation to Generation for the Advancement of Public Good and the Glory of Almighty God"[62]—and in the plans for the university that took shape over the course of the next year. Both McKim's architecture and Low's inscription were intended to send dual messages of a new beginning and a great tradition. In offering a capsule history on the broad attic above the library's Ionic portico, Low hoped that students and visitors alike "shall feel . . . at once to be in the presence of a venerable and historic institution."[63]

McKim and Columbia's blueprint for the future

In late November 1893 the trustees decided that "the fact that Messrs. McKim, Mead & White constitute a firm and represent a certain continuity of existence is an additional consideration in their favor, in view of the long period of time likely to be required for the completion of the undertaking."[64] Pine drew up a contract with the firm in December, but the economic panic that winter dampened enthusiasm for hastening construction and moving the college to its new site by 1895, as originally hoped. While the trustees were eager for more time to seek contributions toward the cost of the site as well as the future buildings–Low himself subscribed for $1 million of the $3 million in 3 percent bonds that Columbia issued against the new land[65]–McKim, Mead & White were simply grateful for the work. By mid-1894, as Leland Roth notes, McKim was complaining to Mead that the firm needed "about a dozen large jobs to keep us out of the poor house."[66] With the time gained, the trustees and McKim, Mead & White spent the next year and a half refining the master plan and the design of the initial buildings before ground was broken. In April 1894 the trustees approved a plan (fig. 18), which was made public in May. But both the architects and the Committee on Site continued to work through the summer, presenting a substantially revised plan to the board of trustees in October, which was in turn approved and published in November (fig. 19).

Increasingly Low took a leading role, developing a close working relationship with McKim, the partner in charge of the Columbia project. McKim was, indeed, perfectly suited to win Low's confidence. He had academic credentials–a year at Harvard's Lawrence Scientific School and three at the Ecole des Beaux-Arts–and his firm was a prototype of the great corporate practices of the twentieth century, run on some of the principles of scientific management that Low sought to bring to both educational and governmental reform.[67] During these very years McKim was forcefully trying to motivate his fellow architects and potential benefactors to underwrite his own educational dream, the American Academy in Rome. Low found thus in McKim a fellow believer in the responsibility of America's cultural elite to build institutions through private philanthropy.

The April 1894 master plan was a direct translation of the committee's growing list of requirements and preferences into the system of freestanding building blocks that McKim was eager to introduce to urban campus design. In emulation of what would soon be called the City Beautiful approach to urban composition, the new site was organized around an axis of entry intersected nearly at its middle by a secondary cross axis. Along these axes McKim positioned the most distinctive functions of the program, those elements that would require individual architectural expression and whose monumental forms he hoped would structure the profile of the university and give variety to his composition. A grand library, planted squarely at the center of the site, or at least of the southern two-thirds of the site upon which McKim and the trustees were now focusing their energies, would provide an ideal symbol of the university as the union of all domains of knowledge with a commitment to research. Terminating the principal (north-south) axis would be a composite building, the largest structure on the campus, which McKim was content to leave as a diagram for the moment. This would combine gymnasium,

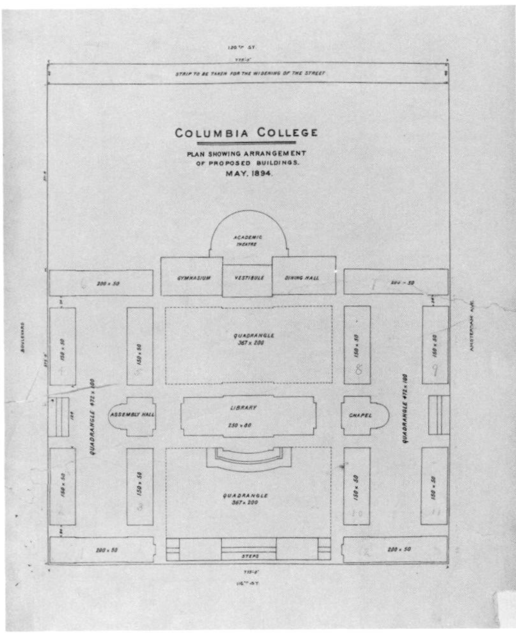

FIGURE 18 *McKim, Mead & White, Master plan for Columbia University, published by the trustees, May 1894 (cat. 13)*

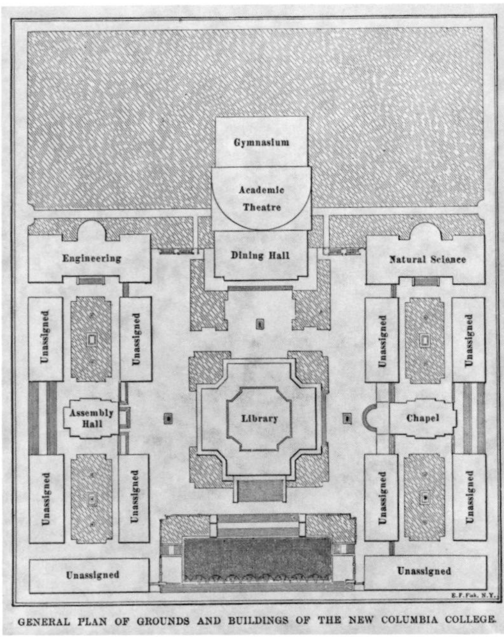

FIGURE 19 *McKim, Mead & White, Revised master plan for Columbia University, adopted by the trustees, October 1894 (reproduced from* Harper's Weekly, *3 November 1894)*

FIGURE 20 *Unknown Central Italian artist,* Ideal City, *late 15th century (Galleria Nazionale delle Marche, Urbino)*

dining hall, and an academic theater, creating a focus of student life such as Harvard had achieved fifteen years earlier with Ware and Van Brunt's Memorial Hall.

On the cross axis the library was flanked by an assembly hall to the west and a chapel to the east, behind which McKim called for broad staircases providing secondary entrances to the campus from the avenues. The chapel and assembly hall also would give spatial rhythm to the two long quadrangles on either side of the site, each bounded by a group of six rectangular "pavilions." These were left unassigned because the trustees were still debating both the distribution of Columbia's schools and departments in this period of curricular growth and the question of whether or not dormitories would be provided on the new site, which was too controversial to resolve rapidly. Designated on the plan only by their dimensions, the long, relatively thin pavilions would respond to the trustees' repeated insistence that the new buildings provide maximum natural daylight and ventilation as well as flexible floor space, all qualities once celebrated but now found wanting in Haight's Gothic buildings at Forty-ninth Street.

McKim's greatest contribution was a clear hierarchy between the large, public scale of the central courtyards, carefully terraced and sequenced, and the enclosed feel and smaller scale of the classroom/residential courts. Most of the buildings appear from this schematic plan to have their entrances on the interior of the site, with the exception of the library, which would be approached with great ceremonial dignity up a flight of stairs reached once the visitor had crossed the great courtyard opening off 116th Street. McKim called it alternatively Columbia's "vestibule" or "atrium" (fig. 5) and explained that it would offer visitors an impressive diorama of the campus's finest buildings and bring them immediately to the very heart of the campus's grand design.

This approach to urban composition—for in the end the campus was something of an ideal city in the spirit of the Chicago exposition—has often been characterized as Beaux-Arts. The hierarchical organization with its major buildings on cross axes and its sequencing of spaces is clearly related to the fundamental principles of architectural planning taught at the Ecole des Beaux-Arts, as is McKim's approach to terracing, which recalls French student analyses of the Renaissance villas of the Roman hills, a subject increasingly popular in the 1860s while McKim himself was studying in Paris. But whereas the French plans invariably interwove the axial organization of the site with the path through the buildings, McKim conceived of his structures as individual blocks to be composed in counterpoint to the axial paths. His work is closer in spirit to Renaissance projections of ideal cities, notably the famous painting now in Urbino, which depicts a paving pattern and a city

FIGURE 21 *Bird's-eye view of the new Columbia campus (reproduced from* King's Views of New York, 1906*)*

developing around a centrally planned structure directly echoed in Columbia's South Court (fig. 20).[68] This was typical of McKim's determination to bypass academic traditions and return directly to historical sources—a belief that was reflected in his efforts to have America open its own academy in Rome and his endowing traveling fellowships for young architects—as well as of his personal tendency to conceive architecture in perspectival and experiential terms. If the strong axes were clear on paper, the buildings would be discovered in a zigzag progression of oblique views, a principle that explains McKim's willingness to imagine his grand formal composition facing a crosstown street of the New York City grid. Whatever it looked like as a plan diagram, or even in the stunning bird's-eye perspectives drawn up by the period's most accomplished architectural renderers (fig. 21), McKim's library would be first experienced in oblique perspective by those approaching the center of the block along 116th Street from either of the avenues. This experience is enhanced today as visitors to Columbia are channeled into the center of the campus through the chasms of College Walk and discover Low Library's looming presence in a sudden oblique view before the power of the campus's geometry exerts its pull toward the central axis, marked by the statue of Alma Mater (fig. 22).

From the very first McKim used a plaster model of the site to work on the Columbia design, which kept his attention continually focused on topography and sculptural effects. These qualities were enhanced in the final master plan, which preoccupied him through much of the summer of 1894. The key difference that leaps to the eye in comparing the schemes of April and November 1894 (figs. 18 & 19) is the redesign of the library, the hub of the plan. At their October 1894 meeting the trustees approved without apparent discussion a resolution "that the shape of the library building be changed from a long rectangle to a Greek cross."[69] As Low later made clear, he was determined that the university's library be an utterly original

FIGURE 22 *Low Library and South Court, ca. 1898 (New-York Historical Society)*

FIGURE 23 *Charles F. McKim, First known sketch of plan and elevation of Low Library, 1894 (cat. 14)*

creation. The rectangular footprint was too close in conception to McKim's acclaimed design for the Boston Public Library, which firmly closed Copley Square, whereas at Columbia the problem was to lead the pedestrian to discover the sequence of subsidiary spaces that lay beyond on the upper platform. By becoming more emphatically freestanding the new building would be the focal point of the campus, less static in form and more distinctly in contrast with the rectilinear academic buildings. The change was momentous, for the building was transformed from a vaguely defined rectangle to a monumental, centrally planned structure that could control the entire composition of the campus from multiple points of view. This was something that had not been seen on an American campus since Jefferson's design for the University of Virginia or Joseph Jacques Ramée's for Union College, although McKim's partner Stanford White was at work in the same years on a rotunda library for the University Heights campus of New York University in the Bronx (fig. 13).[70]

Low would not make his surprise announcement before the trustees of his intent to donate $1 million for the construction of the library until May 1895, but it seems clear from letters that he was working discretely in this direction with McKim at least from the summer of 1894. Only this would explain McKim's decision to conceive a great domed building even as the trustees expressed concern over the price tag of the original design with its "portico and peristyle."[71] Although the president's decision to "adopt" the key piece in the plan and make it a memorial to his father may have been tinged with his desire to leave a memorial of his personal role in reinventing Columbia as a civic institution, it was also a strategic move.[72] All were conscious that the first building would set the style and tone for the rest. Low repeatedly reminded both the architects and the trustees that "it is essential to the accomplishment of our end . . . that unity of purpose shall prevail from the very outset and that the buildings first erected shall serve as the types for those which are to follow,"[73] while Pine, ever mindful of Columbia's balance sheet, reminded Low that "the appearance of the first two or three buildings will greatly effect in assisting or retarding us from raising money for subsequent buildings."[74]

Over the course of the next year McKim and Low worked ever more closely not only on the library but also on the overall composition of South Court. Low served as the intermediary, smoothing McKim's proposals through the meetings of the trustees and defending McKim against Pine's mistrust of architects and of "the risk we run of being led into expenditures much greater than we anticipate or approve."[75] Initially Low was himself a bit unsure of McKim's vision, even penning a sharp critique of the design for South Court. While Pine was alarmed at the expense of the grading and terracing needed simply to prepare for buildings, Low was alarmed at the loss of the site's greenery and reposeful atmosphere and drafted a forceful letter to McKim. "So far as my influence goes," he wrote, "not a single tree or blade of grass shall disappear from that enclosure except upon compulsion. Trees and grass of course must

FIGURE 24 *View of Riverside Park and Morningside Heights, 1903 (cat. 17)*

give way to buildings, but I am opposed to everything like an artificial grading which will substitute for grass and trees a stiff and formal area. If your architecture demands the later, I am prepared to say now that it is not what we want."[76] On second thought Low set the letter aside for a greatly toned-down wait-and-see exposition of his reservations. A few days latter, Low shepherded McKim's preliminary plan through a meeting of the trustees, getting them to agree on the principal grades of the site and the disposition of buildings and indicating that they would reconvene in October to consider "elevations of typical buildings, together with all important information concerning the buildings which should be immediately erected."[77] McKim wrote triumphantly the very evening of the meeting to his friend and future client Thomas Newbold: "I have had a tremendous meeting of the Columbia committee . . . by far the most satisfactory we have had. They endorsed the plan in all its details. . . . I was glad for Mr. Low too, because he was so pleased to have his committee stand by him unanimously. Altogether it has been a red-letter day."[78]

McKim worked on the library through the spring and summer, consulting frequently with Low. "Before leaving the city, I was fortunate enough to hit upon the idea of a Library in consultation with McKim," Low wrote to Pine from Bar Harbor, revealing also that he had shown the preliminary library plans to President Eliot of Harvard, President Gilman of Johns Hopkins, and President Adams "now of Wisconsin University, but who was president of Cornell at the time their new Library was built."[79] On 6 July 1894 McKim wrote to Mead: "The scheme for the Library has undergone many changes. Last week we struck it."[80] On 24 July he was obliged to write to White that he could not join him in Europe on "the delightful journey you laid out for me," since "President Low cut out for me such a lot of work that it simply [has] made my proposed trip out of the question."[81] On the back of the letter (fig. 23) is the first known sketch for the centrally planned, Pantheon-inspired library. McKim conceived a domed building—perhaps influenced by Low's continual insistence on the unity of the university—where the low-profile dome of the Roman Pantheon, which he had already used in his Agriculture Building at the Columbian Exposition, was combined with the high drum of Hunt's Administration Building (fig. 3). Like any Beaux-Arts–trained architect, McKim defined for himself in this preliminary sketch the essence of the problem he was trying to solve architecturally: how to give Columbia the aura of antiquity and a majestic, domed profile for a grand public building in a modern city. McKim's dome would command not only a grand and unified campus but also the emerging monumental landscape of Morningside Heights, where the dome of Grant's Tomb and the lantern of St. Luke's Hospital were already rising and where the great towers of St. John the Divine were projected (fig. 24).

The changed architectural chord struck by the centrally planned and domed library led to subtle adjustments of both the background faculty buildings and the subsidiary accents of the domed Assembly Hall and Chapel, as well as a refinement throughout the plan of the rhythms and patterns between the buildings and open spaces. With its corners chamfered, the footprint of the library building would set up a series of diagonal views. These were marked on McKim's plan, approved in November 1894 (fig. 19), by monuments set before the buildings occupying the cardinal points of the plan. The form of the composite building at the culmination of the principal axis was as yet undecided, but McKim turned it ninety degrees from his original suggestion of a long bar. In this way the building, which would rival Low Library in monumental expression, would come into view only as visitors arrived in the lateral courts before the Assembly Hall and Chapel. These buildings, in turn, were pulled away from the library, giving the whole plan a greater spaciousness and ease and cleanly dividing the lateral quadrangles into a series of four bounded courtyards. McKim was perhaps responding to concerns raised over the density of his plan, which struck several trustees as overcrowding, although Low was quick to point out the dangers of judging a model that "gives us a bird's-eye view of the situation, which in matter of fact will never be had."[82] Later critics would fault this revised plan for failing to terminate the two great paths flanking the library building.[83] It is also possible to argue that here McKim acknowledged that in the future a connection to the lower part of the site—to be left for the present as "a fine grove of oaks and chestnuts"[84]—might exploit these view corridors. He designated stairs to the lower level to be placed here, although as we shall see this was one of the great unresolved features of his plan.

Discussion and reservations from both the trustees and faculty members, including Ware, continued even after ground was broken. In December McKim fended off another attack on the dimensions of the court, as well as suggestions that grassy slopes be used in place of the secondary flights of stairs he imagined rising at either side of the courtyard. As McKim explained, the court was the vestibule not simply to the library but "to the whole University system." "Now, as at Chicago," he tutored Low, "the keynote to the solution of the Columbia site exists in the development of the terrace system and the consequent resulting court on the south, by means of which the center of the plot is immediately brought into contact with 116th Street."[85] He compared it to the piazza of St. Peter's and to Michelangelo's Capitoline Hill in Rome as well as to the forecourt of the Grand Trianon at Versailles.

The design nonetheless was a real challenge to Pine and Low's notion of dividing the program into individual pieces that could attract donors of named memorials. For McKim's "system" involved moving a great deal of earth and doing considerable foundation work, which would considerably raise the costs of the early buildings at the north end of the site. The earth excavated for the South Court was to be transferred to the north end of the site, where it would be used as infill behind a great retaining wall made up in part by the foundations of the three buildings across the northern edge of the plateau. Once he understood the necessity for implementing McKim's plan, Low lobbied the trustees strenuously to complete the court as rapidly as possible: "This will give to the grounds an air of dignity and importance immediately . . . in such a way as to convince the community of our determination to carry our project, great as it is, to a successful issue."[86] By the autumn of 1895 the court was taking shape, and Low was enchanted with the result: "The creation of the platforms on the grade 150' I look upon as a work of genius. More and more, as the scheme works out, this will be seen to remove the plan out of the region of the commonplace, and to stamp the conception as one of those happy suggestions by which the artist makes whole communities his debtor. I count myself fortunate to have been permitted to collaborate with you in such an enterprise."[87] Until his death McKim

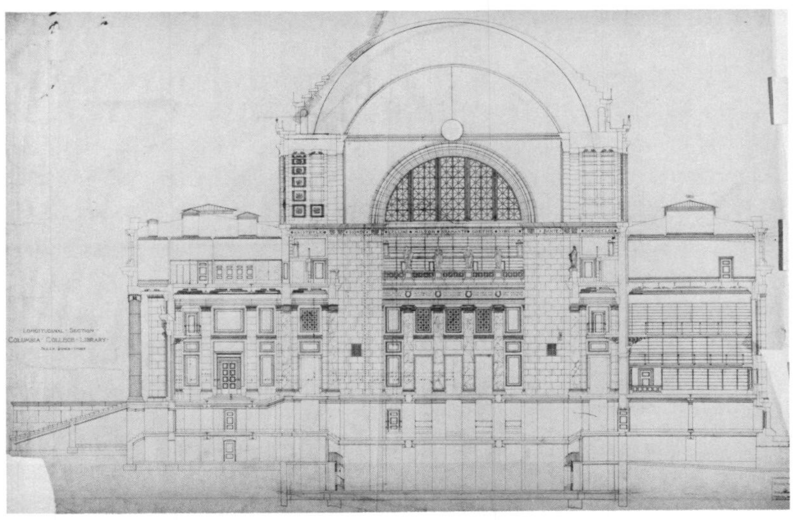

FIGURE 25 *McKim, Mead & White, Low Memorial Library: longitudinal section, 1 March 1895 (Avery Library)*

would fight nearly perennial efforts of the Columbia's directors of building and grounds to overplant South Court with shrubs and vines (fig. 21). He was determined to achieve something of the urban effect by patterning this vestibule and using materials that recalled the urban visions of the Renaissance or the brick patterns of the floor of the Roman Forum, which he cited as inspiration for Columbia's herringbone brick pathways. Even today, on fine spring days, the stairs are at once a forum and an arena for the Columbia community. This civic landscaping, crowned by Low Library, is at once Columbia's greatest architectural asset and most memorable architectural image.

The detailed design, furnishings, and ornamentation of the library–in particular the inscriptions that Low would pen to underscore his vision of the library as the microcosm of the university as coordinated academic disciplines and professional pursuits–would become wholly Low's after he stunned his fellow trustees by interrupting the board meeting on 6 May 1895 to announce his gift of $1 million for the building (fig. 25). A gift of virtually unprecedented size, rivaled only by John D. Rockefeller's recent gift to the University of Chicago, it was celebrated and analyzed in the press for days. "Only Four Men have been so generous as President Low," the *New York Sun* blazoned across its front page: "In the history of this country there are only a dozen men who have given away during a lifetime a million dollars."[88] Later McKim would refer to this great synergy of architecture and philanthropy when he wrote to Low of his first impressions of the Acropolis in Athens, which he visited in the spring of 1896, taking measurements of the Parthenon's great stylobate, or pedestal. "As you can imagine I have studied the subject of platforms wherever I have gone with eager curiosity and without venturing any bold comparisons I look more than ever confidently to the development of yours as a *pedestal* upon which the University may rely for popular as well as actual support."[89]

Low's gamble was successful. Minutes after applause subsided in the trustees' meeting, the president was seconded by William C. Schermerhorn, who offered $300,000 to raise the first of the academic buildings, to be devoted to the natural sciences, growing in importance and prestige since the School of Pure Science had been formed three years earlier. Rising over the great retaining wall forming the northern edge of the pedestal, Schermerhorn Hall and its pendant–the future Havemeyer Hall–would be the largest and most expensive of the faculty buildings, not only because of the extensive foundations required but also because of the apsidal projections at the rear of each providing for large lecture halls. These two buildings, together with University Hall, whose hemicyle was to house the gymnasium and a Greek theater above, would provide powerful foundation walls of massive stone, a sublime effect in the natural setting of the Grove –as the bucolic northern edge of the site was bapitized early on–consonant with the vocabulary of rustic engineering Olmsted had pioneered in New York's parks. While Schermerhorn would have a personal role in many of the details of the first faculty building, both he and his fellow trustees were keenly aware that his building would establish norms for those to follow, some of which would probably be the work of as yet unknown architects specified by future donors. These designers would be held to the guidelines of the master plan to respect volumetric envelope, cornice line and roof profile, and most importantly material.

FIGURE 26 *View of the upper campus shortly after the opening of the university in October 1897 (reproduced from* American Architect and Building News, *1898; Avery Library)*

Creating a vocabulary for Columbia

The design of Schermerhorn Hall (fig. 21) preoccupied the trustees, president, and donor as no other building would for decades to come. Already in the fall of 1894 Low had wondered if the same spirit of simplicity that he and McKim were developing in the monumental library should also prevail in the pavilions. Perhaps these should be ornamented so as to appease the trustees, who were still unsure of Columbia's new scale and classical imagery. "I note what you say in regard to the Faculty buildings and appreciate the importance of winning over the Gothic gentlemen of your committee in all legitimate ways," McKim replied on 8 September 1894. "My experience, however, teaches me that their reasoning is as medieval as their taste, and I honestly believe that the right way is not to sugar-coat our exteriors with compromising features but to meet the problem fairly and squarely in the face as we have, under your leadership hitherto done."[90] By October Low was anticipating McKim in his drive for simplicity and grandeur. Writing to McKim of "our plans," Low warned McKim: "I am afraid that you are allowing your sense of the ornate to dominate you too much. No one of the other buildings seems to me to have the fine simplicity of the Library."[91] McKim fired back a gleeful response to his client and pupil in monumental design: "To make these buildings akin to the Library in design, of course would be to accomplish the most consistent and therefore the most perfect result."[92] McKim was after hierarchy and maintained always that the faculty buildings should form a discrete background foil to the monuments in his ideal city. As Low explained to Pine, fearful of monotony: "'variety' we shall have a-plenty, the Library, the Theater, the Chapel and the Assembly Building are as widely separated from each other in design as in purpose. In addition to this, we have the physical difference in plane between the inner and outer courts, which must necessarily result in numerous and widely different perspectives, so I grow more and more of the opinion that our Faculty buildings will be needed by their simplicity to correct rather than promote variety."[93]

McKim was determined to establish a syntax for these buildings, despite their role as background elements, so that each might be given a subtly different expression both to underscore its place in the larger composition and to allow, through ornamental details, variety as well as reference to the specific functions and donors of each structure. As McKim explained to Low, "the architecture of a new Columbia should be marked by an elastic character, less formal and severe according to the greater or lesser importance of each building."[94] Only the four larger pavilions – Schermerhorn and Havemeyer Halls at the north end of the upper platform and two more planned for 116th Street to frame South Court – would be graced with projecting porches at their central entrances and sometimes by limestone facing on their center bays, at least as McKim envisioned them at this point (fig. 26). These larger masses would be subtly broken up by slightly projecting end pavilions, and their more extensive limestone quoining and trim would create a subtle tonal hierarchy between them. The eight smaller buildings enclosing the courtyards would be somewhat more austere in handling and have a much higher percentage of brick to limestone. All of the pavilions would have overscaled sash windows, which would both allow for maximum light and ventilation, a request common to the list of desiderata submitted by each individual school in 1892, and lend the buildings a monumental, institutional scale.

McKim had suggested to the trustees in 1893 that the pavilions be built of limestone, like the library, but offered that for the sake of economy brick with limestone trim might be substituted. Cost was not, however, the only issue involved; for when the trustees called on the Olmsted firm to review the campus architecture and landscaping in late 1894, they reported back that "the introduction of brick in the walls of the minor buildings . . . is a very reasonable concession to the desire for homeliness and domesticity which some of the trustees very naturally associate with the life of the college."[95] Despite this assessment McKim never waivered from his vision of the pavilions as the Americanized background palazzi in an ideal Renaissance townscape.

In late 1895, as construction was under way on the foundations of Schermerhorn, the precise color of brick and the handling of the mortar joints was still being debated. The yellow brick that White had chosen for the University Heights campus of New York University, and which had the advantage of blending with the stone trim for greater volumetric effect, was quickly passed over. But McKim was eager to steer the trustees away from the somber palette of Haight's Victorian Gothic brickwork at Forty-ninth Street toward the colors and more variegated effects he increasingly admired in American colonial work. Ware argued in favor of a "brownish brick," which would appear as stone, reflecting the aesthetic and palette of an older generation of architects. "The combination of a light colored stone and really red brick presents a contrast so violent as to be difficult of . . . monumental treatment,"[96] he warned, while conceding that McKim's specification of over-burned "Harvard Brick" was an acceptable compromise. For examples McKim pointed the trustees not to Cambridge, Massachusetts, but to some of his firm's recently completed Georgian-style clubhouses and mansions in New York, notably the Harvard Club on Forty-fourth Street. Even during construction the trustees continued to fine tune their choices—since "whatever materials are chosen now must be adhered to through the entire group of buildings."[97] They had McKim lay up different sample courses on trial elevations of Schermerhorn Hall before settling on light colored mortar and raked joints to offset the brick's saturated tones, frequent black accents, and warm texture. Some, including Low, already imagined "ivy . . . trailed upon the brickwork," but McKim was content to leave that battle for later. The trustees' eagerness to capture historical and collegiate overtones is echoed in the pamphlet distributed at the 1896 dedication of the site, which explained that the pavilions "represent . . . a reversion to the best construction of the Colonial period. Schermerhorn Hall offers a pleasing reminder of Old King's College."[98]

Differences in perception resurfaced in the debate over McKim's plan to terminate each pavilion with an emphatic copper cornice, in which the traditional crowning member, or cymatium, would be replaced by broad copper gutters. This detail underscored McKim's conviction that all the elements of classical architectural grammar had contemporary relevance, indeed that even in a building dedicated to scientific research the classics and modern technology were compatible. "The attempt to bring these buildings into relation with the library by crowning them with a conspicuous Greek cymatium, or gutter, seems to me somewhat ill advised," Ware warned. "It hardly suits their almost Colonial character, and enhances rather than disguises the discrepancy of style."[99] Others felt it an unnecessary expense or questioned its efficacy as guttering. McKim defended this detail fiercely, having perspective drawings prepared of Schermerhorn seen from different points of view, and offering comparisons both with and without the crowning element to demonstrate that what might seem to be an insignificant feature was in fact vital to the aesthetic effect of his whole conception.

FIGURE 27 *View of Columbia's Broadway elevation north from 114th Street, 1927 (Columbiana Collection)*

The cornices, which even today are one of the most distinctive and memorable characteristics of the Columbia campus, were indeed no small detail. Their scale was the key to solving one of the most vexing challenges to McKim's quest for pleasing proportions for each individual building and for an architectural language that could accommodate the great discrepancies of height between the interior and exterior facades of the campus. After terracing the site for the library, each of the outer pavilions would have a four-story facade facing the great upper platform, while the street facades would have one to two additional stories to accommodate the contour of the avenues, which crested between 117th and 118th Streets before falling away rapidly toward the north (fig. 27). The emphatic horizontals of the copper cornices and an overscaled, rounded torus molding on the granite bases of the buildings would distract the eye from the great discrepancies in real overall height between the buildings facing the street. In the sweeping oblique views of the campus along Amsterdam Avenue and Broadway, the pavilions appear to sit above a uniform pink granite plinth, demarcated by the moldings continuing across both the lower stories of the buildings and the intervening exterior walls of the vaults that McKim, Mead & White designed between each pavilion. Learning from the latest research on the optical refinements the Greeks introduced into their temples to correct for parallax and other optical distortions, McKim was a master at adjusting curvature in both individual buildings and larger compositions to maximum perspectival effect, even adding an upward curve to the steps of Low Library to counteract parallax.[100] He even specified that the city sidewalks surrounding the campus be laid in the same herringbone brick, both to create a unity of composition on Columbia's city frontages and to reduce glare from the street plane, which would call the eye too strongly to the ground plane.[101]

Equally challenging was the interior disposition of the pavilions, where the harmony of the ensemble and the logic of a standardized type of building would need to be negotiated with the demands of the trustees and faculty for spaces carefully suited to meet the needs of an increasingly diverse and specialized curriculum. "It should be remembered," engineering faculty members noted, "that a modern university is composed of laboratories and workshops and not cloisters, and the utility of the various rooms should not be sacrificed, as it so often is, to attain architectural effect."[102] Laboratories for the young Faculty of Pure Sciences and for the growing engineering departments of the School of Mines were the most pressing need, along with the museum collections, which were vital components of scientific teaching. In addition to lecture rooms, almost all of the university's departments had recently adopted, or looked forward to doing so on Morningside Heights, the seminar system imported from German universities. But while each of the four buildings put into construction in 1895 and 1896 – Schermerhorn, Havemeyer, Fayerweather, and Mines (Mathematics) – was devoted to a single or a related group of scientific or engineering functions, it would be necessary for all the buildings to host a variety of temporary functions for a number of years until additional funds could be raised to begin to fill out the unassigned sites on McKim's plan. This was, of course, equally true of the library, which housed the Schools of Law and of Political Science for over a decade, as well as university administration. All these functions were expected to find future homes in purpose-built buildings.[103] From the beginning flexibility of space was as much a necessity as an ideal for an institution that wished to accommodate progress and change in both the subjects and methods of teaching and research. Schermerhorn Hall, founded as a natural history building, was unique in housing from the start nothing but its intended departments of botany, geology, mineralogy, and zoology. The smaller Fayerweather Hall was intended as the physics building, but it also gave shelter in the early years to the departments of mechanics, astronomy, and mathematics, as well as modern languages, while Havemeyer Hall was officially the chemistry building but housed the School of Architecture on its upper floors. Although each of the schools supplied the architects with their ideal requirements, the trustees requested from their earliest discussions that "the floors should be supported independently of the partitions, as in modern office buildings, so that the partitions may be changed in position as convenience may require; and that the arrangement of windows should be determined with due regard for the uncertainty as to the size and destination of the rooms."[104] The perennial remodeling of McKim's pavilions and the continual musical chairs of departments on the Columbia campus in the century since the first four pavilions were opened is testimony to McKim's success at creating a formal plan and what he called "elastic character." Schermerhorn Hall, unfortunately shorn of its grand stair hall, houses today only one of its original departments, geology, along with two departments, art history and psychology, that did not yet exist in 1897.

Enough of the buildings were in place when classes opened on the new campus in October 1897 to suggest that an entirely new Columbia had been born. The press and the thousands who attended the open houses sponsored that autumn substantiated Low's claims, which he formed both to summarize his achievements and to convince others to contribute the missing pieces:

> Anyone placing a building upon this site, in such a location, may be confident of a memorial at once enduring and useful, and one which will be before the eyes of the people of the United States almost more than any college building in the land. Every stranger that visits New York will certainly visit these heights to see the monumental buildings which will be clustered there; and the people of New York, in showing them to their friends, will become familiar with them, and their affection will dwell upon them as among the most important buildings that minister to their civic pride.[105]

The architecture critic Montgomery Schuyler, who remained steadfast to his credo of architectural truthfulness even as he sought to accommodate skyscraper construction and the new classicism to that ideal framed in the ethics of Victorian Gothicism, confessed nostalgia for Haight's buildings, demolished soon after Columbia sold the Forty-ninth Street site in 1898. "All of us regret, and regret with a mixture of resentment that they should have been superseded by something so different."[106] While he recognized that Columbia's move "coincided with the beginning of the development of a second-class college into a first-class university," he lamented that "architecturally, it was marked by the complete obliteration of the architectural traditions of Columbia."[107] Haight's approach had been purged as Columbia sought to free itself of "Anglicanism," only to fall under a faith less grounded, since the trustees "had been dazzled by the recent and sudden glories of the scenic architecture of the Chicago Fair."[108] Schuyler was not afraid to point out that in the library the quest for a municipal monument had not been compatible with the needs of a library, claiming that a "French friend" maintained that "the library of Columbia is a 'library de luxe and not de books'," but even he could not fail to admit than given the Classical Revival, "the library is, without question, a carefully and successfully studied performance in its own kind."[109] The pavilions were another matter:

> Brick fronts simply do not become specimens of classical architecture because you plaster little porticoes against them, nor even because you erect them on Cyclopean bases of huge slabs of pink granite. . . . The group of Columbia . . . is a failure. One might take it for a hospital, for a group of official buildings, for almost anything but what it is. You may admit that it is "municipal." You cannot possibly maintain that it is "collegiate."[110]

That, of course, was precisely what Low and McKim had set out to avoid.

Growth pains of McKim's master plan

Placing the missing pieces of the puzzle proved harder than Low, Pine, and Schermerhorn had imagined. In spring 1896 the Havemeyer family provided $450,000 for the pendant to Schermerhorn, with its expensive foundations and infrastructure, and proceeds of the Daniel Burton Fayerweather bequest were used to fund a building for physics. But already in 1896 the trustees were forced to build without the benefit of a donor the fourth pavilion they deemed essential from the start – to house the engineering departments (today's Mathematics Hall). Much of President Low's energies in the four years he spent on Morningside Heights before he was elected mayor of New York in 1901 were devoted to fund-raising. If prospective donors found it hard to imagine how their buildings might fit into the "City on a Hill" – as Low characterized Columbia in a memorable speech in 1896 – they could literally choose their benefaction from the large plaster model of the university buildings that the trustees asked McKim, Mead & White to have made. This would serve them not only in their own discussions of design issues but also in their efforts to publicize the university both at home and on the road. In the winter of 1896–1897 the model of Low Memorial Library was put on display at the American Fine Arts Society in New York. A year later, in 1898, it was sent to Omaha, Nebraska, to serve as the centerpiece of the Columbia University exhibition at the Trans-Mississippi Exhibition (fig. 28).[111] When that exhibition was reinstalled in 1899 at the Metropolitan

Museum of Art, existing and projected buildings were added to the model. "A noble memorial awaits the man who will complete the University Building, a model of which is to be seen in the Metropolitan Museum of Art," Low pleaded in his 1899 annual report.[112] Replaced in 1904 by a larger version that included McKim's vision of South Field, the new model was the highlight of the Columbia pavilion designed by McKim, Mead & White at the St. Louis World's Fair in 1904, and it returned to take up residence in a specially built "model house" that stood, until 1911, immediately to the west of the real Low Library (fig. 29).

Early in 1898 the trustees set up a permanent Advisory Commission on Art composed of an architect, a sculptor, and a painter to advise the trustees on the merits and siting of works of art offered by benefactors. Under the initial stewardship of McKim, Daniel Chester French, and Edwin Blashfield, the commission was charged with making certain that Columbia's City Beautiful aesthetic of monumental civic art would not be violated. French's own *Alma Mater*, accepted in 1900 and symbolic in many ways of Low's vision of Columbia's attitude toward the city, was the first major work to be accepted. It was followed in 1907 by Edward Clark's gift of the *Great God Pan* by George Gray Barnard, for which McKim designed a neo-Pompeiian setting at the northeast corner of the campus in the Grove (fig. 30). Two marble lions offered to flank the entrance to the library, however, were refused in 1905 after McKim and French found both the materials and the subject "inharmonious . . . and

FIGURE 28 *Model of Low Library exhibited at the Trans-Mississippi Exhibition, Omaha, Nebraska, 1898 (cat. 15)*

FIGURE 29 *Model of Columbia University and Barnard College on exhibition in the model house, 1908, photograph by A. Fowler (New-York Historical Society)*

FIGURE 30 *McKim's setting for George Gray Barnard's* The Great God Pan, *for the northeast corner of campus, ca. 1903; photograph of a lost rendering by Jules Crow (New-York Historical Society)*

wholly unrelated to the purposes of the Library." Donations from individuals and alumni of the flagpoles, fountains, monumental vases, benches, gates, and even the famous sundial arrived during the first twenty years to adorn the campus. Buildings proved more difficult. By the fall of 1897 Columbia was heavily in debt from its move, and in September of that year Low's bid to serve as mayor of the newly consolidated city was tainted by his opponents' taunts that a college president who had led his college heavily into debt "was not the man to head a great experiment in city government."[113]

University versus donor priorities: Earl Hall and the Chapel

By the time Seth Low left his office in Low Memorial Library in 1901 for a new one in city hall only one new building had been promised, the assembly hall immediately to the west of the library. Since 1897 he had expounded upon Columbia's greatest needs on every available occasion, putting at the top of each wish list the grand university hall building at the head of McKim's grand axis followed by a building for Columbia College. Tellingly, however, the first two buildings bequeathed after the university had settled into its new campus were neither these nor additional classroom buildings. Both the assembly hall and the chapel had been designated by McKim on his master plan as domed structures that would cut a silhouette in Columbia's campus profile, rivaling if not equaling the individual statement of Low Memorial Library. Each would permit a donor to realize a building for substantially less outlay than any of the classroom buildings, estimated in 1896 to cost a minimum of $250,000. McKim's harmonious pavilions were admittedly less appealing; they left only ornamental details to the discretion of donors eager to make their marks on campus, since the trustees insisted that future campus buildings bear either the names of historic figures related to the college or of the disciplines housed within rather than the names of the donor. This policy was, needless to say, short-lived.

William Earl Dodge, who offered $100,000 for Earl Hall (as the assembly hall would be named) in 1900, and Olivia and Caroline Phelps Stokes, who offered $200,000 for the chapel in 1903,[114] were established philanthropists in New York, committed to institutions in which spiritual and moral betterment were allied with social purpose. These donors reacted to Columbia's recent drifting from its religious roots, although neither wanted to underscore Episcopalianism per se. Dodge took a great interest in the use of Columbia's future assembly hall, insisted that it "not be used for distinct dogmatic or denominational teaching,"[115] required a charter that would permit Roman Catholic and Jewish students equal access, arranged with the YMCA of New York to manage the building (an agreement terminated in 1922), and endorsed its frieze inscription: "Erected for the students that religion and learning may go hand in hand and character grow with knowledge." He took an active interest in the conduct of the center and recommended members of Earl Hall's board of directors for years to come; but from the first he was little concerned with details of the architecture. McKim, Mead & White were given considerable freedom to transfer their original sketch for the building, published in the campus dedication pamphlet in 1896, into working drawings.

Although obligatory attendance at chapel had been abandoned with the move to the new site, Low confessed in his 1898 annual report that "I would like to see at an early date a permanent and worthy chapel erected for the University," noting that Columbia had never in fact had a freestanding chapel. Funds for St. Paul's Chapel (1904–1907) were not offered directly by the Misses Stokes but rather by their nephew I. N. Phelps Stokes, who, together with John Mead Howells, would serve as the architect of the building. This was the first time that the assumption that other architects could design the actual building blocks of McKim's master plan was put to the test. Any challenge to McKim, Mead & White's aesthetic precepts was unlikely, however, since not only had both young architects studied at the Ecole des Beaux-Arts, but Stokes had gone there directly from Columbia's architecture school. His architectural partner Howells was a nephew of William R. Mead of McKim, Mead & White. Howells & Stokes thus approached the chapel commission in the collaborative spirit defined first by the architects at the Chicago fair, respecting the footprint and approximating the profile established by McKim in his 1894 plan. Whereas McKim had imagined a building closer to the antique spirit of the High Renaissance, at least to judge by the glimpse of the chapel's Corinthian portico and low dome in a perspective view of the campus published in 1895, Howells & Stokes explored the entire range of classicizing historical styles that a domed central-planned chapel might assume, from the Raventine Early Christian to the Early Renaissance, even exploring the possibility of erecting a campanile so that the chapel's rear facade toward Amsterdam Avenue would offer a beckoning image. They settled finally on a Lombardic Renaissance design, which allowed them to exploit to fullest advantage both the structural and decorative capacities of brick, so that their building might, like Earl Hall, mediate between the monumentality of Low Library and the materials of the background pavilions. Inside they used to splendid effect the Guastavino tile technique that McKim had considered but rejected for the dome of Low Library.[116] For years afterward Stokes remained involved with the chapel, providing designs for memorial tablets so that, like the campus, a harmonic whole would not be disrupted by the wishes of individual donors and as late as the 1920s advising the president and the trustees on the colors and iconography of the stained glass windows in the transepts.

The first of the pavilions to fill one of the many empty sites designated on McKim's 1894 plan was also the work of another architect. In 1904 the mining magnate Adolph Lewisohn offered to donate $250,000 to build the School of Mines (today's Lewisohn Hall), located to the south of Earl Hall, on the condition that Columbia appoint Arnold W. Brunner, one of the city's most prominent Jewish architects. Lewisohn, president of United Metals Selling Company,

FIGURE 31 *Lewisohn Hall (originally School of Mines), ca. 1950 (Columbiana Collection)*

and a leading philanthropist—notably of Columbia's newest neighbor, the Jewish Theological Seminary—was precisely the sort of person Low had in mind when he underscored in his 1899 annual report that "it is rather a noticeable circumstance that two buildings have been given for the advancement of pure science, while only one has been given for the study of the applied sciences. When it is considered that it is the application of scientific laws which produces wealth, rather than the discovery of them, I hope it may occur to some of the many people whose fortunes rest upon the development of the engineering sciences, to do for them what the Havemeyer family have done in erecting the chemistry building."[117] Brunner was an accomplished practitioner of an institutional classicism much akin to McKim's buildings at Columbia. Since 1901 he had been at work on a similar pavilion-style scheme for Mount Sinai Hospital's new uptown site, developing there a pragmatic application of brick and Renaissance detailing to steel frame construction with adaptable interior space. His task, moreover, was facilitated by McKim, who turned over drawings, including those of the engineering building (Mathematics), which the trustees had specified as a model for the new building's exteriors. Brunner stamped his building (fig. 31) nonetheless with the more assertive and ponderous details, particularly in the roof and window brackets and in the cornice, that were signature elements of his designs elsewhere. But when Brunner refused to turn over part of his fee to McKim, the trustees felt obliged to formalize their arrangements with the firm of McKim, Mead & White, appointing them in 1905—eleven years after their master plan was accepted by the trustees—consulting architects of the university and drawing up an agreement of payment for the vast range of services they provided the university both on campus and at the exhibitions where Columbia continued to promote its reputation and seek new benefactors.

Unrealized designs by McKim for college and university halls

Nearly a decade would pass between McKim's initial buildings for Columbia and his next realized designs for the campus. During this time, however, his firm was busy nonetheless with designs to fill in key sites on the plan. These were to be assigned to College and University Halls, both of which were designed, debated, redesigned, and developed into detailed working drawings, even as the old tensions between college and university resurfaced. Neither building would ever be realized as envisioned in the 1890s. "My disappointment is so great as to amount to a personal grief that the College . . . should be shabbily housed," John Howard Van Amringe, dean and ardent defender of the college since the reorganization of the university in early 1891, wrote in an 1899 article. "Amid the splendid edifices that adorn this site and are an ornament to the city, the small and relatively mean building, euphemistically called 'College Hall,' is a reproach. It puts the whole business of the College at a disadvantage. It belittles the importance of undergraduate work, and gives to hundreds of visitors an impression that the College has a very inferior and little esteemed part to play in the great educational movement that is in progress here."[118] It must no doubt have been a disappointment to leave behind the buildings of the former Deaf and Dumb Asylum only to occupy for a decade those of an insane asylum, for the college was headquartered in the former Macy Villa of the Bloomingdale Asylum (today's Buell Hall) and would also, until it was demolished in stages for the construction of Earl Hall from 1901 to 1903, have space in the one wing of the asylum left standing after the completion of Low Library, West Hall. For more than a decade the college remained in temporary quarters while the young science departments commanded respect in purpose-built and architecturally noteworthy structures.

Yet since Columbia's arrival on Morningside Heights, the college, which some had once slated for elimination, watched its enrollments nearly double, reaching 465 in 1900. Van Amringe imagined the college framing the view of the university library above its majestic flight of stairs, housed in the two pavilions to either side of the South Court—which he hoped to have renamed College Court—and entered directly from 116th Street. Trained as he was in classical rhetoric, the dean wondered if it might be possible subtly to subvert the hierarchical code of McKim's syntax for the new Columbia. "College Hall East" and "College Hall West," as he proposed, might "be built of the same material as the Library." While they were to harmonize "with the general scheme of the architecture" in the science pavilions, "their style should be lighter and more ornate than that of the other buildings."[119]

In 1900 after the College Alumni Association launched a building fund, the trustees asked McKim, Mead & White to draw up designs for one or the other site. Low immediately realized that Van Amringe, who bitterly regretted the loss of intimacy and the atmosphere of the old Gothic buildings, had articulated one of the greatest challenges posed by McKim's supposedly "elastic" architectural vocabulary for Columbia, namely, would it be possible to craft an identity for the college within the larger university? Here was raised for the first time a problem at once institutional and architectural that has preoccupied deans and architects ever since as they have sought to give character to components of the university all the while respecting the classical harmony of McKim's original scheme. During his last months in office, the ever diplomatic Low turned again to appeasing old oppositions. "After reflecting upon the elevation of College Hall, I venture to make this suggestion," he wrote to McKim in March 1901. "You are really face to face with an exceedingly delicate problem, for you are trying to recall the Library, which is our most formal and stately building, in the College Hall, which ought to be the most domestic building of the group, the very abode of Alma Mater. I do not know whether the two ideas can be made to harmonize in any fashion." The options were admittedly limited. "I think the effect will be much improved if you will use the long rounded windows in the wings and for the central window between the columns, and substitute for

FIGURE 32 *View of the northern end of campus and of Teachers College, showing the incomplete University Hall, ca. 1910–14 (cat. 67)*

FIGURE 33 *McKim, Mead & White, First project for University Hall, 1896 (cat. 63)*

these long windows individual windows in the low-ceilinged rooms of the main and mezzanine floors. I do not know what canons of art this suggestion may violate; but it will at least conform to this canon, which you and I have assented to pretty generally heretofore that the outside fenestration should reveal the inside arrangement."[120]

McKim submitted a final proposal later that month, recommending that the building be located at the Broadway corner of 116th Street, since according to the announcement that year of the first line of the subway this corner was likely to make the first impression of Columbia in coming years.[121] A domestic feeling was, however, out of the question, and the trustees sought to reassure the college's advocates that even if the building would be "perfectly consistent with the buildings already erected," it would "on account of its conspicuous position . . . possess the character and dignity to which it is entitled on account of its importance historically."[122] Nevertheless, the site posed a nearly insurmountable financial challenge, for in order to achieve four stories on the level of the platform, the building would in fact have to be six stories in height, the lower two continuing the plinth along Broadway onto 116th Street. While this provided an additional two floors supplied with direct natural light on two facades, it also pushed up the estimated cost from $250,000 to $400,000 or more, at a moment when as Low admitted the university would need "to adhere firmly to the safe rule of expanding only as the funds are in hand."[123]

The hall for the college was not the only building to register escalating construction costs, exacerbated by the foundations required for building on the upper platform of the university. During these years Low stepped up appeals to alumni for Columbia's grandest unrealized project–University Hall, which was the singularly most complex and expensive component of McKim's grand design (figs. 32 & 33). Intended as the culmination of the site's principal axis, and planned as the social center for both students and faculty, the building was to incorporate a variety of functions into a single structure: dining hall, auditorium-theater for commencement and other large assemblies, and gymnasium. In addition it was to provide space for Columbia's growing administrative offices and to house the campus power plant. In both his April and November 1894 plans McKim had done little more than sketch a diagram, but by the time construction had begun in 1895 it was realized that at least the lower levels of the building would be required, both as an integral part of the great retaining wall separating the upper platform from the wooded northern end of the campus and to put the boiler house under cover. Not only would construction need to start in anticipation of a donor, but if this key building were to possess the unity of conception and grandeur required by its position in the plan, McKim would also need to prepare a design complete in most details. When the university opened in the fall of 1897, the lower parts of University Hall, up to the 150-foot grade of the campus platform, were completed, with a distinctive round apsed design rather than the squared off design projected in the earliest schemes (plate 4). The incomplete building housed McKim's extraordinary Grecian gym and swimming pool–briefly honored as the most modern of college athletic facilities–as well as the coal boiler, all under a temporary roof.

How to create architectural unity on a site with such a steep and significant drop in grade between its front and rear elevation, and in a building that was to house such a variety of complex functions, each requiring a monumental interior space, was a challenge both to McKim's capacities as a designer and to Low's and Pine's mastery of the new art of speculative philanthropy. McKim's design would go through extensive revisions over the course of the next decade as scheme after scheme was reviewed by the trustees each time a prospective donor or a new surge in alumni giving appeared on the horizon. McKim took Roman bath complexes as his controlling metaphor, for not only did these ancient buildings have a grandeur that he was eager to instill in American architecture–and ultimately would in New York's Pennsylvania Station (1902–1911)–but they had served as the veritable social centers of ancient Roman cities. Bringing together the most diverse spaces and functions, Roman architects had combined great assembly halls with sport and bathing facilities. For the great dining hall McKim proposed a lofty vaulted Roman bath space, entered through a broad Corinthian portico spanning the front of the building and announced, at least in his first design for the project, by a large-scale thermal window echoing the great windows in the drum of Low Library's dome.

While this part of the building was perched on the edge of the upper platform, the rear of the building was to be a soaring affair, beginning with a multilevel gymnasium and terminating in a great semicircle housing a theater based on a Grecian amphitheater. The lower level was pierced by a tunnel allowing 119th Street to pass through the site. Reconfigured by the university rather than dictated by the city commissioners, the street made a picturesque sweep through the Grove, much as Olmsted's carriage paths did through New York's parks. This was one of the few entrances to the campus accessible by vehicles, and those who know it today only as the service road for deliveries and trash removal will perhaps have difficulty imagining the alternative scenario that Pine sketched for a prospective donor in 1895: "The road . . . will pass under the academic theater so that the people will alight from their carriages as they do in the Vienna Opera House." He was quick to qualify, however, that the theater would be used "for public lectures, for the meetings of scientific societies, for fine concerts and oratories," while "its use for the purpose of amusement will be very limited indeed. The students may occasionally give a play there."[124]

Funding was indeed a challenge. The cost seemed to escalate with each new estimate: $500,000 in Pine's 1895 draft appeal, $600,000 for the lower stories only in Low's 1895 annual report, $1.5 million for the entire structure to a revised design in June 1896, by 1925 $3.5 million to complete the building. The trustees were confronted with a cost for the first time that seemed beyond the means of any single individual. Pine and Low devised a scheme whereby the alumni would be asked to fund the dining hall, renamed in Low's 1895 report Alumni Memorial Hall, which was to be "designed to make it the Valhalla of the University," filled with plaques and memorials of former students. The remaining functions and costs might be assumed by a single donor, as Pine explained in a form letter drafted in 1895: "The northern facade, as it has been designed, is, in my opinion, exceedingly graceful, and from the north nobody would be conscious that the building contained other functions than those of the gymnasium and the theater." While each new discussion led to a reappraisal of McKim's designs, even Professor Ware, one of the most skeptical viewers of the project, admitted its importance to the university's monumental presence on Morningside Heights: "The big sweep of the rear is dignified and imposing, and the enormous mass of the whole building, in its conspicuous position, would be a fine object for miles around."[125] Indeed, the design of University Hall was essential to provide the university a northern facade opposite Teachers College, since McKim's plan left this part of the campus unresolved in his great attention to his grand entrance from the south.

By 1897 Pine had devised a new scheme, which he was eager to put before the alumni. In exchange for a small contribution each alumnus would have his name included on tablets lining the walls of the dining room to be known as Memorial Hall; "there are very few graduates who will not pay $25 for immortality," he noted.[126] Money trickled in but never caught up with the escalating cost. In 1899 the trustees decided to build, as a temporary measure, the first story of the four projected above the 150-foot grade of the upper platform. This would provide a dining hall and a kitchen, which were absolutely necessary, since Morningside Heights was only just showing the first signs of residential and commercial development. In addition the vast footprint allowed for a large lecture hall for 1,500 students and offices for the superintendent of buildings and grounds, and the bursar, the first of the university's expanding central administrative functions to outgrow Low Library. This temporary floor, topped by two enormous smokestacks of the university's coal boiler, became an anticlimactic ending to McKim's grand axis; rebuilt after a fire in 1914 and rather pathetically crowned with ornamental vases in the 1930s, it stood as a perennial plea of presidential annual reports and a continuous embarrassment to the university's fund-raising efforts until it was demolished in 1962 to make way for Uris Hall.

The dormitory debate and a scheme for the Grove

It was neither lack of enthusiasm nor parsimony that defeated the president and the trustees' bid to the alumni in the 1890s, however, but a difference in opinion over Columbia's priorities. In 1894 Pine had already warned Low, who was planning a speech to the Alumni Association for the funding of various projects, not to allow the debate to move toward a vote: "If the matter is put to a popular vote among the alumni, the verdict will be practically unanimous in favor of a dormitory."[127] Indeed, so strong was alumni support for the idea that Columbia might at long last become a residential college on the new site, engendering not only a sense of "college life" but also a less local student body, that a scheme was even proposed whereby the alumni would endeavor to raise $400,000 to be split equally between the Alumni Memorial Dining Hall and a dormitory, with the proviso that the dining hall be financed and built first. The issue again boiled down to diametrical points of view that were in open opposition not only at Columbia but also at many other colleges, with powerful administrators embracing the ideal of the research university at the expense of the traditional nineteenth-century residential college. Dormitories, which were frequently a focus of alumni giving on many campuses, became the rallying cry of those who sought to reinforce the college tradition as opposed to those who felt that a university should take little interest in the students' lives outside the classroom.[128]

In private Low admitted that he was dead set against building dormitories on the campus, although he was not opposed to the development of student housing by the private market, even a private market in which the university or its trustees acted as investors. He was concerned about the college's extending its in loco parentis duties and was eager to keep the unused space on the campus for growth of the schools and the departments and to maintain the Green or Grove, as the wooded frontage on 120th Street was alternatively called, as recreational space. Both he and Pine were confident that the real estate market would provide dormitories once the need became pressing enough. A full year before Columbia moved to the new site, a joint stock company had been set up to build near the campus a dormitory to be called Hamilton Court. "I assume you are planning to secure control of a majority of the stock," Pine wrote to Low, expressing his concern that the project had been leaked to the press. "The newspaper statements seem to me unfortunate, viz.: in giving the impression that Hamilton Court is to be practically a hotel. . . . In so far as Hamilton Court departs from the usual idea of a college dormitory, it should be spoken of and considered as a club, for the club idea is as popular as the hotel is the reverse, and the club system of individual responsibility and respect for the rights of others is the one that should govern the administration of the Court."[129] Hamilton Court failed, as did a number of other projects in these years, including one for the corner of Amsterdam Avenue and 116th Street.

By 1898 Low had conceded halfheartedly to commission a study of on-campus dormitories. "The demand for [dormitories], as the sentiment reaches me, is almost universal, among young and old," the president noted in his 1898 annual report, admitting that while dormitories in the neighborhood would solve both the housing and proximity issues, as well as offer a sound investment for the owners, they could never "fully meet the wishes of those who want dormitories for the sake of their influence upon college life."[130] In late spring 1898 Low and Pine studied the question

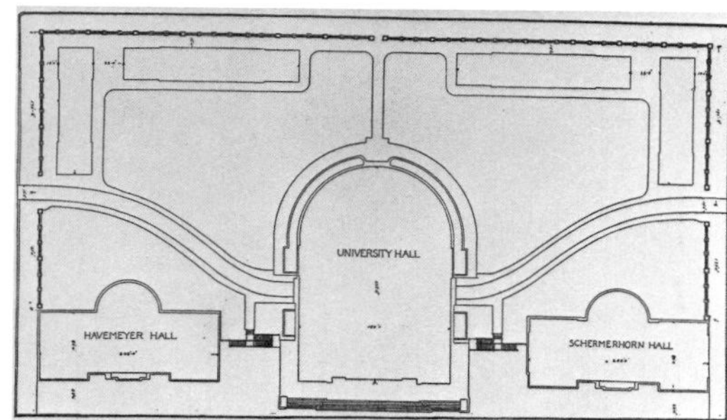

FIGURE 34 *McKim, Mead & White, Site plan for dormitories on the Grove, 120th Street from Broadway to Amsterdam, 1898 (Columbiana Collection)*

FIGURE 35 *McKim, Mead & White, Perspective view of a dormitory for the Grove, 1898 (Columbiana Collection)*

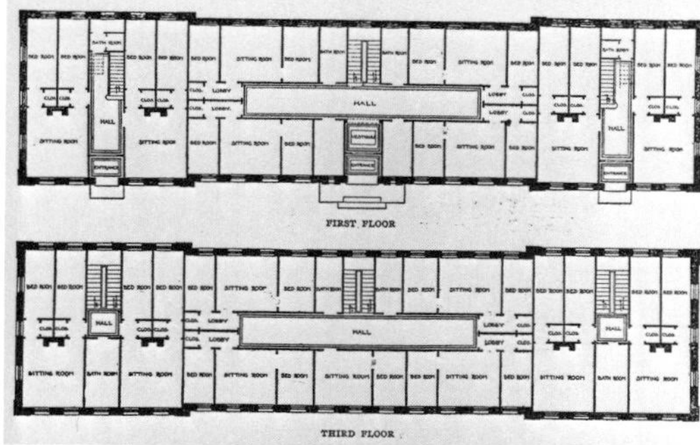

FIGURE 36 *McKim, Mead & White, Model floor plans for dormitories on the Grove, 1898 (Columbiana Collection)*

with McKim and Mead, weighing the practical and architectural advantages of two possible approaches to building dormitories on the new campus: assigning some of the unused sites of the Quadrangle, as it was now proposed to call the campus plateau, or sacrificing the open space of the Grove to create a residential precinct. The first option was quickly eliminated. Dormitories on the Quadrangle would violate the distinction Low had underscored a year earlier when he wrote to Pine that "the upper plateau must be consecrated . . . to dignity and silence" while "the lower plateau will serve its best purpose . . . if it is dedicated to the informal use of students. . . . It is absolutely impracticable to keep them on dress parade all the time," he added.[131] McKim, moreover, had quickly abandoned sketching ideas for developing any of the pavilions as a dormitory because he found it impossible to intermix the large scale of the existing faculty buildings with the multiplication of floor levels and smaller windows of a residential building. As Low concluded, this would only result "in marring the harmonious architectural effects which have been so happily secured."[132]

By summer 1898 McKim, working this time with Mead,[133] had in hand studies of the interior layout and the site planning for developing the Grove as a residential quadrangle, which were published in the *Columbia University Quarterly* (figs. 34–36) and worked up by Hughson Hawley as a bird's-eye view to show how the development might give a northern face to Columbia (plate 5). For this lower lying site McKim developed a repeatable pavilion type for the dormitories that was suitable to accommodating a maximum number of sitting room and bedroom suites with good light and ventilation and yet bore a strong family relationship to Columbia's established architectural vocabulary. At five stories, four large dormitories could house a sizable population—a total of 460 students—all the while deferring to the more monumental architectural composition above. McKim in fact seized the occasion to propose how Columbia might have a secondary facade to the city, a more domestic one to be sure but one that was no less hierarchical in the build-up of volumes and decorative detail, from the simple brick blocks of dormitories to the great swelling roofs of University Hall and Low Library, which would now be clearly visible as the hub of the campus from the north as well as it was from the south. The siting was also carefully studied to draw distinctions. Whereas Columbia's classroom pavilions created a formidable cliff to the avenues, the dormitories would be set back sixteen feet from the street behind the iron fence and 20-foot-high granite posts erected in 1897, which would be compared by the trustees to "the fence that surrounds the Garden of the Tuileries."[134] They would align in height with Milbank Hall, Barnard's first building erected in 1896 (architects Lamb and Rich) on the one-block site it had acquired across Broadway from Columbia at 120th Street. Like Milbank, the new dormitories would defer to the grander Columbia buildings atop the hill. To create a sense of community separate from the surrounding neighborhood, the dormitory entrances – three per pavilion in order to reduce interior corridors to a minimum – would all face inward to a wooded lawn.

The dormitory pavilions would achieve a more domestic tone by their simpler architectural detail, which McKim imagined as a more American neo-Georgian, and by tall chimneys. While he was eager to achieve a sense of seclusion and craft an intimate interior green space, McKim specifically rejected the perimeter block quadrangle approach recently pioneered to much praise by the architects Cope & Stewardson at the University of Pennsylvania, although he emulated their internal arrangements.[135] Not only was such an approach incompatible with the classical language of freestanding building blocks that he had defined for Columbia, and redolent of precisely the cloistered imagery that Low was eager to avoid at all costs, but large-scale building blocks also allowed McKim to imagine a large open space at the center of 120th Street as he had on 116th Street, thus providing at once a stunning view of the aligned volumes of University Hall and Low Library and a wooded entry to the campus at the north in contrast to the formality of South Court.

It was not only the values of college life versus the vision of a metropolitan research university that were at stake, however, in the standoff over these dormitories. The discussion over creating a residential college on Columbia's site raised the issues, destined to be perennial, of preserving open space and of Columbia's ability to control development in the surrounding neighborhood. Even before Columbia moved to Morningside Heights, both designed and left over open space was beginning to seem a precious commodity. Low warned that the Grove must be jealously protected: "If you will try to realize how quickly the city builds up when the march of improvement definitely reaches a specific quarter, you will appreciate, I am sure, how important it is to have space available," he wrote to Pine in April 1897.[136]

Instead of developing a collegiate atmosphere around dormitories in the Grove, the president hoped that a joint stock company might finally be successful in building dormitories immediately adjacent to the campus, perhaps even on part of the block immediately north of 120th Street, which Teachers College was consolidating at just that point. The possibility of a joint dormitory project between these two institutions in uneasy alliance had already been raised, and Low was happy to report that Teachers College's great benefactor and treasurer, Grace H. Dodge, seemed disposed toward collaboration: "I have seen Miss Dodge and she tells me that for the first time since they have been looking into the problem, their real estate agents inform them that every piece of property upon the block not controlled by themselves can be bought if prompt action is taken. This is a result greatly to be desired; for it would not only give us command of ample space for dormitories as conveniently located as possible, but it would permanently protect our northern front from objectionable neighbors."[137]

The threat, of course, was by no means confined to the north. Shortly after McKim's master plan had been adopted by the trustees, the Olmsted firm had reminded them that tabula rasa was a fleeting condition on Manhattan Island:

> As a further development of the general idea of the South Court, we think it will be a very great advantage if the buildings to be erected hereafter on the south side of the street, could be set back ten or twenty feet (or, if possible, even fifty or sixty feet), from the street line throughout the whole length of the court, and if you find it impracticable to obtain the consent of the present owners to such an arrangement, we would suggest that the trustees of the college purchase the property facing the College on the south side of 116th Street, or at least the part opposite the South Court, as an investment, and that if the land is leased for building purposes, the necessary restrictions for carrying out the court idea on the south side of the street, should be embodied in the leases.[138]

Five years later, by which time the neighborhood's streets were filling rapidly not only with town houses but also with the first apartment houses, an editorial in the *Columbia University Quarterly* sounded an alarm: "The erection [on the south side of 116th Street] . . . of commonplace or ugly buildings or of lofty structures would tend greatly to diminish the beauty and effectiveness of the present approach to the University."[139]

The addition of South Field

The president and trustees maintained a watchful eye on the blocks south of the new campus from the day construction began on the new site. The first line of the subway, begun in 1900 and opened in 1904, would follow Broadway and pass under Morningside Heights. It helped to fuel an already heated real estate market. In 1900 the trustees began negotiations with the hospital for an option on the two blocks south of 116th Street, which the students were using, by consent of the hospital, as playing fields. Although the trustees were not certain that it would be needed in the foreseeable future, they contemplated leasing the land, profiting from both rents and the power to issue restrictive leases, which would allow the university a say in the layout of its immediate surroundings and a control over the view from South Court, just then being outfitted with fountains and the first plantings. "It is probable that on the expiration of the leases and their renewals, say forty-two years hence, the ownership of the property would then be of the utmost advantage, either in connection with the extension of the University or as a continued investment," they concluded in autumn 1901.[140] One year later, however, forty-two years was reduced to tomorrow as a new sense of urgency colored President Nicholas Murray Butler's first annual report. He compared Columbia financially to "a giant in bonds" and insisted that "the area of the site now occupied on Morningside Heights will be entirely insufficient for the work of the University in the very near future. The growth of the past few years has been so unexpectedly great, and the demands on our resources are multiplying so rapidly, that it is the part of wisdom to consider how we may acquire possession of additional land. . . . Yet burdened with heavy debt . . . the purchase of additional land is out of the question unless funds are given for that purpose." While Butler already forecast Columbia's twentieth-century expansion, he also realized the greatest challenge to it: "While land in the vicinity of Harvard . . . can be purchased for about $18,000 an acre, and in the vicinity of the University of Chicago for about $50,000 an acre, land adjoining the present site of Columbia University is valued at more than $200,000 an acre."[141]

By the time Butler was writing his report, a group of wealthy businessmen had acquired the 9.3-acre site and agreed to hold it until 1 July 1903, while the trustees devised a scheme to purchase it. The trustees discussed the option of developing much of the plot as rental property, reserving the northern edge, facing Low Library, for dormitories, but Butler had a grander vision. Scarcely a month after the purchase was approved by the trustees, he wrote to Professor A. D. F. Hamlin, the newly appointed acting director of the School of Architecture, suggesting that the autumn-term studios of the architecture school "try their ingenuity on the development of the so-called South Field."[142] Butler didn't hesitate to sketch in words a detailed architectural program, as he would for nearly every new building added to the Columbia campus during his forty-three years in the president's office: "They might assume, for example, that the main entrance will be in the middle of the south boundary line of the property, and that the edge of the property will be occupied by dormitories on the east and west sides and for a certain distance along the north and south edges as well. It might be assumed, I think, that these dormitories will abut on the sidewalk, so as to make fences unnecessary. It would also be wise to assume that we shall want as much free space within the quadrangle formed by these dormitories as possible, perhaps finding place for an adequate College Hall at some point in the plan."[143] In his annual report he noted, "It should always be borne in mind that a dormitory is the one type of building used by a university from which an income is derived. A gift of $40,000, for example, if used for the building of dormitories, would provide, in perpetuity, an annual income of between $18,000 and $20,000 for the university."[144]

The Grove, meanwhile, was once again declared sacred. Pine called it "one of the natural beauties of the site" and stipulated that "this portion of the land is being reserved for unforeseen needs of the future,"[145] while the trustees, turning to the Olmsted firm for a landscaping plan, noted that it "bears some resemblance to the academic gardens of the old world, and it will one day be the pride of the University and of the city, if it can be treated with the care and attention that it should now have."[146] As the northern end of the campus was enhanced in its picturesque qualities, South Field—which enlarged the area of the campus by a full 50 percent—was to be developed as a dense extension, not as a contrast, to Columbia's grand composition.

McKim's institutional classicism reached its high water mark of influence during these years, and nowhere more than at Columbia, where Butler was aggressively courting McKim to take over the architecture school, which many felt had languished in recent years under Ware's inflexibility.[147] The year 1904 was celebrated not only as the 150th anniversary of the founding of

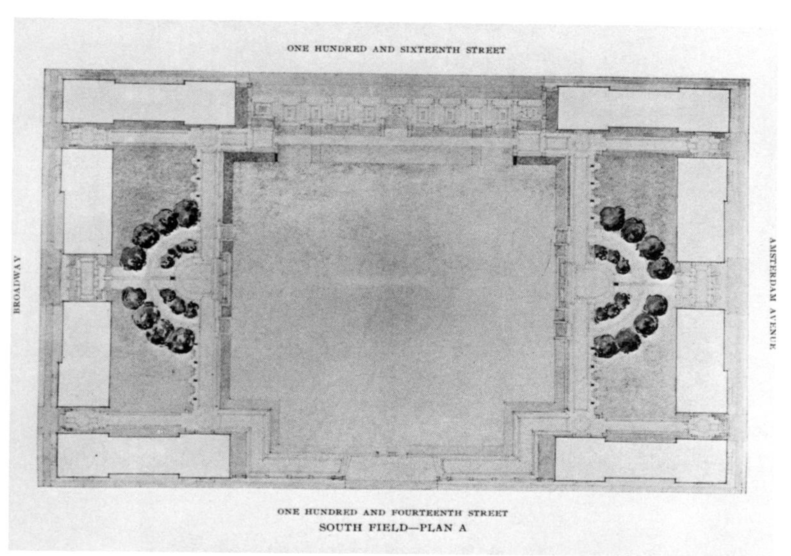

FIGURE 37 *Student project for South Field, 1902 (Columbiana Collection)*

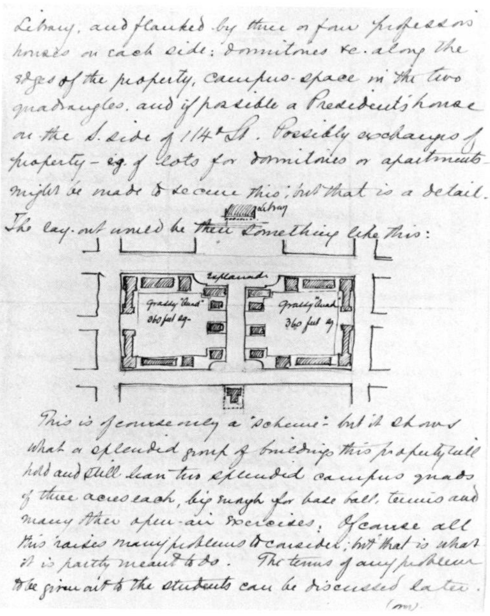

> Library, and flanked by three or four professors' houses on each side: dormitories &c. along the edges of the property, campus-space in the two quadrangles, and if possible a President's house on the S. side of 114th St. Possibly exchanges of property—e.g. of lots for dormitories or apartments—might be made to secure this; but that is a detail. The lay-out would be then something like this:
>
> Library
> Esplanade
> Grassy "Quad" 360 feet sq.
> Grassy "Quad" 360 feet sq.
>
> This is of course only a "scheme"—but it shows what a splendid group of buildings this property will hold and still leave two splendid campus quads of three acres each, big enough for base ball, tennis and many other open-air exercises. Of course all this raises many problems to consider; but that is what it is partly meant to do. The terms of any problem to be given out to the students can be discussed later.

FIGURE 39 *A. D. F. Hamlin, Plan for the development of South Field, as sketched in a letter of July 1902 to President Nicholas Murray Butler (cat. 51)*

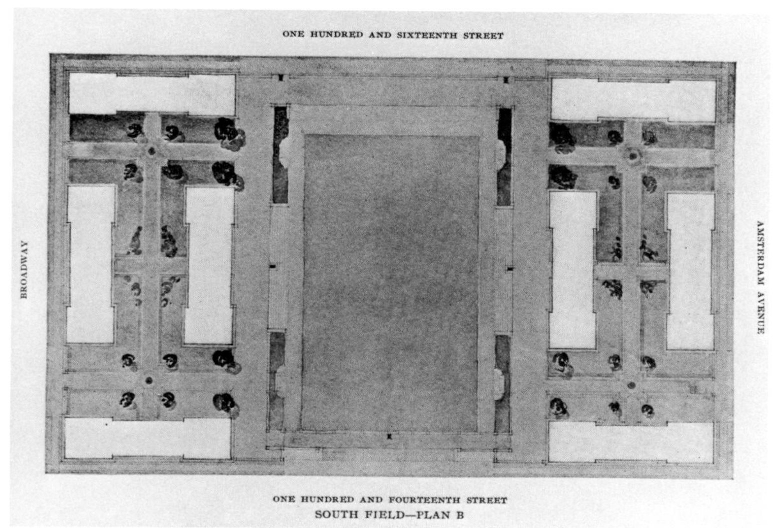

FIGURE 38 *Student project for South Field, 1902 (Columbiana Collection)*

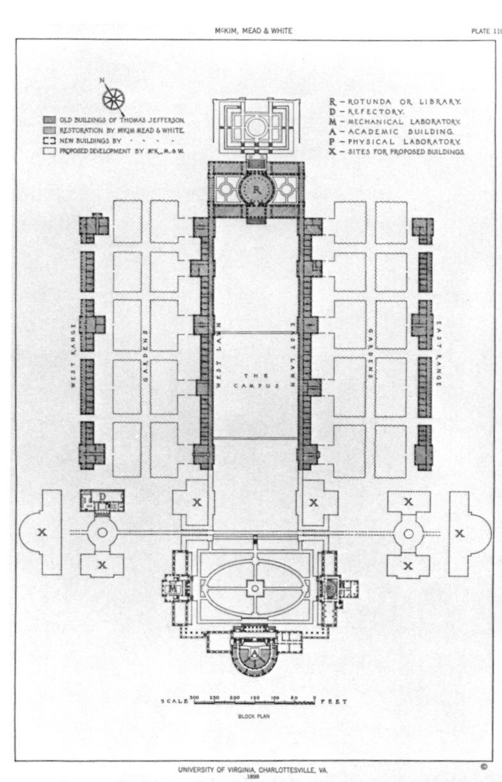

FIGURE 40 *McKim, Mead & White, Plan of the University of Virginia showing the firm's addition of Campbell Hall which closed the famous perspective of Jefferson's campus design (reproduced from* Monograph of the Work of McKim, Mead & White *[1915])*

King's College, inaugurating a renewed rhetorical insistence on Columbia's place in America's revolutionary mission, which would gain in rhetorical flourish and force with every year of Butler's presidency, but also as a new beginning for the expanding university. At commencement in May, McKim was awarded an honorary degree. By autumn cornerstones had been laid for the first two buildings that his firm would erect on their quickly accepted master plan for South Field. And the grand vision of an expanded Columbia was being celebrated at the St. Louis World's Fair with a new plaster model in McKim's specially designed Columbia Pavilion (fig. 29).

Although McKim declined the directorship of Columbia's School of Architecture, he agreed to open, in 1905, one of the three external ateliers by which the school set out to emulate more closely the French Beaux-Arts method of training. Given McKim's stature at Columbia, and the extent to which the planning of the campus was upheld as an exemplar of urban design in these years,[148] it is hardly surprising that the student designs for South Field in 1902 and 1903 bear such a strong resemblance to the alternatives explored by McKim's own office just a few months later (figs. 37 & 38). The most striking difference, aside from a less assured proportioning of open and built spaces, is the enormous amount of space left open by the students at the center of the site by which they sought at all costs to preserve the sports fields.

The only discordant voice was Hamlin himself, who had already sketched an idea for the site two days after Butler proposed that the architecture school take up the challenge (fig. 39). "My suggestion involves the sacrifice of the athletic field feature, which must inevitably go in time, as land becomes more and more valuable," Hamlin noted, warning Columbia not to compromise the potential of the site by making a temporary use determinant. Such foresight, moreover, would offer "the incomparable advantage of a worthy *approach* to the esplanade [as he called 116th Street] and the library."[149] A processional approach and distant axial view of Low Library would thus be obtained, something all but impossible in the New York City grid plan, except where large blocks of land could be assembled to obtain views down side streets (which had determined, for instance, the siting in 1897 of Carrère & Hastings's New York Public Library). While the large scale of McKim's pavilions would be continued south along Broadway and Amsterdam with blocks of dormitories forming a periphery, the two new blocks would be bisected in the middle by an eighty-foot-wide avenue leading to the library, flanked by houses for professors. The other end of the axis was to be occupied by the Presi-

FIGURE 41 *Palmer and Hornbostel, Plan of stadium in the Hudson River off Riverside Park at the foot of 116th Street (Avery Library)*

FIGURE 42 *Palmer and Hornbostel, Perspective view of a stadium for Riverside Park (Avery Library)*

dent's House on the south side of 114th Street, on land that Hamlin proposed the university also acquire, possibly by exchange. This arrangement would provide for a domestic scale at the center, while the edges of the block, developed as dormitories, would shield from the surrounding neighborhood both the professors' houses and the two 360-foot-square "grassy quads," which might be used for recreation. In both its mix of faculty and student housing and its formal organization Hamlin's scheme was an imaginative sketch of a different Columbia, an urban interpretation of Thomas Jefferson's "academical village" at the University of Virginia, with its small-scale pavilions forming a broad grassy court before a rotunda library (fig. 40).

Although McKim, Mead & White had only recently completed their restoration of Jefferson's library, taking the controversial step of closing UVA's lawn at the other end, McKim saw little relation between Charlottesville and Manhattan. Pine was quick to note that while Columbia might learn from other campuses then constructing dormitories, "we cannot expect to find a ready-made model in any other university."[150] McKim and his assistant William Kendall experimented with the size and number of dormitory and classroom blocks to be accommodated on Columbia's new land, and drew plans for the future treatment of the central area as a formal garden with statuary, hedged enclosures, and exedral benches. But all of their various schemes retained a system of enclosed quadrangles with large-scale buildings conforming to the cornice and rooflines established above 116th Street that would continue the arrangement of a double ring of buildings. Jules Crow's stunning bird's-eye perspective (plate 6), based on one of these variants, is the clearest image of a Columbia built to the full density that Butler and McKim envisioned, showing not only the four bounded quadrangles of classroom buildings on the upper campus around Low Library, but also its full development as well on South Field with U-shaped dormitory blocks tightly arranged around double quadrangles. "The quadrangular system," Pine explained "has the great practical advantage of permitting gradual development along the lines of the streets and the avenues, thus preserving for many years, if not indefinitely, an extensive campus within the great quadrangle."[151] Competitive and recreational sports were to be moved definitively off campus. Columbia was actively canvassing support to have the city extend Riverside Park eastward to Claremont Avenue, where it would form a grassy forecourt to Barnard College, which had recently published a scheme for an extension of three blocks to the south of its original one-block campus on 119th Street; and in the same year a group of Columbia alumni, including the architect Henry Hornbostel, a brilliant designer and former instructor in the School of Architecture, had floated their scheme for a grand university stadium in the Hudson River off Riverside Park at the foot of 116th Street (figs. 41 & 42).[152]

By July 1903 McKim had established guiding principles for developing the new site. He insisted first of all that the center of the block south of 116th Street be developed

FIGURE 43 *Columbia University campus looking north from 114th Street, ca. 1918. South Field was used until the 1950s as a playing field; the sundial, installed in 1910 on the south side of 116th Street, is visible in the center. (New-York Historical Society)*

as "civic" space, for he imagined mirroring the plaza of South Court on the other side of 116th Street so as to weave the two parts of the campus together across this single city street interrupting Columbia's six-block site. Since the new land sloped gently toward the south, being 13½ feet lower at 114th Street, this terrace would be a raised plaza with ornamental paving from which flights of stairs would descend both to a series of parterres in the center of South Field and to the flanking quadrangles. The two buildings facing 116th Street were to be virtual duplicates of the projected academic pavilions on the north side of the street, leaving room for eight dormitory buildings forming the two quadrangles. All of this was quickly agreed upon and rapidly set in stone, or more accurately limestone and brick, with the cornerstones of Hartley and Livingston Halls, Columbia's first dormitories, being laid in fall 1904. But the southern boundary remained open to negotiation. The trustees wondered if at least for the time being this city frontage might be developed using revenue generated by leaseholds. Although McKim drew several variants of how the university's new edge might be handled in the future, none of these schemes was ever voted on by the trustees, and the plaster model, at one time displayed at Columbia, left this key edge of the campus unfilled.

There was indeed room for anxiety. The handling of the south edge of Columbia's extended campus was perhaps the most decisive moment in the university's planning since it had arrived on Morningside Heights. While the landscaping of the central third of South Field extended the monumental vista of Low Library, even creating a distant frontal view (fig. 43) of Columbia's grand civic monument that could not even have been imagined a decade earlier, closing or leaving open the 114th Street frontage would inescapably involve reevaluating Columbia's relation to the surrounding city. McKim hesitated, proposing in his most completely rendered schemes (fig. 123) variously shaped building blocks each featuring a colonnaded opening on their ground floor, a sort of propylaeum to the Morningside acropolis that would permit framed glimpses of the campus as a visitor approached from the south. But 114th Street, unlike 116th, was a narrow crosstown street, and even with a *cour d'honneur* before the new building on McKim's grand axis the Columbia campus was destined to become an inward-focused composition, entered from its long sides along 116th Street. Rather than a grandly open forum, the campus would now be reached from the avenues through alleys of closely planted trees. First proposed in McKim's 1903 master plan these were put in place after 1910, when with the completion of Kent and Hamilton Halls the trustees' Committee on Buildings and Grounds under John Pine's leadership became concerned over "the need of some greenness to relieve the present monotony or hardness of brick, stone and asphalt" and ordered the planting of forty-four trees to give the "principle approach . . . the character of a parkway,"[153] thus evoking one of the standard forms by which Olmsted had sought to soften the grid plans of America's cities.

FIGURE 44 *McKim, Mead & White, Master plan for Columbia with landscaping suggestions for South Field. The possible future development of additional classroom buildings at the northern perimeter of the site was not included on the plan reproduced as the frontispiece of this catalogue. (New-York Historical Society)*

Despite Pine's insistence that the Grove at the north be left for future generations, McKim and Kendall included a revised building plan for the north end of the campus in their presentation to the trustees in 1903 (fig. 44). The set-back blocks proposed in 1898 when the site was studied for dormitories were replaced by academic buildings flush with the street line, the three blocks lining 120th Street set so as to close the axes established by the openings of the three larger buildings on 114th Street. For the next decade, however, buildings added to the campus on both sides of 116th Street–Hamilton (1907), Kent (1910), Avery (1911), Philosophy (1911), and Journalism (1913)–all avoided the northern and southern edges of the plan. But despite some hesitation about closing the vista from Low Library, the principle of Columbia's closed perimeter had been established.

McKim's most radical visions of the transformation of the Columbia campus encompassing its southern extension are offered in a series of three panoramas of possible future vistas from the top of Low Library's steps (plate 7). Although these are neither signed nor dated, they are fully in the spirit of the Renaissance ideal city views that inspired McKim a decade earlier. Like his original projects for Columbia on Morningside they evoke the Renaissance piazza and, in turn, the ancient Roman Forum, thus situating Columbia in that tradition of classical values and communal exchange; but now they had a vital difference. These new views of Columbia as a veritable academic agora, are now views from within the campus, whereas all of McKim's earlier perspectives were views toward the campus from outside city streets. The open view of the city from the plaza of Low Library of 1895 is now closed, the haphazard development of the cityscape in nearby Morningside Heights and beyond carefully screened. Little had been decided about the future use of the new low-lying southern edge of the campus, but these watercolor visions are prophetic. They imagine a university carving a zone apart from the city, controlling now its own horizons. The theatrical backdrop to the newly enclosed campus, its perimeter carefully closed on both north and south as it had been earlier only on its flanks, would now provide a screen wall to the city. And for the first time the prospect of a high-rise campus perimeter was considered. Nothing as spectacular as the twin domed towers or the Italian Renaissance villas striving to the height of Manhattan's new office buildings sketched in these views—perhaps based on suggestions made by Columbia trustees or architecture professors—was, of course, ever built.

Over the next twenty years the scale of Columbia's buildings would grow to meet, even to surpass, this vision. As it did, Butler would portray Columbia in speeches, as well as in the increasingly rhetorical preludes to his annual reports, as an urban university of national stature. Thomas Bender has argued that this emphasis would be at the expense of the university's openness to its local setting, as Columbia became decidedly *in*, rather than *of*, the City of New York.[154]

The most immediate beneficiary of this dual expansion and enhanced seclusion was Columbia College, for the sudden increase in building sites permitted a complete rethinking of the university's growth. It suddenly seemed more strategic to relocate buildings that the trustees had been poised to place on key sites on the upper campus. President Butler's announcement in 1905 of an anonymous gift of $500,000—from the bequest of John Stewart Kennedy—for the long-desired College Hall was the catalyst for rationalizing the spatial and social organization of both curriculum and campus. College Hall, which was originally planned for the north side of 116th Street at Broadway, would now be moved across the street and shifted east to Amsterdam Avenue, adjacent to the two dormitories under construction. This would lock in place the principle that South Field with its great residential density and sense of enclosure be developed as a "Columbia College Campus," thus answering Van Amringe's fears that without a space clearly set aside for it, Columbia College would face "extinction." The college's new home, baptized Hamilton Hall (fig. 45) both in memory of the founding father and college alumnus Alexander Hamilton and to recall the college's home on Madison Avenue, was to be set apart from the family of brick pavilions by a richer treatment of both its facades and its interiors,

FIGURE 45 *Hamilton Hall photographed shortly after its completion in 1907 (Columbiana Collection)*

most notably by decorative and emblematic details and its two-story columnar portico, which McKim then developed for all four of the buildings flanking 116th Street. At the opening in 1907, Van Amringe declared the new building "the outward and visible sign that the College is to remain an entity. . . . Its serious work, its undergraduate life, its very soul, are now provided with a habitation which will in time develop into a stately quadrangle, the very sight of which will prove to the most casual observer that Columbia College stands proudly by itself. It is of the University, yet is not lost within the University."[155] Most college classes were to be moved to Hamilton—projected for four times the college's enrollment in 1905—and over the next few years fierce defenders of the college's distinct identity would refuse every challenge to the initial designation of Hamilton Hall as the exclusive precinct of the college, and most adamantly as an all-male environment.

At the same time the upper campus was to take on a more distinctly "university" atmosphere, zoned so that future growth might not obscure a clear logic already discernible: The west side of the campus would be devoted to "instruction in applied science and to the engineering laboratories," while the future development of graduate and professional education in nonscientific areas would be directed to the eastern side of the campus. Thus the site facing Hamilton was assigned to the School of Law and the Faculty of Political Science (Kent Hall) and the smaller building perpendicular to it considered as a future home for the Department of Philosophy, another key division of the graduate faculties on the German model. A building for the new journalism school had been considered at several possible sites on the upper campus but was moved to the southeast corner of 116th Street and Broadway when it became clear that the bequest from Joseph Pulitzer was not sufficient to pay for the large auditorium theater the trustees wanted to house in the lower stories of the building on the site's opposite corner (today's Dodge Hall), adjacent to the entrance of the new subway. Because in its early years the School of Journalism had a largely undergraduate curriculum, it seemed a suitable pendant to Hamilton Hall.

In 1916, with the founding of the School of Business, William Kendall—the design partner in charge of Columbia since McKim's death in 1909—took up once again the site at the northeast corner of 116th and Broadway, which his firm had already studied twice, once for the college and once for the School of Journalism. Above an auditorium to seat a thousand, the building would contain the university's youngest and fastest growing divisions: Business and University Extension.

Reporting back to the full body of the trustees in December 1916, the Committee on Buildings and Grounds weighed the advantages of filling the last corner of McKim's original master plan, "one of the most priceless of the University's possessions as it is the largest and most conspicuous [site] remaining on the campus."[156] The vast hall, which it was hoped "would resemble in some respects the well-known and very useful hall at Cooper Union," would attract large evening crowds to the campus, and it was thought equally desirable to concentrate in one spot, near the main entrance, the diverse occasional students brought to campus by University Extension (today's School of General Studies).

The School of Business (renamed Dodge Hall after Business took up residence in Uris Hall in 1964) was not built until 1923 to 1924. Construction was delayed by its high price tag—estimated at $600,000 in 1916, it came in at $1,005,957—and by World War I. As a species the McKim pavilion had, by then, evolved a great deal. Kendall was disheartened that Columbia's tight budgets rarely allowed him to develop the exterior expression with the full richness of Renaissance articulation; indeed, one drawing of the projected Business School in the firm's archive is annotated "Original Scheme as desired by Mr. Kendall before building was cheapened by omission of ornament" (fig. 46). But exterior conformity disguised a great deal of innovation within. Not only had the firm introduced splendidly detailed and lofty vaulted libraries for Law and Architecture on the lower levels of Kent and Avery Halls, but the increased sophistication of steel-frame construction now allowed the creation of large volumes within the buildings in which spaces were literally hung from the frame, including the architectural studio spaces on the upper floors of Avery and the balconies of the McMillin Theater (now the Miller Theatre), which was housed within the massive basement stories of the School of Business. The School of Business was the last of the pavilions to be built. By the time it was inaugurated in 1924 Kendall and his associates at McKim, Mead & White were designing buildings for Columbia such as McKim had never imagined.

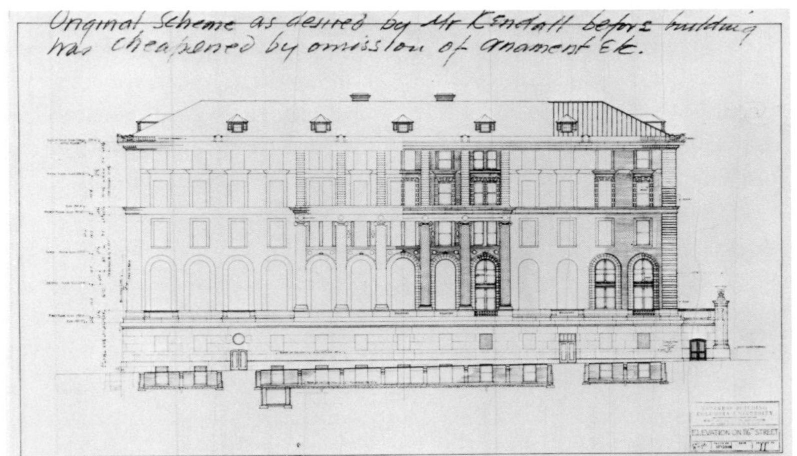

FIGURE 46 *McKim, Mead & White (William Kendall, designer; J. C. McGowan draftsman), Project for the School of Business (now Dodge Hall), 116th Street elevation, ca. 1916 with later notations (New-York Historical Society)*

III. TWENTIETH-CENTURY REVOLUTIONS AND THE FATE OF MᶜKIM'S MASTER PLAN AFTER WORLD WAR I

> If I were President of the United States Steel Corporation and you were its Board of Directors, or if I were President of the New York Central Railroad and you were its Board of Directors, I should be before you with a proposal to increase our capital stock by 40 percent, or to issue debentures for a large amount. We are, however, precluded from these particular methods of increasing our capital resources. Yet we have arrived at a point where they must be increased unless we are going to stand still, and we cannot stand still, because to stand still in this particular endeavor means to fall back.[157]
>
> —*Nicholas Murray Butler, speech to the trustees, 3 January 1921*

Nicholas Murray Butler had been speaking of Columbia's need for expansion almost since the day he was appointed university president in 1902, but after World War I he pursued that program with a single-minded determination that fully underscored his claim to a seat among Thorstein Veblen's "captains of erudition," as that acerbic critic labeled the presidents of America's elite research universities.[158] By 1921 Butler had fully articulated a vision both of Columbia and of himself as a breed apart. "Conditions are steadily and rapidly bringing Columbia University to occupy a place peculiarly its own," he insisted as early as 1911, comparable he added only to the universities of Paris and Berlin for its stature and importance in the affairs of both its city and nation.[159] A decade later he reminded faculty, trustees, and the public once again that his own stature was no less distinct. Unlike his predecessors, Barnard and Low, Butler relied on a complex hierarchical structure of deans and a growing administration concerned with the day-to-day requirements of the university. From now on Columbia's president "must live largely in the future, and must concern himself with those major policies and acts that affect the prosperity, the influence and the prestige of the University as a whole."[160] Although Butler remained deeply competitive with the presidents of other Ivy League institutions and of the growing megaliths of the state universities—notably Michigan, Illinois, Minnesota, and California, which were expanding rapidly in those years—these too, he maintained, were unsuitable comparisons. The president's "duties," Butler explained "may best be stated in terms of the English political system as those of the prime minister holding the portfolios of foreign affairs and of the treasury. . . . In the strict sense of the word, the administrative head of Columbia University is neither a college president nor even a university president; he is President of Columbia University. His duties and occupations are unique because Columbia is unique."[161] If Butler saw his office in political terms—paralleled by his failed attempts, such as in 1920, to win the Republican party's nomination for president of the United States, and his personal moment of glory, when he addressed the German Reichstag in 1930—his critics saw his portfolio of board memberships on the city's banks and insurance companies as part of an empire, one that merited Upton

Sinclair's epithet for Columbia as "the university of the House of Morgan."[162] By the time Butler retired in 1945—the longest term of office of any major university president in the twentieth century—he had raised, by his own calculation, $120 million for Columbia's buildings and endowment.

The 1919 building program

As soon as the American economy had recovered from World War I, Butler began to articulate a strategy for Columbia's first organized building campaign since the original laying out of the campus between 1894 and 1897. The "building program" was presented as a pressing emergency in the president's annual report of 1919, in which he recommended that Columbia purchase or lease property in the neighborhood as a temporary solution if escalating costs of construction made it impossible to complete the campus's many unfilled sites in the immediate future. "It is plain," he noted, "that unless the work of the University is to be thrown into confusion, immediate steps must be taken to provide new buildings both for academic work and for residence."[163] By 1921, when Butler spelled out his vision in greater detail, Columbia had launched a two-pronged response to the tightening real estate market on Morningside Heights. While new campus buildings would be highly visible and prominent in their unprecedented bulk or height, a less readily apparent horizontal expansion of the university into neighboring blocks would provide both apartments for faculty, who were increasingly forced to leave the city in search of affordable living quarters, and sites for future campus expansion. Four years later, in 1925, Columbia was building not only on all sides of its "McKim" campus but also on three new sites in Upper Manhattan. The East Field block, bounded by Amsterdam and Morningside Avenues, and 116th and 117th Streets, originally acquired for $1 million in 1910 for the Medical School, was now to be developed as an integral part of the Morningside campus for functions that could not be housed on McKim's original master plan. For in 1921 a collaborative agreement with Presbyterian Hospital had been hammered out and an ample site for a new medical center had been acquired on Washington Heights at 168th Street. On 31 January 1925, Butler opened Columbia's first dormitory for women, Johnson Hall, on East Field in the morning and laid the cornerstone for the Columbia-Presbyterian Medical Center, designed by James Gamble Rogers, in the afternoon.[164] In the same year work was completed on a stadium named for George Baker, who had purchased for Columbia at the northern tip of Manhattan Island a few years earlier a large tract of land for the athletic facilities that alumni and students had been wanting for decades. By the time the stock market crashed in 1929 the square footage of classroom and dormitory space on the Morningside Heights campus alone had been increased by nearly 40 percent, and Butler had raised more than $20 million for new construction. In that same year Columbia took under its wing St. Stephen's (later Bard) College at Annandale-on-Hudson, the first of a string of upstate satellite sites, to which the

FIGURE 47 *Evans, Moore and Woodbridge, Project for the expansion of Bard College, Annandale-on-Hudson, NY. From the 1920s Bard was an affiliated school of Columbia University. (Bard College)*

Nevis estate at Irvington would be added in 1935 (fig. 47).[165]

Butler's vision of an expanded Columbia was unwavering. The list of requirements laid out in 1919 would guide the development of the campus for the next twenty years and was frustrated only by Butler's inability to finance the completion of University Hall, which remained throughout his reign Columbia's white elephant. The architectural and planning narrative of the 1920s (fig. 48) is one of a continual spatial adjustment and renegotiation of Butler's initial program, set against the background of Columbia's rapidly growing graduate and professional divisions. At the same time concerted efforts to attract a national rather than local undergraduate population, at once more geographically diverse though still socially homogenous, were launched that Columbia College might vie with its fellow Ivy League schools as a coveted pedigree.[166] Enrollments continued to climb in all divisions. The most spectacular increases were in scientific and engineering research, which were increasingly tied to American industry and even to national politics. "The European war has served at least one good purpose," Butler pointed out already in 1916, "in arousing our industrial managers and public men from their long sleep of indifference to scientific inquiry and to scientific progress. . . . The future of American industry is bound up with the future of American science."[167]

The university's needs, if it was to compete, were enormous; and each was described as urgent. "The gravest emergency arises in connection with the provision of additional residence halls for students," Butler noted, suggesting not only two new dormitories on the 114th Street corners of South Field–permitting that the athletic field remained undisturbed for the time being (fig. 48)–but also calling for the first time for a women's dormitory. In addition both a large building to

FIGURE 48 *Aerial photograph of Columbia, before the addition of buildings on 114th and 120th Streets, ca. 1925 (New-York Historical Society)*

house a university commons and quarters for student organizations and activities were required, perhaps to be set between the two dormitories on 114th Street. A new faculty club, "a necessity of our metropolitan academic life," should be built to replace the makeshift one in one of the asylum buildings still standing near the northeast corner of Broadway and 116th Street, today occupied by Dodge Hall. "On the academic side the most pressing need is for the erection of a building for the School of Business," but no less demanding of attention were the overcrowded conditions in the scientific laboratories, particularly those of chemistry and chemical engineering, both of which would require new buildings, as would botany, zoology, and physics. The Graduate School too was bursting at the seams with "the rapid multiplication of courses and students in the advanced fields of Philosophy, Political Science and Pure Science . . . putting severe pressure upon the accommodations of Kent Hall and Philosophy Hall." Not surprisingly all this growth had caused an equivalent shortage of space for the burgeoning central administration. "Such a building program as that indicated, which leaves untouched the completion of University Hall or the building of the Hudson River Stadium, will call for several millions of dollars," Butler concluded.[168]

In matching his analysis of pressing needs to available space, Butler assigned first priority to the open corners of the campus, designating the southeast and southwest corners of South Field for new residence halls and the edges of the Grove for new laboratory space in both the pure and applied sciences. To fill the unused inner sites on the upper campus–only Avery Hall had been built of the four buildings intended to form the academic courtyards of McKim's 1894 plan–Butler envisioned buildings for individual departments, perhaps with office space on certain ground floors, thus creating a domino effect as departments were moved from overcrowded older buildings. That three of the four peripheral sites were built by the end of the decade while not a single new pavilion arose to fill out McKim's plans is telling.

All of the new buildings erected in the 1920s rose above the datum of McKim's copper cornices, and even the smallest of them–Chandler Laboratories–had 50 percent more floor area than the inner pavilions would have permitted. Driven by the rapidly changing needs of laboratory science–highly detailed requirements were drawn up for the architects by some of the most prominent of Columbia's scientists for Chandler (1925), Pupin (1925), and Schermerhorn Extension (1928) –the new buildings also required a much higher percentage of fenestration, a more flexible compartmentalization of space, and easy access to loading docks for sometimes heavy equipment, none of which would be possible in the close imitations of Avery Hall as indicated for the upper campus on the master plan. The small teaching labs and museums of the 1890s had already been superseded by a new ethos of large-scale laboratory research (fig. 49). Although Butler would continue well into the 1930s to propose uses for the unbuilt inner sites on McKim's plan–including Pierce Hall (plate 8), which was proposed

FIGURE 49 *Laboratory of Geology and Palaeontology, Schermerhorn Hall, ca. 1904 (cat. 37)*

in 1927 as an addition to the School of Engineering and would be a pendant for Avery—in its appropriateness to scientific research the pavilion species had become extinct only twenty-five years after Schermerhorn Hall had been inaugurated in as a state-of-the-art natural science building. Of the four original pavilions completed in the 1890s only Havemeyer Hall, the chemistry building, still housed a science department seventy-five years later. Although demands of scientific research have predominantly driven each generation of new academic buildings on the Columbia campus—as on so many others—McKim's 1897 pavilion type has in fact proven remarkably resilient. Remodeled progressively over the years, sometimes to the detriment of their original scale, sometimes to restore it, the academic pavilions have confounded every attempt to proclaim them defunct by the laws of natural selection. Nonetheless, it was in the 1920s that attention turned away from the inner campus, leaving a legacy of unintended picturesque irregularity and open verdant space among Columbia's density that McKim never imagined.

Expanding laboratories and towers for 120th Street

The struggle to reconcile Columbia's bid for a prime place among the emerging elite of research universities with the legacy of McKim's harmonious but incomplete composition led to the first major rethinking of the master plan since the addition of South Field in 1903. Between 1924 and 1927 McKim, Mead & White, under Kendall's direction, explored a series of alternatives for the development of the Grove at the north end of campus and of its 120th Street frontage (plate 10 and figs. 50–52). While Butler, in 1919, called simply for extensions to the rear of Havemeyer and Schermerhorn to create modern laboratory annexes for chemistry and biology, Kendall studied a series of approaches to developing a grand northern skyline for Columbia that could provide a series of tall buildings of much higher density than McKim's buildings, ample enough, he hoped, to accommodate the growing science departments for decades to come. He imagined filling the site to capacity with no fewer than seven new buildings, arranged so as to compose harmoniously when viewed as the backdrop to Low Library, especially as seen from the sundial, the symbolic center of the campus since its placement in 1910, on the south side of 116th Street.[169]

Study of the problem began in autumn 1924 with pragmatic proposals for one or two new buildings for chemistry and chemical engineering along Broadway immediately to the north of Havemeyer (figs. 53 & 54). Working directly on photographs of the existing view of Columbia looking north along Broadway, the architects extrapolated the perspective lines of the granite bases and copper cornices—as well as principal intermediate moldings—of the existing Broadway facades to interweave the new scale and density required for laboratory buildings with the existing compositional grid of the campus. Tied to the old buildings by continuity of principal divisions and by the palette of materials—granite bases, brick facades with limestone trim—the additions to the campus would translate the essentially horizontal phrasing of the original buildings into a more vertical expression. In place of McKim's brick walls punctured with overscaled double-hung windows, Kendall's new buildings featured closely spaced brick piers and a setback honeycomb of standard sash windows, a facade expression of steel-cage construction common in tall office buildings since it had been given its classic definition by Louis Sullivan in the 1890s. McKim had been an outspoken enemy of the emerging skyscraper, but after his death, particularly in the towering New York Municipal Building of 1907–1916, Kendall developed a highly influential classical interpretation of the new species of urban building, which sought to reconcile advances in steel framing with the neo-Renaissance precepts of his late

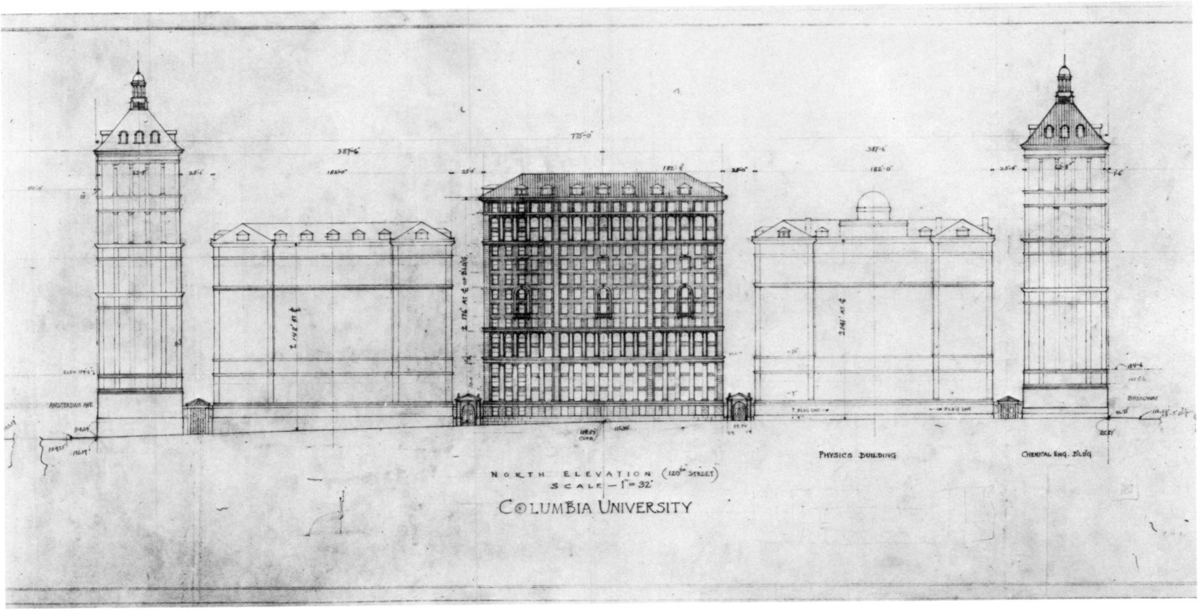

FIGURE 50 *McKim, Mead & White, Project for the development of the 120th Street expansion of the science departments, 1924 (cat. 70)*

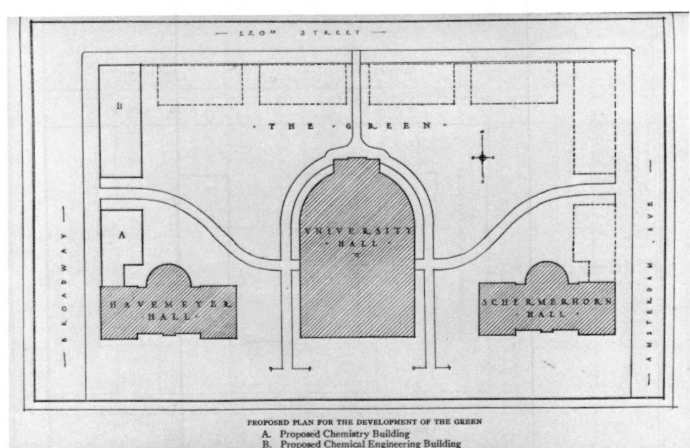

FIGURE 51 *McKim, Mead & White, Site plan for the development of the Grove (the Green) in the 1920s (Columbiana Collection)*

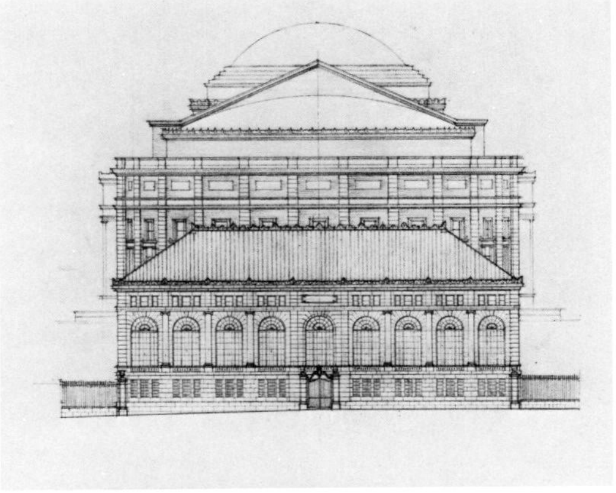

FIGURE 52 *McKim, Mead & White, Elevation study for the center of 120th Street showing the juxtaposition of a proposed art gallery, University Hall, and Low Library, 1929 (New-York Historical Society)*

FIGURE 53 *Columbia's Broadway frontage looking north (Mathematics and Havemeyer Halls), 1924, photograph used by McKim, Mead & White to study the insertion of Chandler Laboratories (note pencil lines) 1924 (New-York Historical Society)*

mentor. Columbia's Chandler Laboratories is said to be the first completely steel-supported structure ever realized for a chemical laboratory in the United States.[170] Emphatic horizontal continuity with the older buildings allowed Kendall to introduce more stories–made possible by increased reliance on mechanical ventilation systems, which permitted lower ceiling heights–without losing the largeness of scale that was such an important feature of McKim's brick pavilions. This interweaving also permitted the introduction of an additional two or three stories above the emphatic cornice line; here the stories were tied together by a series of brick arcades so that the upper stories appear somewhat more open and thus lighter, reducing the overall impression of bulk, a technique ultimately derived from the belvederes frequently set above the massive projecting cornices of Renaissance palaces.

As soon as the cornerstone of Chandler Hall was laid in 1925, Kendall began to reflect on how this new type of building block might be used as a system for developing the north end of the campus. Returning to McKim's 1903 master plan, he explored the possibility that the line of buildings then projected along 120th Street might be developed as a staccato rhythm of towers and slabs, a high-rise response to the fact that Columbia was running out of space on its campus much more rapidly than anyone had been able to imagine two decades earlier. In addition, by the 1920s ten-story apartment houses lined Riverside Drive and Claremont Avenue, and buildings approaching that height had appeared on the side streets. The commanding views both of and from Low Library had disappeared within a generation. As it was completed the university's perimeter would thus respond to a new set of requirements, at once shielding the campus from views of competing buildings and raising Columbia's skyline in the neighborhood to new heights (fig. 137).

FIGURE 54 *McKim, Mead & White, Project for Chandler Laboratories, 1924, engraving by Fritz Steffens. This engraving was based on the photograph shown in fig. 53. (New-York Historical Society)*

Pupin Hall (1924–1927) and Schermerhorn Extension (1928) were the only other buildings of Kendall's scheme to be completed. While both buildings respected Kendall's new master plan, by the end of the decade even he admitted that the new demands made on McKim's vocabulary had stretched it almost to the breaking point. During construction, quibbles over details revealed fault lines in the confidence underlying Columbia's classical enterprise. In the spring of 1925 an exchange with Henry Lee Norris, Columbia's superintendent of buildings, over the depth of the limestone windowsills on Pupin Hall is a first sign of trouble. To suit their new height and to meet the increasingly demanding budgets, the new buildings shared the stripping down of classical detail common in much office construction of the day. But Kendall feared that the windows, reduced to a mere four inches in depth, as Norris proposed, "would give a meager and insubstantial appearance" to the entire building. "This brings up the whole question of the policy to be pursued in relation to the new buildings now being erected at Columbia," he explained. The new buildings, "are, we are aware, on an entirely different basis from the point of view of design, from the older buildings. Still we should regret to depart any further than absolutely necessary from the character of the latter."[171] Kendall gave in on Pupin (fig. 55), convincing himself that the individual building, as always at Columbia, could be corrected by the ensemble. But in the process he was forced to admit that new construction methods led naturally away from the weighty brick-and-stone aesthetic of McKim's original campus design. A year later Kendall wrote directly to President Butler that

> the Physics Building, has not as much stone work in it as we could have wished, but we were given to understand that the appropriation would allow no more elaboration than we have made. The result is, in my opinion, a perfectly good building, but not quite up to the standard of the older Columbia buildings. This would, in fact, have been impossible in a building of that height without making an excessive cost. In the general scheme of the 120th Street elevation, our idea is to make the corner and central buildings more important architecturally as to their ornamentation, and to the use of stone, thus making a composition in which the central building is flanked by two plain buildings, the end building being in the same class as that in the center. Furthermore, in the building east of the central building we should use a little more stone and ornamentation than we have in the Physics building. I am confident that the result would be an architectural composition worthy to stand par with those of the older buildings, in spite of the greater extent of the undecorated brick wall. The corner towers have the desired strong accent, and the central building of equal elaboration, would have increased importance, owing to its plainer neighbors.[172]

The threshold between the classical dignity that Columbia announced with its original plan and the commercial background buildings of the city had become dangerously narrow. Perhaps something of Kendall's anxieties registered already with Butler and the trustees. When Butler encouraged them, in 1928, to allocate funds for new laboratory space for biological research, the Committee on Buildings and Grounds assured him that their budget allocations would be sufficient to permit "a building the

FIGURE 55 *Pupin Hall (Physics) under construction, ca. 1927 (New-York Historical Society)*

exterior of which will be satisfactory and will conform to the original design of the buildings on campus."[173]

Schermerhorn Extension is the pendant on the east side of campus of Chandler on the west, but it is not a precise mirror image. Not only did the steeper grade on Amsterdam allow a taller building, but Kendall was authorized to incorporate considerably more ornament and more three-dimensional stone trim in this new design. Most notable is the return of the bulging torus molding of McKim's original buildings, carried directly over from the original Schermerhorn and continued around all three exposed facades of the new building; this key detail had been reduced to a shallow two-dimensional strip on Chandler. Yet despite these enhancements the steep downhill slope of Amsterdam Avenue at this point meant that the continuation of Columbia's plinth–McKim's 150-foot datum line–in the facade of a building whose exterior entrance is tucked away on its side elevation, facing the service road, created an ever more formidable fortress wall toward the neighborhood growing up around the university. With its new height Columbia was turning emphatically inward; none of the buildings that Kendall projected along 120th Street had entrances directly onto the sidewalk.

Students Hall and the emergence of a new type of Columbia dormitory

A grand university commons, combining dining hall with facilities for clubs and activities that would lend Columbia something of that ever elusive spirit of campus life that its students perennially envied in more bucolically situated universities, was a key component of Butler's 1919 program. These were functions that McKim and Low had envisioned grouped together in University Hall, but since the addition of South Field the central axis of the university had two poles vying for attention. Increasingly Butler's attention was focused on Columbia's southern horizon, the view not coincidentally from his office in Low Memorial Library. From the library atop its plinth, Columbia College's incomplete quadrangles and the popular but makeshift stadium on South Field appeared against a backdrop of run-of-the mill apartment houses recently completed on the south side of 114th Street (see fig. 48). By 1921, the building that Butler envisioned closing this vista had grown in both scale and ambition; it would now include "a new and thoroughly modern gymnasium, rectangular in shape." McKim's Grecian reverie, a gymnasium and swimming pool in the shape of a Greek amphitheater in the foundation stories of University Hall, could easily be converted to an auditorium, Butler suggested. The upper stories of the building could be planned "to make provision for student life and student organizations which are so important a part of the total educational influence that the University, and particularly the College exerts."[174] This would concentrate "everything pertaining to . . . the domestic life of the University" below 116th Street. In the same annual report Butler suggested that Low Library, which had reached capacity and been supplemented by numerous departmental libraries, might be extended by including book stacks and a new reading room in the projected upper stories of University Hall, since the great dining hall originally projected there by McKim and Low had now been shifted to South Field in Butler's vision of Columbia.

In 1922 McKim, Mead & White drew up a scheme for a building that could both accommodate this ever growing list of functions–in that year Butler added "studies, reading rooms and class rooms as shall relieve the pressure on Hamilton Hall"[175] to the list–and provide a suitable pendant to Low Library itself (fig. 56). They envisioned an overscaled palazzo-style structure that would rise above the roofline of the existing South Field buildings, and whose facade would include a great Ionic colonnade, three stories tall, set above an exceptionally tall basement calculated to be seen in its full height and splendor even from the upper platform. This was to be the starting point nine years later for James Gamble Rogers's South Hall on this same spot (fig. 57), although Rogers rejected the mannerist intermixing of scales and decorative vocabularies that the McKim, Mead & White firm suggested as a means of creating a building that could mediate between Columbia's grand axis and the brick facades and smaller domestic-scale floors and openings of the dormitories. Over the next year the firm continued to revise this design in consultation with Dean Hawkes of the college, but by the end of 1923, when the architects' estimates had reached $4.5 million and their design fees nearly $100,000, even Butler was forced to admit that the project should be shelved.

Meanwhile the demand for dormitory space had reached a crisis point. Not only was there "a waiting list of students wishing rooms long enough to fill completely another dormitory as large as Furnald Hall," but a year earlier, in 1922, the housing dilemma facing Columbia's growing population of women graduate students had also been exacerbated by the decision to end the wartime use of Furnald as a

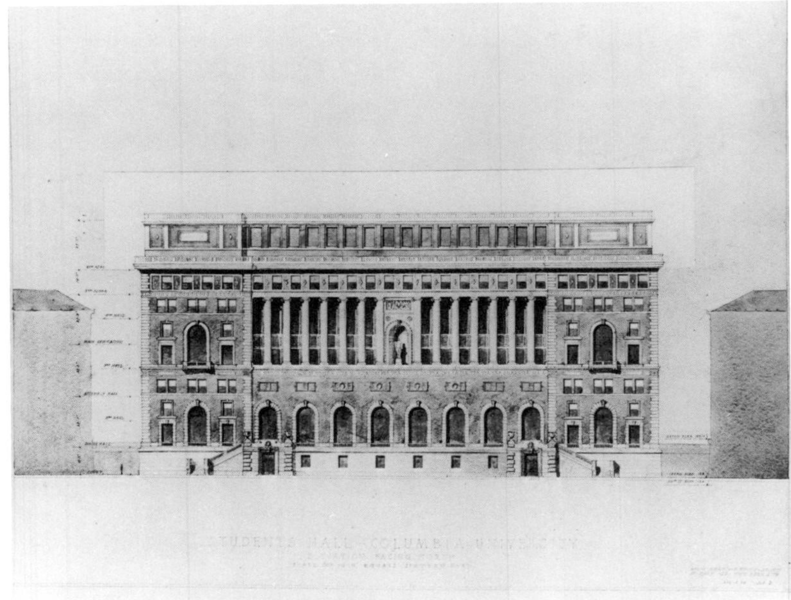

FIGURE 56 *McKim, Mead & White, Design for Students Hall for South Field, 1923, photograph of a lost design (cat. 56)*

FIGURE 57 *James Gamble Rogers, Preliminary design for South Hall, probably early 1931, prior to budget reductions. This design included a three-door entrance and Corinthian columns and did not yet feature the frieze of famous philosophers. It also includes colonnaded links to John Jay Hall and a projected pendant. (Avery Library)*

FIGURE 58 *McKim, Mead & White, Johnson Hall (now Wien) soon after completion, ca. 1925 (New-York Historical Society)*

women's dormitory. Five sites remained open on McKim's 1903 plan to replicate Furnald Hall. But just as McKim's academic pavilions could not accommodate the university's academic expansion, so his prewar dormitory type now seemed ill-suited to Columbia's residential expansion, made all the more urgent by escalating rents in the neighborhood. Johnson Hall (today's Wien Hall) for women and John Jay Hall for men established not only a new high-rise scale but also a new type of dormitory (fig. 58). Both would house dining halls, kitchens, and rooms for student activities–and in the case of Johnson an infirmary–on their ground floors, and both would have staffs devoted to counseling and organizing activities to look after the moral and social welfare of the residents. For Johnson Hall, Butler turned to Virginia Gildersleeve, Barnard's formidable president, for advice on a head resident. "We are agreed," Gildersleeve noted, "that some woman of intellectual distinction, presence and charm should be placed at the head of the hall and given every opportunity to make it a delightful center of scholarly and social life."[176] Dean Hawkes of the college wrote to Butler that these services were not luxuries but fundamental to Columbia's policies of selective admissions. "As you know," he wrote in the spring of 1924, it is very difficult for the students, graduates, or faculty to urge boys from good families, especially from outside New York, to come to Columbia College when there is no place in which they may get suitable board. Until this is provided it will be difficult to attract, and still more difficult to retain, the kind of student we desire." John Jay, built at the corner of 114th and Amsterdam in 1925 and 1926, took over the dining and club facilities originally planned for Students' Hall, announced a new scale for Columbia's southern edge, and promised a new collegiate atmosphere for undergraduate life.

From the moment the idea of a women's residence hall was raised in June 1922 it was agreed it should be the first building block of an ambitious master plan for the East Field (today East Campus) site that Columbia had originally assembled, with the help of William Vanderbilt, for the medical school. By then James Gamble Rogers had been at work for over a year developing innovative principles for institutional planning at the Columbia-Presbyterian Medical Center, and something of his approach there of interconnected high-rise buildings resonates in Kendall's sketches for this eastward expansion of the Morningside campus. The prestigious frontage of the site along Morningside Drive, with sweeping open views to the east, had already been developed on a residential scale with the four-story President's House (1911–1912) and its pendant, the Faculty House, then under construction (fig. 59). This left the lion's share of a city block to be developed with the high densities now considered a necessity on Columbia's scarce land. Kendall placed a new twelve-story residence hall, later named Johnson Hall (1924–1925) and today Wien Hall, perpendicular to 116th Street. This would not only screen the President's House and Faculty Club from the new campus rising behind (fig. 60), but it would also form one wing of an enormous courtyard–U-shaped or E-shaped in variant schemes–to be developed so that the new block maximized habitation without entirely sacrificing open space. Once all the wings were completed the new east block would form a grand south-facing foyer to the university echoing to a certain extent Low Library's South Court and acknowledging that the university had outgrown the capacity to house all its departments and students along radial vistas back to Low Library (figs. 141–143).

Kendall studied a variety of massing solutions and crowning elements drawn alternatively from the Renaissance vocabulary of Columbia's original pavilions and from the tower imagery of the projected 120th Street frontage. The new residence hall was considerably lighter in decorative details than Columbia's other brick buildings, evoking at once Italian Renaissance palaces and the American Federal period, notably in the handsome fan windows of the ground floor dining room and lounges. Perhaps this was intended to lend a more graceful touch, even, as Andrew Dolkart suggests, a self-conscious feminine inflection; perhaps Kendall also saw this subtle variant as a way of defining a new dialect for Columbia's high-rise site. Although the East Campus master plan would be revised numerous times in the coming years, both for projected dormitories and even for an ambitious arts center to be designed by James Gamble Rogers around a gallery,[177] Johnson Hall remained for many years a marooned fragment of a grand vision.

Or perhaps the vision was not grand enough. By the late 1920s the trustees had gone a long way toward acquiring most of the city block to the north, converting, along the north side of 117th Street between Amsterdam Avenue and Morningside Drive, brownstones but a generation old into a series of national language houses, institutes, offices, and houses for the college dean and the chaplain. The flagship of these foreign centers, and the only new building on the block, was Casa Italiana (1926–1927), an exquisitely proportioned and finely detailed Italian Renaissance palazzo, the first building since Low Library to be faced in limestone (fig. 61). Its exceptionally finely detailed construction and materials were the

FIGURE 59 *President's House and Faculty House seen from Morningside Drive, 1927 (Columbiana Collection)*

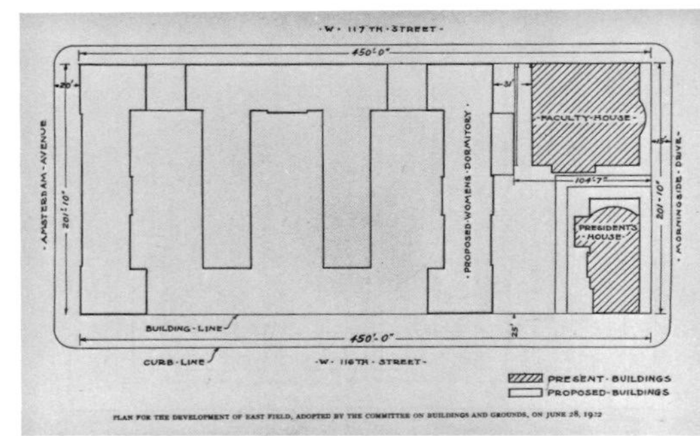

FIGURE 60 *Plan for the development of East Field as adopted by the trustees in 1922, based on projects by William Kendall of McKim, Mead & White (Columbia University Archives)*

FIGURE 61 *McKim, Mead & White, Project for Casa Italiana with suggestions for the development of West 117th Street, ca. 1925, engraving by Fritz Steffens (New-York Historical Society)*

signature as much of its architect, William Kendall, who considered it one of his finest designs, as its builder, Joseph Paterno, a real estate developer and Morningside Heights resident (in the splendid curved apartment house that his firm had built on the northeast corner of 116th Street and Riverside Drive). Paterno offered in 1925 not only to subscribe the remaining amount necessary for the building fund but also to undertake the entire project himself, including the immediate demolition of the Hotel LaPorte on this site, opposite the apse of St. Paul's Chapel. With the exception of the asylum buildings, this was the first time one of Columbia's buildings involved the demolition of a neighborhood building; not insignificantly it removed an inexpensive hotel from the block, and reflected Columbia's perennial anxiety about the social mix of its immediate neighborhood.

"Since this building will, in some measure at least, determine the architectural development of the block on which it stands, the Committee have requested the architects to make, as speedily as may be, an outline sketch of a projected development, including particularly the skyline of the buildings that are likely to be placed on the north side of 117th Street," the trustees noted in accepting Paterno's offer. They posed but two conditions, that "the foundations of the proposed building should be deep enough and strong enough, and the structural steel used heavy enough, to make possible the subsequent addition of several stories," and that the six-story building conform "in general style and structure to the established architectural system of the University."[178] Certainly for McKim these two desires would have been mutually exclusive, and even Kendall was beginning to have his doubts. In any case these contradictory demands were prophetic of the future of East Campus.

Butler Library and the end of McKim's vision

At their June 1929 meeting the trustees' Committee on Buildings and Grounds, worried that Columbia's rapid expansion was threatening the quality of its classical campus, passed a resolution: "RESOLVED, that this committee is agreed that in the erection of new buildings or additions to our present buildings, the architectural designs thereof should not be inferior to the designs of buildings erected for the University during the life of the late Charles F. McKim."[179] McKim had died twenty years earlier and was commemorated in 1910 with a Latin inscription set at the very center of the Renaissance-style paving of South Court: CHARLES FOLLEN McKIM ARCHITECT MDCCCXLVII–MDCCCCIX DESVPER ARTIFICIS SPECTANT MONVMENTA PER ANNOS (the monuments [of an artist] look down upon us through the ages).[180] Kendall's victory, however, was Pyrrhic, although he could not have known it immediately. He would continue to advise Butler on design for buildings and landscape until his death in 1941; but the firm of McKim, Mead & White, formally dissolved in 1956, would never again erect more than a temporary structure for Columbia. Four months after the trustees' resolution, the stock market crash all but brought to a halt Butler's grand architectural visions.

The one exception was the grand new library that, after 1946, bore his name and definitively closed the vista from Low Library. South Hall (figs. 57 & 62), as the new library was originally called, was the only permanent building undertaken on Morningside Heights by Columbia in the fifteen years between the onset of the Great Depression and the end of World War II. But it was also, at $3.5 million, the most expensive building that Columbia had yet constructed, and by far the largest building on the campus when it was completed in 1934. Despite its innovative services and spacious accommodations, the bulky block of Butler Library has never found many enthusiasts. As its most recent historian, Michael Stoller, has noted, "The new building . . . was the product of compromise–financial, architectural, and operational. The story of its design and construction illustrates both the scale of Columbia's vision and the limits of its resources."[181] While it is impossible to retrace that story fully here, the principal episodes form a key chapter in the continued saga of McKim's grand axis and the ultimate fate of his master plan in a period when the classical image he had honed at Columbia was increasingly under attack by younger members of the architectural profession.

That McKim and Low had simply neglected one of the original stipulations of the program presented to Columbia's prospective architects back in 1893, namely that the great central library be planned to allow future expansion, become painfully clear by the early 1920s. "The present University Library, one of McKim's greatest creations, is in reality a magnificent monument, but ill-adapted to its purpose," Butler confided to Edward S. Harkness late in 1930 as his decade-long courtship of the legendary millionaire and philanthropist seemed on the verge of adding a modern library building to the rich dowry Harkness had already established for Columbia.[182] Since 1921, when Harkness had skillfully matched Columbia's College of Physicians and Surgeons with the Presbyterian Hospital, ending years of protracted and complex merger negotiations, he had almost single-handedly underwritten the cost of the enormous complex of buildings for the Medical Center designed by his friend and architect James Gamble Rogers. In 1930 Harkness and Rogers had thrown in a fourteen-story dormitory tower for the medical students, Bard Hall (1929–1930), for good measure. This was a last addition, moreover, to Harkness's lifelong commitment to reforming the residential life of

FIGURE 62 *South Hall (Butler Library) under construction, 6 February 1933 (cat. 59)*

America's elite institutions, most famously the nearly $26 million he had split a decade earlier between Harvard and Yale—his alma mater—for the creation of their systems, respectively, of residential houses and colleges.

In 1926, as the Medical Center was under construction at 168th Street, Butler broached the possibility of an additional benefaction from Harkness for the Morningside Heights campus, outlining his dream that University Hall might finally be completed to serve as an enormous annex to Low Library. Discreetly Butler turned to Rogers, asking him to work with the newly appointed director of Columbia's chaotic library system, Charles Williamson, to study schemes for a library that could correct Low Library's notorious deficiencies and face up to the daunting statistics of Columbia's expansion. "Each year there are some 10,000 different individuals who come to Morningside Heights as graduate students," Butler noted, comparing a library to a laboratory for nonscientific fields of research. "At the moment there is not only no adequate place, but literally no place whatever for most of them to do their work."[183] Williamson recommended that a new building be planned for a minimum of four million volumes, which "should provide for the growth of forty years at least," but he advised that "the still more distant future also be taken into account."[184] With an estimated budget of $7 million, Harkness and Rogers were at work at the very moment on the finishing touches in the designs for Yale's new Sterling Memorial Library.

Harkness had been hesitant about Columbia's library project, indicating in 1926 that he would prefer to give a "more useful" building to Columbia, but he finally conceded to review his decision if in a specific architectural proposal Rogers and Columbia could keep costs down.[185] In 1930 Rogers studied and revised a design to fill McKim's projected envelope for University Hall with the state-of-the art library that Williamson dreamed of creating. Connecting the two grandest buildings on the campus with an enormous bridge, Rogers proposed converting Low Library into a grand vestibule to the reading room, book stacks, and private studies to be housed in the upper floors of University Hall and in the linking building. The generous spaciousness of this new library would be enjoyed all over campus, since Williamson suggested centralizing most of the departmental libraries, which had proliferated in McKim's pavilions over the last three decades. The spaces they would leave free could, in turn, be reassigned to relieve overcrowding in nearly every department. "In one building there are sixteen men teachers who are assigned to a single office room," Butler wrote to Harkness at his Fifth Avenue mansion.[186]

But by the time Harkness agreed on a figure of $3 million in December 1930 it was altogether apparent that the University Hall scheme could not be made to work. Butler himself had reluctantly arrived at that conclusion the preceding summer, after engineers reported that the idea of constructing steel book stacks atop the university's gym and swimming pool would be enormously complicated and prohibitively expensive. Even if the athletic facilities were to be moved to

South Field, as the president had proposed a few years earlier, the lower stories of the 1897 building would need to be rebuilt to accommodate the new loads. In addition there was, as Rogers himself pointed out, the logistical challenge of the power plant housed in the existing lower level, which ruled out a workable elevator connection to a street-level loading dock. Rogers himself was ready to throw in the towel, admitting that even "utilizing every scheme of architectural deception, I do not believe that we could . . . house more than 1,800,000 volumes," or for that matter fulfill any of the other desiderata for the new library. Not that he was opposed to architectural deception, for at the very moment he was weathering a tempest that had brewed up at Yale over his neo-Gothic cladding of Sterling Library's towering steel frame book stack, a controversy that received new force from architectural spokesmen as prominent as Henry Russell Hitchcock, Lewis Mumford, and Frank Lloyd Wright.[187] For Rogers the issue of style and modernity were not inextricably linked however. In October 1930 he outlined an approach to Columbia's dilemma that he was confident would not violate the trustees' recent pledge of allegiance to the spirit of McKim:

> As long as you have asked my opinion, I will state that I believe that the best method of handling the library question would be to leave the present library almost as it is, utilizing the large reading room as a grand exhibition hall and the other space in the library for special collections of books. Then, have your working library made in the manner of the modern office building giving the facilities as you want them, with an architecture that could be utilized for such a variety of purpose, carrying that building to any height desired. This could be built from the ground up introducing all the improved methods that have been going into library buildings in the last twenty-five years.[188]

Rogers directed Butler's attention back to South Field, proposing that starting afresh it might indeed be possible to combine gymnasium and library. Not only would such a combined building fit the spirit of the times–whereas Low Memorial Library reflected a period "when the Library was the proper expression for education . . . [today's] college students are generally as fully engaged in athletics as in their books"–it was also in keeping with modern technology's capacities to house the most diverse functions in a unified structure. This new hybrid "Mens Sana in Corpore Sano building" would rightfully find its place "in the center of the students' residential quarters," the architect concluded his appeal.[189]

Less than two months after Harkness pledged $3 million, Rogers was ready with a preliminary design (fig. 57) for an enormous rectangular block on South Field with a series of one story colonnades to link it to flanking dormitories, John Jay and an imagined twin on the corner of 114th and Broadway. Drawing inspiration from McKim's earlier sketch of 1923 for Students Hall (see fig. 56), he proposed an enormous block, whose scale, ironically enough, was to be *reduced* by a great multistory Ionic colonnade inspired by that of Low Library and carried aloft so it would be best appreciated when viewed from the 150-foot elevation of McKim's upper campus terrace. An integral steel frame building with a central book stack to house 2.9 million volumes on fifteen tiers, the whole was clad in limestone and brick, with proportionally more limestone at the center to echo Low, while at its extremities brick dominated to blend in with McKim's dormitories. Even though the new library had nearly three times the floor area of Low, Rogers boasted to Butler of its deferential architectural demeanor: "You will notice that the style of architecture is quite similar to Low Library and in itself imposing. However the fact that this new working library is at a much lower level makes me feel quite sure that this new building will in no way detract from the dominance of the beautiful Low Library. Rather, on the other hand, it will enhance the appearance of that masterpiece of beauty."[190] The same day he reconfirmed his reputation among his professional colleagues as a consummate gentleman by writing to Kendall, to underscore what Butler had already explained to Columbia's consulting architects, namely that Columbia had sought out Rogers and commissioned architectural designs to please its potential donor and not vice versa. "Whether they will meet with success I do not know but I am writing to assure you that I did not make any effort to encroach on what I considered your field and further, to explain that I have endeavored in my plans not to interfere with the scheme of your general plan."[191] This could only be understood figuratively, since as Rogers himself admitted to Butler, "We do however come further north into South Field than was originally planned."[192] This was no small matter, for the projection of the new library facade far beyond the building line McKim and his associates had contemplated for the southern edge of South Field changed the spatial dynamics of the central campus in a fundamental way.

Although few could be so churlish as to overlook the tremendous improvement the new library made in Columbia's intellectual life, all were disappointed and all realized that the building had been achieved at a price. Harkness stood fast that he would not expend more than $3 million on the building; at the same time he refused to abide by the university's policy of hiring contractors through competitive bidding. When the builders designated by Harkness, Marc Eidlitz & Sons, came back with estimates hovering around $5 million, Rogers was sent back to the drawing board to simplify his project. By early April he had shaved the cost to $3.9 million literally by shrinking the design. The new design was "smaller . . . and is made in a much more compact form."[193] Although it would now accommodate only 2.89 million volumes–forcing Columbia to retain many of its departmental libraries–Rogers explained that he had strengthened the book stack enough to take six additional tiers in the future. Not only would this still fall shy of Williamson's minimum requirement of four million volumes, but Rogers also made no attempt to explain how the system of proportions he had respected in occupying the most prominent location on McKim's plan could accommodate such a future enlargement. The professional and popular press alike were no more entranced by the result, even the 1939 *WPA Guide to New York* ended its tour of Columbia's campus with the note that John Jay had destroyed "the harmony of the whole lower end of the campus," and Rogers had but added insult to injury, since "the new library, fits badly into the group, largely because it clashes in scale with near-by buildings."[194]

Despite President Butler's insistent explanations of its importance, Harkness continually barred any discussion of a tunnel connecting the new building to Low Library. It is difficult to imagine that such a lengthy underground connection would have been practical, but its elimination essentially sealed Low Library's fate as a monument in search of a purpose. Low Memorial Library started life as an extraordinary hybrid where the students passed the president's and trustees' rooms to get to the reading room and to the various classrooms and seminar rooms that had been planned to disappear as the new pavilions were completed. But after the books left, the period in which the activities of students and administrators crisscrossed one another's paths came to an end. Some collections remained for a while. But progressively book stacks gave way to administrative functions, and in the mid-1930s Rogers, rather than Kendall, was asked to complete the building's transformation into an office building and ill-adapted exhibition hall and ceremonial space.

Even Butler had reservations about the new library. Once the final project was approved in the spring of 1931 he admitted that adjustments would need to be made to the South Field master plan in deference to the bulk of the new building. Any structures facing Hartley and Livingston would need to be a little lower he thought (an opinion, it might be noted, evoked in the recent discussions concerning Lerner Hall). He was sure that the new monument would look fine once a landscaped approach could be conceived, but Harkness refused to pay for this and the students and alumni resisted all suggestions that the playing fields yield to parterres. Butler's most imaginative suggestion was that the new library's flat roof be used as a roof garden, an idea he took perhaps from the gardens atop some of the buildings under construction at Columbia's Rockefeller Center site. "Every time I see a new building going up in this crowded city," he wrote to Rogers, "I hope that it might be planned with a flat roof and that the roof might be made available to use . . . by those who are going to have no end of difficulty in finding all the light and air that they need as this city grows more and more tightly packed."[195]

Columbia's classicism and debates over modernism in architecture

Butler was no student of Le Corbusier, the Swiss-French architect who had made roof gardens a veritable sine qua non of modernism in his seminal *Vers une architecture (Toward a New Architecture)*, published in 1923. But by the time the new library opened its doors the building had become something of a reference point in the emerging debate over modernism and the Beaux-Arts heritage in American architectural education. After a long period of soul-searching and much outside advice, on 6 February 1933, Butler appointed the progressive young architect Joseph Hudnut as acting dean of Columbia's School of Architecture. Although Hudnut remained only two years in his post before leaving for Harvard, his major overhaul of Columbia's architectural curriculum, with his effort to wean students of stylistic analogies and the classical orders of architecture as starting points for design solutions, is a celebrated threshold in the history of architectural modernism in America.[196] On the day of his appointment Hudnut could look across campus to South Hall (later Butler Library) nearing completion (see fig. 62) and witness its great cage of steel disappearing behind a robust screen of classical columns, that had not even a nominal structural role in the building, which was monumental evidence of everything Hudnut felt was wrong with American architecture. After South Hall's first year in service, Hudnut used it as an entirely negative case in point in his "Notes on Educational Policy in the School of Architecture," which accompanied a confidential list of possible successors to his deanship, submitted to the president in 1935:

> There exists among American architects two different and opposing viewpoints in respect to the relation of aesthetic effects to the structure of buildings. One group (the traditional, or conservative group) believes that structure and aesthetic effects may be more or less unrelated except that the first serves to sustain or hold in place the elements of the latter. This point of view is exemplified in the Riverside Church where the structure is steel and yet there is no suggestion of steel in the appearance of the building. The idea is exemplified also in the new library (South Hall) which has the aspect of a stone palace although built of steel and concrete.[197]

Hudnut counted his own pedagogical crusade as key to advancing a second point of view. Although he considered it to be in opposition to Columbia's traditionalism, in retrospect it seems a more middle-of-the-road stance in the expanding field of architectural philosophies. Hudnut made no reference to European avant-garde architecture, which had been exhibited at the Museum of Modern Art on Fifth Avenue three years earlier and laid down in Henry Russell Hitchcock and Philip Johnson's influential primer *The International Style* that same year. Rather he pointed to a group of American architects who, without denying "the beauty of the old architectures [feel] that our buildings would be more expressive and ultimately more beautiful if we could discover some aesthetic values in the structure rather than add these on in the name of architecture. An example of such a building is the Empire State Building in which the exterior is obviously a thin membrane-like covering for a steel frame."[198]

The long period in which the campus had provided lessons and examples for Columbia's architectural students–lessons carried far afield moreover by the prominent place accorded Columbia's master plan in the widely influential student edition of the *Monograph of the Work of McKim, Mead & White*, assembled by Kendall and the other partners in the firm between 1915 and 1920–was over. The last project that McKim, Mead & White drew for Columbia, in 1929, was a small art gallery and fine arts building to occupy the site at the north end of the central axis, that is, at the middle of 120th Street (fig. 63), once a donor could be found.[199] This was a charming throwback to McKim's original scale, a point made espe-

FIGURE 63 *McKim, Mead & White, Proposed art gallery on 120th Street, 1928 (cat. 73)*

cially clear in the careful pencil sketch that the office prepared to show the calibrated classical build-up of volumes from the art gallery to a faithfully completed University Hall to Low Library, still crowning the academic acropolis (see fig. 52).

The School of Architecture was already moving in a different direction. In 1932, as Dean Boring was preparing to retire, the jury of the school's Charles Follen McKim Fellowship–comprising many of the New York architects who later served on the search committee that chose Hudnut–awarded both first and second prize to designs for a thirty-story skyscraper to be erected atop University Hall, which Rogers and Butler had just abandoned as a site (fig. 64)! With a great deal of irony, and as a parting gesture, Architecture Dean William Boring–a McKim, Mead & White employee many years earlier–submitted his own version to President Butler, suggesting he publish it in his next annual report (figs. 134 & 135). Carefully calculated as a backdrop to McKim's classical composition and as "the logical solution of the campus Building problem," Boring explained that the tower could be built immediately but only outfitted floor by floor as required. This would eliminate the need for new architecture for decades to come, since such a tower "would contain the equivalent of all space now on the campus which is used for educational activities."[200] Here was a model of the urban university that had been recently realized with considerable bravura for the University of Pittsburgh–Charles Klauder's famous 1925 Cathedral of Learning–which was the veritable antithesis of McKim's Columbia.

One cannot help wondering if Nicholas Murray Butler was derisive or tempted when he received Boring's sketch and description which was discussed later that year by the trustees' Committee on Buildings and Grounds. Increasingly it would seem Butler wished Columbia would reflect something of his own stature in the international worlds of education, diplomacy, and charitable organizations. In 1930, Butler did not hesitate to impress on Harkness, for instance, the urgency of decisions about the new library, writing that he hoped a donation might be announced quickly to the trustees, and in any case before his departure: "On March 8 I am sailing with my wife and daughter . . . for Europe, to be gone some weeks on business connected with the Carnegie Endowment. I have some important conferences at the Vatican and have accepted the invitation of the German Government to address the Reichstag."[201] A decade later Butler asked the university's recently reorganized Department of Buildings to study an "automobile approach to the upper campus," so that dignitaries could be dropped off directly at Low Library rather than at the foot of McKim's daunting stairs on 116th Street.[202] Variants for a "motor entrance" weaving between St. Paul's Chapel and Avery or looping up from Broadway around Earl Hall to reach Low Library's entrances were studied. For a brief moment McKim's master plan was imperiled, at risk of being transformed prophetically into a microcosm of the highways that would soon rip asunder the fabric of America's cities. But in 1953, eight years after Butler's retire-

FIGURE 64 *Howard Bahr, Skyscraper to rise above the lower stories of University Hall, Charles Follen McKim Fellowship design, School of Architecture, 1932 (Avery Library)*

ment, the trustees negotiated with the city for the closing of 116th Street to traffic, which was transformed into College Walk. The two halves of McKim's master plan were united for the first time into an uninterrupted academic precinct in the midst of the city. By then, however, all the principles McKim stood for were the subjects of profound doubt and challenges.

Columbia stuck between tradition and modernity: the 1940s and early 1950s

For nearly a decade after World War II Columbia seemed adrift, and nowhere more prominently than in architecture and planning. Three years after Butler retired in 1945, the university was still in search of a president, and the trustees and Acting President Frank Fackenthal wondered aloud how architectural decisions should be made; open competitions and jettisoning the long-standing policy of not awarding commissions to architecture school faculty were both considered but rejected. Launching the new Development Program for Columbia University before the Alumni Federation in January 1948, Chairman of the Trustees Douglas M. Black admitted that "for as long as most of us can remember, planning and development of the University have been identified with our beloved Dr. Butler. . . . the trustees were a little inclined to look to him for almost everything."[203] They were not confident simply to fall back on the firm of McKim, Mead & White, however. William Kendall, who had taken responsibility for Columbia for more than thirty years–beginning even before 1906, when McKim's health and spirit failed after the assassination of Stanford White atop Madison Square Garden–had died in 1941. By then he had not built for Columbia for over a decade, in large measure due to the slump of the Great Depression, and a year earlier Butler himself had passed him over for designs for a new experimental theater to be named after longtime Columbia professor and theater critic Brander Matthews. The building, erected on the East Campus, was experimental only in name, for the trustees endorsed the choice of one of the period's more stylistically conservative large firms, Eggers & Higgins; both of the principals were pupils of John Russell Pope, whose name epitomizes conservative classicism in the mid-twentieth century, and who had taught briefly in Columbia's School of Architecture decades earlier.

In the postwar years McKim's reputation was at low ebb, even among Columbia's leading intellectuals. In John Kouwenhoven's widely read polemic *Made in America: The Arts in Modern Civilization,* published in 1948 with a preface by Columbia's famed Mark Van Doren, few aspects of American architecture were so summarily dismissed: "The work of men like McKim . . . had less relation to the vital contemporary forces of American life, and to its future, than even the crudest, least ingratiating examples of small-town dwellings or the most materialistically functional office buildings."[204] The university's own image was far from brilliant during these years; tourists to the campus could contemplate Columbia's new scale while reading a description in the 1939 *WPA Guide to New York* of the institution as a veritable factory, a quality detected too in many of the buildings of the 1920s: "Columbia has not escaped the accusation of applying mass production methods to higher education. . . . Certainly a corporation that has six thousand employees, thirty thousand customers, an annual budget of more than ten million dollars, and is one of the largest landowners in the city, cannot avoid the appearance of an industry. . . . One of the innovations credited to [its president] is the use of modern publicity methods in the field of learning. For every student enrolled in Columbia when Dr. Butler became president, today there are seven."[205]

Alumni spirits too were glum. In 1947 College alumnus Howard Coon published a highly polemical history of Columbia–the only substantial one issued between the 150th anniversary in 1904 and the bicentennial in 1954–containing a hard-nosed and acerbic attack on the legacy of Butler, Inc., which laid out the dilemma facing "Columbia University at the End of an Era." "For nearly half a century [Nicholas Murray Butler] enjoyed delusions of grandeur, some of which became realities in brick and stone. For forty-four years he confused Morningside Heights with Mount St. Geneviève or the Acropolis."[206] Coon counseled Columbia to return to its roots, admonishing the trustees that the college must be at the heart of its concerns with "the development of college-mindedness in contrast to the university-mindedness which has existed."[207] He looked to the development of the Contemporary Civilization curriculum and the stable of famous teachers in the college, including Lionel Trilling, Mark Van Doren, Jacques Barzun, and Harry Carman, the last soon to take up the deanship of the college, as leading intellectual and moral forces that should stamp the larger institution. By the early 1950s Columbia College had responded with a major fund-raising effort and plans to develop a series of new buildings on South Field, which would be designated as the "Columbia College Campus" after 116th Street was closed in 1954 and the area relandscaped.

By 1948 the trustees decided to take the situation in hand. Even before they offered the presidency to Dwight D. Eisenhower in 1948–a strategy to capitalize on the general's enormously popular reputation–they had drawn up plans for campus expansion that they hoped would be a vital wedge in attacking the much discussed "decline" of Manhattan's West Side. In this they were not departing from Butler's vision. For already in one of his final letters to the trustees, in September 1945, Butler, nearly blind, put the situation in terms not quite black and white:

> It has always been my ambition to have the University own all the property between 114th and 122nd Streets, Amsterdam Avenue and Morningside Drive, in order that it might be made part of the campus for development in years to come. In this way we should unify Morningside and lay the basis for the solution of the difficult problems which will confront our successors, but we should also protect ourselves against invasion from Harlem or from the North. Morningside Park is, so far as it goes, a helpful protection, but the pressure upon Harlem for extension of its area is very great and at any time we might find an apartment house on Morningside Heights has been pur-

chased to be occupied by Harlem tenants. The investment of University funds in these buildings would, in my judgment, be excellent and would produce a somewhat larger income than those which come from ordinary investments in securities. Moreover, by owning the title of all of this property . . . we should achieve that unity of Morningside Heights which I have had in mind for a half century.[208]

In 1947 Columbia took a leading role, along with fourteen other neighborhood institutions, in organizing Morningside Heights, Inc., "a nonprofit agency promoting neighborhood conservation and redevelopment," under the presidency of David Rockefeller which sponsored a $75,000 study on the neighborhood's housing conditions. As Robert A. M. Stern notes, "In 1951, when Morningside Heights Inc. recognized in the Title I provisions of the 1949 Housing Act a way to promulgate physical change benefiting the middle class constituency that was the backbone of the area's institutional employment group, the organization became the sponsor of the city's first Title I redevelopment project, Morningside-Manhattanville."[209] Subsequent modifications to this legislation–which permitted the federal government to take land declared blighted–were made under President Eisenhower once he left Columbia's President's House overlooking Morningside Park for 1600 Pennsylvania Avenue in 1950. The stage was set for Columbia's neighborhood policies and for the redevelopment of its own campus with both the optimism and the ultimate paradoxes of urban renewal, which would culminate in the now famous standoffs of 1968.[210]

The emergence of the superblock idea in Columbia's planning

By the late 1940s the "grand compositions" of campus planning were under attack within the architectural profession, spearheaded by Columbia's former architecture dean Joseph Hudnut, who portrayed them in an article on college planning as "corseting the body of a live and unpredictable creature."[211] In 1948, a year after his analysis, the trustees revamped the structure of architectural decision making at Columbia, appointing an outside consulting architect, Fritz Woodbridge, to work with the university's Department of Buildings and Grounds, which was growing into a veritable planning agency. In 1956 President Grayson Kirk established a Senior Architects Advisory Council including the dean of the Architecture School and several established New York City practitioners. Unlike McKim, Mead & White, the new consultants–the stylistically conservative firm of Adams and Woodbridge–were not the default designers but rather merely coordinators of the huge anticipated expansion of the university. Individual commissions would be awarded to firms with specific expertise in one of the diverse types of buildings required by the increasingly broad range of activities and fields of research of the postwar research university, which included everything from advanced laboratories for nuclear research–Columbia had, of course, been the site of much of the research for the Manhattan Project in the early 1940s–to performing arts centers, administrative buildings, and expanded sports facilities, not to mention classrooms for evermore diverse teaching, sometimes involving audiovisual equipment, and student and faculty housing. The idea of a neutral shell in which any university function could be accommodated—the very principle of McKim's campus—was replaced by the developing modernist ethos during the late 1940s that diverse and complex functions should lead to highly particularized solutions and even distinctive architectural forms for different types of study and research.

Voorhees, Walker, Foley & Smith, specialists in laboratory design for both universities and private corporations, had begun to study the expansion of Columbia's School of Engineering, promised since the 1920s. In the early 1950s they undertook studies for an extensive off-campus Engineering Center, finally concentrating their efforts on a site at the end of 125th Street near the Hudson River piers, which could be exploited for the delivery of the heavy equipment increasingly required for engineering research,[212] before turning their attention finally back to the northeast corner of the campus. Eggers & Higgins, whose style was evolving toward a middle-of-the road modernism, studied sites on the north campus for a new gymnasium (fig. 65) and proposed completing University Hall as an administrative annex to Low Library—a project also studied by Adams and Woodbridge (plate 12). For the college, Shreve, Lamb and Harmon—best known as architects of the Empire State Building—studied various South Field sites for a Citizenship Center as the long desired student center was rebaptized in the early 1950s in direct response to President Eisenhower's impassioned appeals that America's schools and colleges take a role in preparing the nation's youth to form a citizen's army, the country's "first line of defense" against the "lengthening shadow of world communism."[213] While none of these buildings was undertaken until many years later, each of these firms would ultimately, sometimes after countless changes of site and program, see their studies turn into additions to the campus. Each ultimately would face the challenge of finding a suitable expression within the framework of McKim's master plan even as its classical underpinnings were no longer broadly subscribed to as articles of faith in American architecture. Shreve, Lamb and Harmon's unrealized projects of 1948 and 1953 for a Citizenship Center, for instance, were the first of numerous essays in these years in which a compromise between the stylistic idiom of American modernist design and the contextual designs of McKim's strictly ordered geometric master plan was sought (figs. 66 & 67). Their Citizenship Center would not only complete Van Am Quadrangle, and thus create a sense of enclosure the college had been missing since Columbia left Midtown, but would respond very directly to President Butler's remark upon the completion of South Hall (Butler Library) that any future buildings upon South Field would need to be lower to compensate for the scale and bulk of James Gamble Rogers's building.

At first glance the projects that Voorhees, Walker, Smith, Smith & Haines developed for the School of Engineering and Applied Science,

FIGURE 65 *Eggers & Higgins, Project for a new gymnasium at the northwest corner of campus, behind Chandler Hall, March 1947 (cat. 74)*

FIGURE 66 *Shreve, Lamb and Harmon, Design for a Citizenship Center on South Field, 1948, photograph of a lost rendering (cat. 93)*

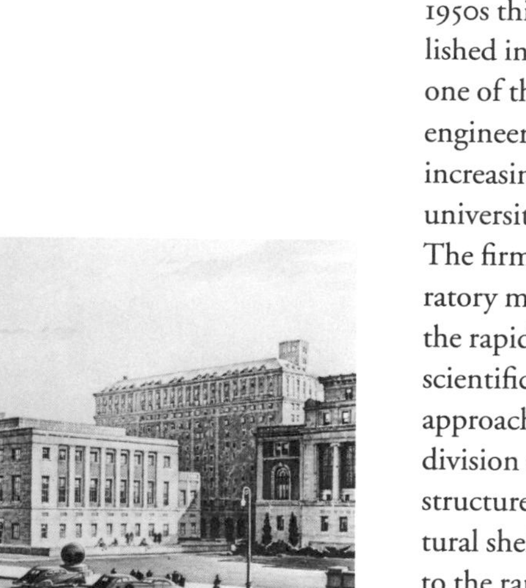

FIGURE 67 *Shreve, Lamb and Harmon, Design for a Citizenship Center on South Field, 1953, photograph of a lost rendering (cat. 94)*

once it was decided to develop new laboratory space on the campus itself, seem equally products of a negotiation between a more modern expression and the general lines of McKim's grand composition, as it had already been updated by Kendall in the 1920s. By the mid-1950s this firm, which was established in the 1930s, had emerged as one of the leading designers of engineering laboratories for the increasingly intertwined worlds of universities and private industry. The firm elaborated a flexible "laboratory module approach" to fight the rapid obsolescence endemic in scientific research buildings, an approach in which both spatial subdivision and the equipment infrastructure were free from the structural shell and thus easily adaptable to the rapidly changing demands of advanced scientific research.[214]

Their first building for Columbia, the George B. Pegram Laboratory, an annex to Pupin Hall completed in 1955 (and now demolished) to house an advanced positive ion accelerator, was a modest essay in a new functionalist iteration of McKim's brick-and-limestone language. In the same year they presented a three-phase proposal for the development of the entire northeast corner of the campus as an Engineering Center, anchored at the corner of 120th Street and Amsterdam Avenue by an enormous slab, faced in brick, whose overall massing and footprint respected more or less Kendall's 1920s proposals for the development of Columbia's northern elevation. If the Seeley W. Mudd Building, as phase one was baptized upon completion, echoed the height of Pupin Hall and made nominal reference to the older buildings in its use of granite facing at sidewalk level and a residual use of limestone trim, it introduced a new principle to Columbia planning that was to have dramatic consequences both for the form of the campus and for the university's relation to the neighborhood for decades to come. The Engineering School's fourteen stories of functionalist space rose as a setback slab over a three-story base flush with the streetline. While Kendall projected that the tall buildings along 120th Street would all be entered on ground level directly from the Grove, Voorhees, Walker, Smith, Smith & Haines proposed to use the base of their building to raise the ground level of the north campus to the 150-foot datum of McKim's upper terrace. The shallow terrace created by the set back after the fourth floor–optimistically verdant and populated with researchers taking a moment's respite in the sun in the official rendering of the building (fig. 68)–was to be extended southward in a second phase of construction as the Engineering Terrace, the roof of which would bridge the gap between the northern edge of McKim's terrace and Seeley W. Mudd (fig. 69).

The brick pathways of McKim's campus were thus to be brought to a new precipitous end, overlooking now not the park of Columbia's disappearing Grove but the city streets far below the level of the campus. From one point of view it could be said that McKim's insistence on a subtle hierarchy and progression of levels was to be severely compromised by transforming his classically bounded plinth into a fragment of the meandering plaza of the modernist city with its desire to sink even existing streets into canyons. On the other it might well be argued that from the moment in 1894 when McKim left the northern third of his master plan blank, he failed to address one of the most dramatic of the site's topographical conditions. Although there was an asymmetrically placed entrance to the Engineering Center on 120th Street, from the first the principal entry would be on campus level. The Engineering Terrace would contain structural steel members dimensioned to carry a second slab set perpendicular to the first (redesigned in 1963), and be the first of Columbia's buildings in which the roof is actually the floor of the campus. This principle was emulated twenty years later when the new gymnasium (1974) filled in yet more of the Grove and led to a retrofitting of Pupin, with its entrance moved to an upper floor.

The East Campus development

By the time these projects were in development the trustees had decided to formulate an overall plan for campus expansion in preparation for an ambitious fund-raising drive launched in the wake of the university's bicentennial celebrations in 1954. In that year Harrison & Abramovitz were commissioned to prepare a planning study that would encompass possible expansion to the east of Amsterdam Avenue, where the vast majority of the property had been acquired by the university since the 1920s, and to the south of 114th Street, where considerably more of the property was in private hands. Wallace K. Harrison was a former employee of McKim, Mead & White, and Max Abramovitz was a 1932 alumnus of the architecture school (plate 9); but most importantly they had played a key role among the teams of architects who collaborated on Rockefeller Center, which was begun in 1929 and since 1941 was again under study for expansion to the west side of Sixth Avenue.[215] Not only was Rockefeller

FIGURE 68 *Voorhees, Walker, Smith, & Smith, Design for an Engineering Center (Seeley W. Mudd Building) as seen from 120th Street, ca. 1958, photograph of a lost rendering (Columbiana Collection)*

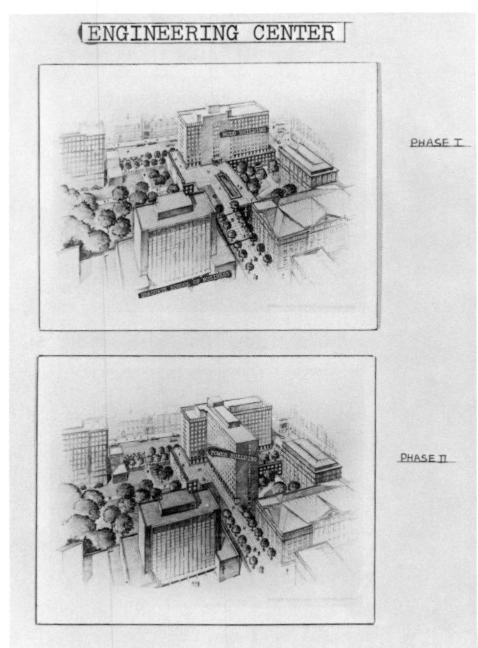

FIGURE 69 *Voorhees, Walker, Smith, Smith & Haines, Design for an Engineering Center, 1962 (cat. 91)*

Center one of Columbia's principle sources of institutional wealth, but the approach pioneered there of multilevel superblock planning seemed the ideal architectural prototype for a campus eager for ever greater victories over Manhattan's grid plan.

Harrison & Abramovitz advised the trustees to focus their energies to the east where the blocks from 115th to 120th Streets between Amsterdam and Morningside could be developed not as a parallel campus—as Kendall and Gamble Rogers had sketched out for a more constrained East Campus in the 1920s and 1930s—but as a nearly seamless extension of the existing campus. They proposed returning to the city, which had allowed Columbia to close 116th Street between Broadway and Amsterdam Avenue in 1953 to create the pedestrian College Walk, for permission to close four more streets: 116th, 117th, 118th, and 119th, between Amsterdam Avenue and Morningside Drive. Whereas 116th Street would be extended as a pedestrian way right to the edge of the esplanade overlooking Morningside Park, the other streets would be eliminated. This would create a superblock whose raised terrace would provide a great level plinth, even as the ground fell away sharply toward the north. The space within the plinth could be used for services and for extensive garage space for the growing percentage of university staff and faculty who were joining the exodus to the suburbs, while above classroom buildings and office high-rises could be positioned on a four-block plane set free from the constraints and hazards of New York City's streets and grid plan.

Harrison & Abramovitz did not limit themselves to the eastern expansion, where they had been invited to make specific architectural proposals, but proposed that the principle suggested by Voorhees, Walker, Smith, Smith & Haines embodied in the Engineering Terrace be extended to retrofit the "present main campus [by] raising the entire area (except for two service courts) of the old Grove to the level of the upper campus and leveling off the upper portions of University Hall to provide one vast open space, comparable to South Court and South Field. . . . The extremely difficult problem presented by University Hall" was to be solved by burying it permanently within the plinth.[216]

Raising the level of North Campus

While Harrison & Abramovitz packaged the emerging modernist ethos of the raised pedestrian plaza with building slabs set freely and asymmetrically in large open spaces—so universal in postwar urban redevelopment—as the logical extension, even the culmination, of McKim's master plan, the consulting architects, Adams & Woodbridge, were skeptical. They objected in particular to expanding the open space behind Low Library, underscoring that the proportions and sequences of open spaces were key to McKim's conception, and that without University Hall forming a courtyard Low Library itself would be hopelessly set adrift from McKim's carefully anchored patterns of built and open space. Reviewing Harrison & Abramovitz's plans on behalf of the trustees, they underscored that University Hall was the singularly most important "aesthetic consideration." Even if all the practical factors concerning relocating the power house, gymnasium, and swimming pool currently housed in the incomplete building's lower stories could be resolved, they still felt that a building to complete McKim's grand axis was a necessity as "an attractive central feature of the entire group," even though they conceded that it would inevitably assume a different shape than that projected a half century earlier by McKim.[217] They were in no way slavishly attached to McKim's original vision, however, even granting that "a change in scale in any additions to University Hall would be permissible because it is a central, axial building and would not be considered against a matching building opposite to it," an argument embodied in their own proposal for this key site (plate 12). They unwittingly provided the rationale for the approach taken seven years later when construction began on the banal slab of Uris Hall (1962–1964), which rises far above the height of McKim's projected Roman-bath assembly hall for this site.

Adams & Woodbridge applauded the idea of a consistent modernist remaking of the northern reaches of the campus, as long as it was developed in a symmetrical way that continued the circulation of McKim's original plan. The great plinth proposed for the engineering building should be echoed on the other side of the campus, the whole developed with sunken courtyards in which great curtain wall facades could allow the rooms contained within the plinth to enjoy views out to the surviving sylvan fragments of the Grove, notably the center of the site where they were emphatic that no building should–as the recently completed Morris A. Schapiro Center for Engineering and Physical Science Research (1989–1991) has –obstruct the view of McKim's ruggedly rusticated University Hall and its verdant forecourt. Perhaps the most striking of their recommendations was that McKim's upper campus should be frozen, with no further consideration given to the planned inner pavilions. They even remarked that "it would be better if Avery had not been built in its present location." McKim's pavilions with their overly generous floor-to-floor heights could not be justified in contemporary economic terms, and the unintended openness of the upper campus was now considered a quality of the campus design to be jealously protected. They concluded their report by noting that while "the proposals for raising the ground level of extensive areas may seem at first glance a fantastic and uneconomical idea" they were at once eminently practical in creating enormous underground service areas and were the only hope for "finally producing one magnificent unified campus for Columbia."[218]

The marriage of urban redevelopment and Columbia's expansion

By March 1956, the trustees were ready to unveil the first phase of the great superblock project for East Campus, limited for the time being to the two blocks bounded by 116th and 118th Streets, since the city had agreed in March of 1955 to close 117th Street between Amsterdam Avenue and Morningside Drive and convey title for the land to Columbia. At a press conference in New York's City Hall, Columbia's future was celebrated as a collaborative effort of the city and the university.[219] Mayor Robert F. Wagner,

FIGURE 70 *Harrison & Abramovitz, Bird's-eye view of East Campus superblock, 1956, photograph of a lost rendering (Columbiana Collection)*

and Robert Moses, an alumnus of Columbia's Graduate School of Arts and Sciences (Ph.D. 1914) and mastermind of numerous collaborations between the city's institutions and the proponents of slum clearance, praised Harrison & Abramovitz's designs for a projected $17-million group of three buildings. Captured in bird's-eye perspective renderings (fig. 70 and plates 11 & 13) by Robert E. Schwartz (a 1950 alumnus of the School of Architecture), the scheme called for three large buildings composed asymmetrically above a large raised plaza, which would provide a common base of services for the buildings and connect them to the McKim campus via a broad bridge-plaza spanning Amsterdam Avenue for a full city block. In addition to new quarters for the Law School at the 116th Street corner of the site – the only piece of the project to be built roughly as projected (1959–1961) – the superblock was to include an office building for 200 faculty members and, at Morningside Drive north of the Faculty House, a men's residence hall for 742 graduate students in engineering, law, and business. Harrison & Abramovitz projected a gleaming white expanded campus in which reinforced concrete framing would be exploited for ever greater flexibility of interior planning and called for the development of a modernist expression of institutional monumentality, all belying the logic of postwar office design that prevailed within.

At the press conference President Grayson Kirk reassured any traditionalists or nostalgic alumni lurking in the audience that the designs were preliminary and that "any approved final design will call for a predominance of red brick and Indiana limestone, the materials of the present neo-Renaissance campus buildings." But to many observers it was all too apparent that new projects, no matter what they were sheathed in, were premised on a highly ambiguous attitude toward both the traditional campus and the traditional city. As Robert Stern notes, "the visually acute sociologist Nathan Glazer," responding to *New York Times* editorials praising "a new happy relationship between the city and the University" in the larger schemes of the urban redevelopment of Manhattan's West Side, dismissed the proposal as "depressing." "He objected particularly to the elimination of part of 117th Street which he considered 'one of the pleasantest streets in the Columbia neighborhood' . . . and suggested that the completion of McKim's original scheme for the campus as a series of tight internal courtyards would be a superior alternative to expansion."[220] By 1959 117th Street had begun to disappear under a plaza extending the paths flanking St. Paul's Chapel all the way to Morningside Drive, leaving the entrances to Johnson Hall and the Faculty House sunken below the new gleaming and planted plazas of the East Campus. Not only would any reference to McKim's vocabulary be abandoned once the final design of Harrison & Abramovitz's Law School, with its facade of vertical concrete louvers separated by strips of green-tinted glass, was unveiled in 1961, but Abramovitz himself quickly reassured President Kirk every time he seemed on the brink of a failure of nerve. Early in 1963 approvals were finally in hand for the oft-delayed bridge over Amsterdam Avenue, named Revson Plaza in honor of its principal donor, the chairman of Revlon, the cosmetics manufacturer. Although the $1-million bridge required an awkward ramp connection grazing the side elevation of Philosophy Hall, Abramovitz revealed in a letter to Kirk that this was but a temporary inconvenience, destined to disappear once McKim's campus could be corrected according to more contemporary planning principles:

> My reason for this letter is to stress my intense feeling that the project should be pressed to completion . . . because I personally believe it is one of the most important visible features Columbia can make towards the development of its future physical growth. . . . It should be built essentially as planned without reduction in its finishes–its landscape and its size. It should be done with a proudness and if we are to be criticized in the future it may likely be for not building it of finer materials than we have proposed.
>
> In fact as a great planning feature I would even venture to say that someday it will be worthwhile to demolish Philosophy Hall and turn it into an open landscaped space and have the great group of Columbia to the East of Amsterdam visible to all who enter the heart of the Columbia complex on the way to Low Library.[221]

Ferris Booth and Carman Halls and the rise of student activism

Shortly after the March 1956 press conference at city hall, Columbia College announced that funding was finally in hand for a new building on South Field. Shreve, Lamb and Harmon were called back to campus to reconsider the design of the Citizenship Center which they had studied in various guises between 1948 and 1953 as the final component of the so-called Van Am Quad in front of Hamilton. The Fund for Columbia College, which had been at work for nearly a decade to form a distinct identity for the college within the university, had attracted major donations for the patriotically named student center, and a scheme was at hand to tie it to construction of the first new dormitory to rise since the 1920s. The dormitory would be the first of several the college hoped to build to accommodate a projected increase in enrollment and to counteract the growth in commuting students; it would rise at the northeast corner of 114th Street and Broadway, the last gap in the southern periphery of the campus. The site had been studied repeatedly over the years by McKim, Mead & White, first as a low-rise pavilion and then as a pendant to John Jay. The thirteen-story slab of New Hall (renamed Carman Hall after College Dean Harry Carman in 1965) would also serve as the backdrop to the student center, which combined a four-story building on Broadway with a two-story glass-fronted extension, angled toward South Field. Named Ferris Booth Hall for the late son (A.B. 1924) of the donors, Mr. and Mrs. Willis H. Booth, the new student center had a relatively ample budget of $4.27 million, which would allow for considerable attention to interior finishes and materials. But the strict provisions of the dormitory loan pro-

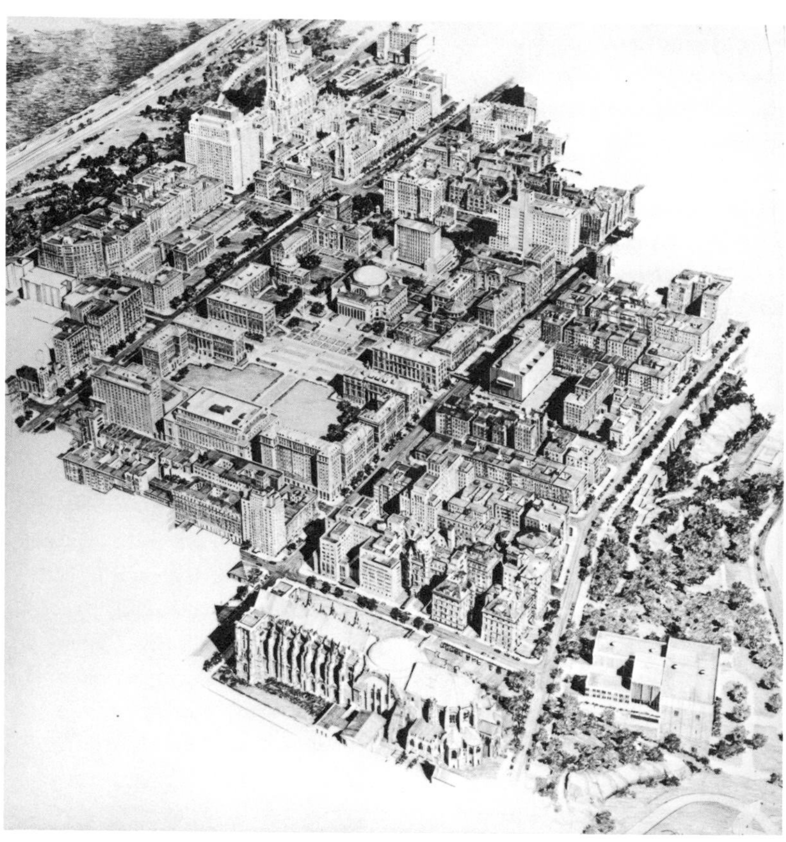

FIGURE 71 *Aerial view of the Columbia University campus and neighboring Morningside Heights with projected gymnasium designed by Eggers & Higgins for Morningside Park, ca. 1965. Also visible are Columbia's recently built Carman Hall (center left) and Uris Hall. Photograph of a lost drawing (cat. 96)*

gram of the Federal Housing and Home Agency, which supplied a $3-million loan for New Hall required that there be no link between the dormitory and the student center–the loan program forbade any feature that reinforced what it called a "country club atmosphere" on college campuses–and thus set a tone of austerity that designer Harvey Clarkson applied to the exteriors of both buildings. Ferris Booth Hall's glass curtain wall provided sweeping views of McKim's campus, but from the exterior its emphatic diagonal was a flagrant disregard of the master plan's compositional principles and classical syntax, which even Gamble Rogers had respected in advancing South Hall far into McKim's field. Not only did the architects make no effort to match the overburned red-brick palette of McKim's campus, but as Robert Stern notes with apt disdain, "the facades contrasted vertical piers with horizontal bands in a misguided attempt to update McKim's classicism."[222] Few were eager to celebrate the addition of Carman and Ferris Booth Halls as either contextually sensitive or innovatively modern–a challenge taken up anew in Bernard Tschumi's design for Lerner Hall, currently replacing Ferris Booth–and from the beginning the dormitory fell to the lowest rank among student housing preferences.

Ironically enough the Citizenship Center–first planned under Eisenhower–was announced as vital to the college's program "to develop in the undergraduates, as part of their college experience, a greater sense of obligation and responsibility to the community." But even before the foundations were begun Shreve, Lamb and Harmon's design unleashed outspoken protests–the first of many in coming years–which quickly moved from the realm of architectural aesthetics to ethics, as students and faculty expressed skepticism concerning the sense of obligation and responsibility the Columbia administration and trustees themselves felt toward either the campus or the neighborhood. In 1957 students and faculty protested the demolition of the gatekeeper's lodge, a picturesque Victorian fragment of the old Bloomingdale Asylum; Dustin Rice, a professor of art history, maintained that it possessed far greater architectural character than McKim's "emasculated Renaissance." By the time Ferris Booth Hall was completed in 1961 pointed barbs from students had appeared not only in campus publications–the *Columbia Owl* devoted an entire issue, largely satirical in tone, to Columbia's recent architecture–but also had been picked up by the New York daily newspapers. Architecture students derided Ferris Booth's marble-and-flagstone detailing as "Bad Miami Decor," while the new dormitory's lounge called to mind "a bus station with Muzak." Perhaps most damning, and most frequently quoted in the press, was the caustic appraisal of the new campus architecture penned by the architecture critic and alumnus Allan Temko in the alumni magazine *Columbia College Today*. With its "lounge of a would-be Hilton Hotel," he labeled Ferris Booth "a horror embarrassingly bureaucratic in mood," while the new dormitory's concrete-block double bedrooms and long corridors evoked a "Victorian reformatory." For comparison critics evoked the important buildings by major figures in contemporary architecture that were not only bringing challenging design but also new ideas about housing and social life to other campuses, notably Eero Saarinen's new colleges at Yale and dormitories at Penn. When, in 1961, the student radio station, WKCR, invited professor Percival Goodman from the School of Architecture to comment on the new campus architecture, the administration confiscated the tapes, since, as the *New York Times* later reported, "it was feared that some of Professor Goodman's remarks might be libelous."[223]

Columbia's stubborn refusal to respond to escalating criticism of its plans to build a gymnasium on public lands in Morningside Park–an idea first broached in conversation between Columbia President Grayson Kirk and Park Commissioner Robert Moses in 1954 and given final city and state approval in 1960[224]–ultimately triggered the riots of April 1968 (fig. 71). But the perception that the university's poor judgment in architectural and planning matters reflected a more deep-seated lack of concern about the institution's role and responsibilities in the neighborhood and in society at large had already been reinforced in the years leading up to those famous events by a series of increasingly confrontational disputes over Columbia's designs both on the campus and in the neighborhood.

An important catalyst was the announcement by the trustees in 1962 of the design to finish, at long last, University Hall, the culminating element of McKim's master plan. Sensibly scaled and detailed, if none too imaginative, projects by Eggers & Higgins for an administration building on this site were shelved since it was decided to use this prestigious location for new quarters for the rapidly expanding School of Business, which was bursting the seams of the last of McKim's pavilions (renamed Dodge Hall in 1965). University Trustee Percy Uris (M.B.A. 1920), who had been serving since 1957 as executive assistant to the president for new construction, offered $2.5 million (later raised to $3 million) toward the new building, a gesture not without echoes of Low's generous patronage almost seventy years earlier. But when Moore & Hutchins's design was unveiled, many wondered aloud if Uris had not accidentally substituted one of the run-of-the-mill Midtown office buildings that had made the fortune of his Uris Buildings Corporation rather than commissioning a suitable closure of McKim's great axis.

Much attention had been paid to the engineering challenges involved in raising an eight-story office slab above McKim's foundations without interrupting the activities of either the pool or boiler house, but all too little attention was paid to issues of design. "Low Library is a marble pantheon of full-scaled dignity," Ada Louise Huxtable wrote, "Uris Hall, by either design or irony, since it is the gift of one of the city's largest builders, whose insensitivity to architectural standards has been matched only by his commercial success, enshrines the tin-type of speculative construction in Columbia's academic groves."[225] While a spokesman for the trustees later defended the building as a background design intended not to upstage McKim, few were convinced that the feeble attempt to relate the lower classroom wings to the volumes of flanking Schermerhorn and Havemeyer Halls was sufficient compensation for the lack of imagination in the bland, even dreary, aluminum-trimmed curtain wall of the eight-story slab rising on axis with McKim's Rotunda. "We thought bad architecture might pass like a nightmare," architecture student Harry Parnass told the *New York Times.* "But when the university came up with the School of Business and held a ground-breaking ceremony to lionize the design–it was too much. We had protested other buildings on campus without reaction so we decided to picket this one."[226]

On 18 April 1962, the university's carefully orchestrated ground-breaking ceremony was turned on its head by an equally skillfully plotted piece of architectural guerrilla tactics worthy of the current theories of the radical Situationists in Paris! The Department of Buildings and Grounds had arranged an amphitheater of chairs facing the new site, exploiting the one-story fragment of University Hall as a theatrical backdrop. On the stage provided by the broad steps spanning the front of the building were placed two easels, one with the architects' perspective rendering of the projected structure, the other with a photograph of McKim's never realized design. As the denouement of the afternoon, after speeches were completed, President Grayson Kirk and Business School Dean Courtney C. Brown were to take a sledgehammer to the photograph of McKim's project, officially launching the new construction project. At precisely the moment when this solemn assassination of McKim's ambitions arrived, the official drama was upstaged by a group of architecture students who had slipped quietly out of nearby Avery Hall and positioned themselves behind the seated guests with placards carrying slogans–We Protest Bad Design, Ban

FIGURE 72 *Protesters from the School of Architecture picketing the ground-breaking ceremony for Uris Hall, 18 April 1962 (Columbia University Archives)*

THE BUILDING, and NO MORE UGLIES (fig. 72).[227] The story was given prominent coverage in the next day's *Times*, where one student was quoted as saying, "If we designed like that they would throw us out of this school."[228] Alan Lapidus, the president of the student organization of the School of Architecture, blasted Uris's bland modernity: "It looks backwards rather than forward – it is mock monumental, eclectic, manneristic and awkward, a junior skyscraper. . . . The building should have some image relating to the students who work in it. The building looks no different from a post office or a branch office of an insurance company."[229]

At this point architecture faculty, who honored the AIA code of ethics prohibiting one professional from criticizing the work of another by refusing to be identified, chimed in by pointing the finger at the university's procedures in selecting designs. One who did speak up in name was Professor James Marston Fitch, who would soon launch at Columbia the nation's first program in architectural preservation. He bemoaned the fact that, with the exception of the dean, the School of Architecture's faculty was never consulted. "We're qualified enough to give degrees in this field, but apparently they don't consider us qualified enough for consultation," Fitch told the *Times*, explaining that "Columbia doesn't have a really comprehensive plan of development. . . . This is particularly serious," he continued, "because the university is in the process of expanding a campus not meant for expansion,"[230] pointing at once to a shortcoming of the master plan and a failure of vision of the present administration. While many recognized the necessity of facing the challenge, few were convinced that Columbia's officials were aware of just what sophistication would be required of their designers.

Peter Blake, the managing editor of *Architectural Forum* and an ardent advocate of modern expression in architecture, was even more blunt: "If Columbia can do no better in this idiom that the drawings of its proposed business school, then it should go back to neoclassical prototypes and thus produce a coherent campus." *Progressive Architecture* editor James T. Burns Jr. admitted that "a scholastic version of a 1950s Uris Brothers office building" was all well and good "for acclimatizing its graduates for their future lives, but it hardly plays fair with other denizens of Columbia who have to live with it," and cited a larger failure of planning in that the building completely sidestepped the possibility of creating a new "dynamic pedestrian traffic pattern at this point of the campus." Had the designers created a suitable monumental entrance from 120th Street around the great curve of University Hall (now crowned by the Business Library), "think . . . [of a] series of grand ramps leading from 120th Street, sweeping around Uris Hall to emerge on the plaza in front of Low! Such a series of levels and outdoor spaces could have been a truly exhilarating experience." (The proposal had in fact been made in the mid-1950s by Adams and Woodbridge [plate 12] but long forgotten). The article concluded with a damning assessment of Columbia's recent architecture in general: "Will it continue in the present vein, leaving Yale to become a veritable museum of buildings by contemporary architectural giants and Harvard to furnish the U.S. with the first building by Le Corbuiser? Great buildings usually do not cost much more than run-of-the-mill ones, and if they sometimes do, who is to put a dollar sign on what superb architecture will mean for generations to come? 'In Thy Light Shall We See Light' proclaims the Columbia motto. With heightened and verbal interest of student and faculty, perhaps the Almighty might cast a ray of hope for architecture and planning at the University in years to come."[231]

In a prescient analysis the *Times* noted that the protest over Uris reflected recent protests against "dull and ugly academic buildings" planned at other rapidly expanding campuses, including Princeton and Trinity College, Hartford, and was part of "a growing trend toward active student participation in public affairs evident on the nation's campuses." The bad publicity came home to roost in the fall when *Columbia College Today* devoted its entire issue to the distressing state of Columbia's architecture and warned that it could only serve as an obstacle to alumni loyalty and generosity.

Tensions between Columbia, the city, and the neighborhood

During the course of the next two years controversy spilled into the nearby neighborhood as the university picked up the pace of acquiring new buildings–108 purchased between 1940 and 1966 at a cost of more than $23 million–and emptied, often with means that bordered on harassment, residential properties in the path of new projects, in particular those for the East Campus superblock. In January 1964 the *Times* reported that despite all the improvements Columbia and Morningside Heights, Inc., had brought to the area–including new playing fields and a track for joint college/community use in the southern end of Morningside Park –the university was viewed with enormous suspicion. This was largely because of the great secrecy that surrounded its projects: "as the painted white X marks appear on condemned buildings, many old-time residents feel themselves threatened," the *Times* noted, in reporting on the first organized rally called by neighborhood residents groups against Columbia.[232]

Although the university had hammered out with city officials many of their earlier expansion plans, and in particular the hundred-year lease on a precipitous cliffside site in Morningside Park, for which Eggers & Higgins had drawn up the latest project for a new gymnasium (see fig. 71), with the arrival of Mayor John Lindsay's administration Columbia began to lose friends in city hall. At the same time Manhattan Borough President Constance Baker Motley called the whole alliance between urban redevelopment and Columbia's expansion into question. In April 1965 the city discussed a renewal plan for the Upper West Side that would freeze institutional expansion on Morningside Heights for a decade, exempting only projects that had already been publicly announced. The day before the board of estimate met to vote on this plan, Columbia hurriedly unveiled eleven new projects, bringing the total of

FIGURE 73 *Harrison & Abramovitz, Preliminary project for the School of International Affairs and plaza, ca. 1966, photograph of a lost model (Avery Library)*

new projects announced since 1962 to twenty. These included an arts center to be built south of the Law School and connected to East Campus by a bridge, a project first proposed in the mid-1950s, as well as ten classroom or dormitory buildings on neighborhood sites that the university had already acquired. While many applauded Columbia's role in attacking the spread of slum areas on the West Side, a growing number sympathized with the plight of tenants faced with relocation, and many loudly accused Columbia of racism, since the buildings were overwhelmingly occupied by black and Puerto Rican tenants, who were living in some instances in notorious SRO conditions.

Over the next few years the university sought simultaneously to program its expansion and to appease its most vociferous critics, both those calling for a halt to the replacement of neighborhood housing with university facilities and those who attacked the lack of coordination and vision in institutional planning. A grant of $10.9 million from the Ford Foundation earmarked for World Studies, announced in January 1965, led to the decision to complete the second of the buildings called for in Harrison & Abramovitz's superblock plan. While the university began the work of clearing faculty and student tenants from the brownstones on 117th and 118th Streets to prepare the site, Harrison and Abramovitz redesigned the building (fig. 73), originally intended as a faculty office tower, to house the School of International Affairs (built 1967–1970). In November of the following year dreams of an expansion to the south, first broached in Harrison & Abramovitz's plans a decade earlier, seemed several steps closer to reality as the university launched a three-year fund-raising campaign for $200 million for expansion and in order to maintain a first-rate faculty and student body. The Ford Foundation responded almost immediately with a pledge of $35 million, "the largest amount ever granted to a single university by the foundation at one time." This included $25 million as a matching challenge grant to be awarded once the university had reached one half of its goal and $10 million for developing programs in urban and minority affairs, intended for joint work by the university and the Ford Foundation concerning problems of "the city and the Negro." "It is sort of ironic that Columbia got that $10 million to work with minority groups," said Franz S. Leichter, the Democratic district leader and longtime Columbia critic. "So far Columbia's solution has been to move minority groups away from their doorstep."[233]

The $200-million campaign was announced with great fanfare on 1 November 1966, and a new master plan unveiled that included the entire neighborhood from 109th to 125th Street, from Riverside Drive to Morningside Park, in a project of ambitious scope drawn up by the University Office of Architectural Planning (fig. 74). Although several new buildings were proposed on the unbuilt sites of Kendall's 1920s master plan for the north end of the campus, once again for expanding the chemistry and biology departments, no building was proposed for any other site on the main campus between 114th and 120th Streets.

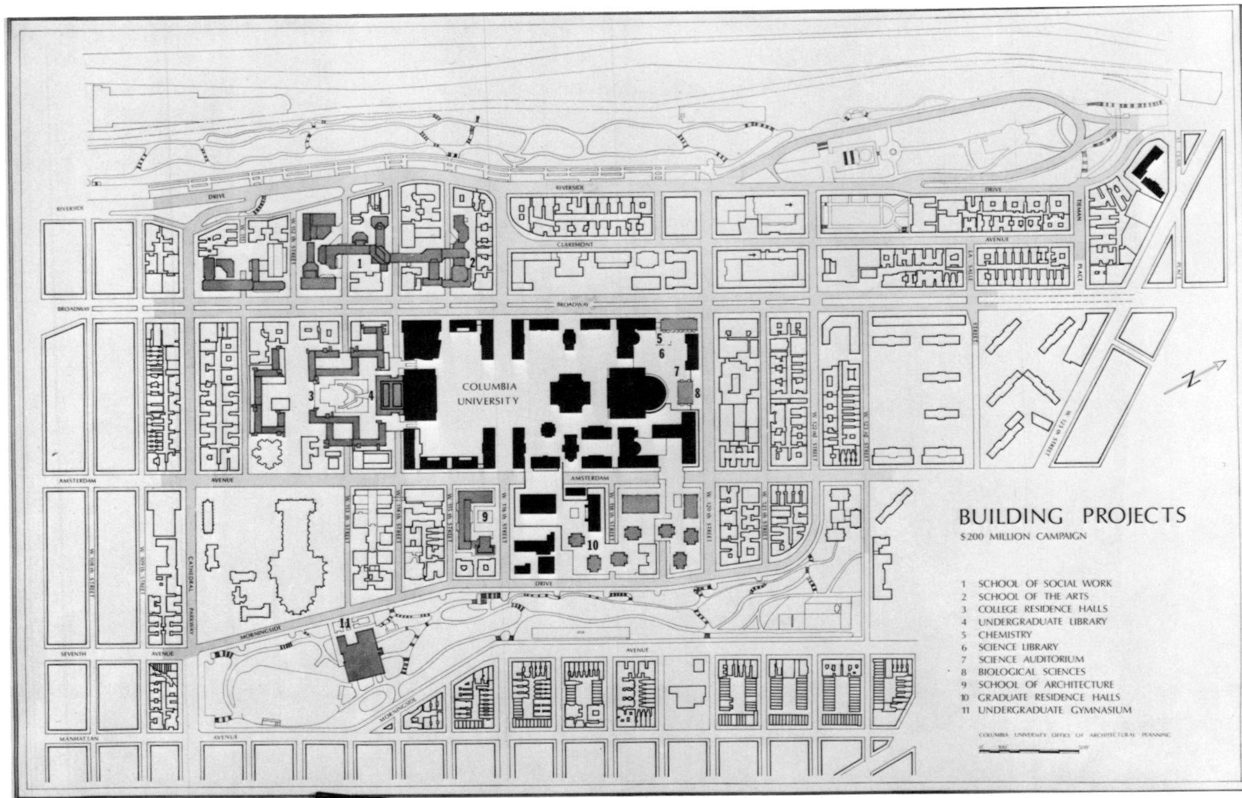

FIGURE 74 *Columbia University Office of Architectural Planning, Building projects for the $200-million campaign, 1966 (cat. 95)*

Rather the university's enormous growth would take place to the east, south, and west, much of it on city blocks that had never before been discussed for institutional development. The East Campus superblock was to be extended to the north with new graduate student housing, closing and bridging streets up to 120th Street, as Harrison and Abramovitz had proposed a decade earlier. And the controversial gym in Morningside Park at 113th Street, under attack by the new parks commissioner Thomas Hoving since he assumed office in January, was defiantly included.

What was new in the 1966 master plan was a major project for extending the campus to the south in the blocks between 114th and 111th Streets on both sides of Broadway to accommodate projects for an entirely residential college and buildings for the university's School of the Arts and the Graduate School of Social Work. All of these projects involved a radical restructuring of city blocks, particularly between Amsterdam and Broadway, where 112th and 113th Streets were to be largely erased or bridged over in order to create an inward-facing residential campus for undergraduates centered around a large undergraduate library appended to the south flank of Butler Library and a new auditorium. On the west side of Broadway, buildings for the Arts and Social Work would snake their way across streets, filling midblock sites while leaving largely intact the Broadway and Riverside Drive frontages, the latter having been increasingly converted to faculty housing. Finally, a new building for the School of Architecture was to be erected on the block south of the Law School, leaving Avery Hall entirely to Avery Library, as intended by Samuel Putnam Avery's original bequest. While the schematic plan suggested that the university's architectural office was eager to explore some of the current architectural and social experimentation with superblocks as well as with structures that interwove built and garden space within the traditional city fabric, only a few projects undertaken by the Architecture School's studios, most famously one for a massive mid-rise megastructure (fig. 75), ever posited a form for this grand vision. The architecture students in fact proposed extending the campus as far south as 105th Street, with a science center—left undesigned in their "future growth plan"—occupying the blocks south of 110th Street.

Just days after the $200-million campaign was announced the *New York Times* architecture critic Ada Louise Huxtable published a penetrating and damning analysis of Columbia's bureaucratic planning and poor track record of community relations. Columbia's proposal for fourteen new buildings, she noted, "make clear in dollars and cents what the Morningside Heights neighborhood has always feared—that Columbia is the maker and shaper of a considerable chunk of the urban environment." She continued:

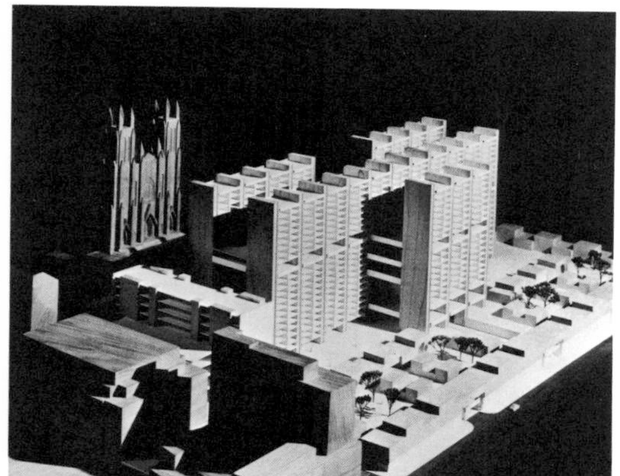

FIGURE 75 *Columbia University South Campus Study, 1963, produced as a studio project in the School of Architecture*

> Since Columbia is obviously in the large-scale planning business to stay, the question arises as to the quality of the university's planning and building record. . . . Results visible now, after almost a decade of construction are so uncoordinated and undistinguished that they suggest to critics a kind of do-it-yourself planning based on a lack of administrative understanding of urban planning as a process, or as a source of superior design. If the present system and standards continue, they predict that the next ten years will produce a great deal more of the same. . . . All of this adds up to a large planning package of radical physical change. But Columbia's vision of planning is a curiously restricted and unprofessional one. It operates as a purely administrative process with architectural afterthoughts. . . . At this early stage, when the university should already be translating its requirements into the most stimulating and suitable environmental concepts, it settles for lists, timetables and room counts, rather than three-dimensional ideas. . . . it is the proven inability of the university to see the environment as a whole and to recognize the need for the highest level of professional vision that threatens its development program and the Morningside Heights neighborhood with planning disaster.[234]

Huxtable's critique soon found echoes among architectural faculty, including the prominent young architect Romaldo Giurgola, who had recently moved to Columbia from Penn and lashed out against the "University's lack of consistent planning [which] has resulted in architectural chaos."[235] Scarcely three months later it seemed Columbia would weather this latest onslaught of sharply critical press, and the trustees proudly announced, on 23 January 1967, that Percy Uris had donated $2 million to the fund drive. By then the controversy over the gym was reaching a boiling point, with Percy Sutton and Charles B. Rangel in Albany calling for a renegotiation of the lease and Columbia conceding to add a swimming pool to the community gym in a vain attempt to appease critics of the separate-but-not-equal facilities for the neighborhood planned for the building's

FIGURE 76 *Construction site for gymnasium in Morningside Park, near 113th Street, 25 April 1968 (cat. 97)*

lower stories. By summer the West Harlem Community Organization was predicting riots over what the *Westside News* had recently baptized "Gym Crow," but the Columbia administration stood its ground and refused to abandon the project – for which fund-raising was making great strides. In July 1967 fifty picketers marched back and forth in front of the President's House in mourning carrying tombstones for buildings "killed" by Columbia, similar to the protest marchers carrying death statistics in Vietnam in the period's antiwar demonstrations. Even those who found merit in Eggers & Higgins's design or endorsed the benefit of the new community facilities without calculating the percentage of space they occupied in the overall scheme were frustrated at Columbia's inflexibility. Instead of listening and seeking to compromise with its neighbors, the university, one alumnus noted in a letter to the *Spectator*, "rather continues to wave the contract in the face of the community very much like Lyndon Johnson quoting the Gulf of Tonkin resolutions."[236]

The events that rocked the Columbia campus in the spring of 1968 – too well known and frequently analyzed to be chronicled once again here[237] – were incited by the arrival of bulldozers in late February atop the cliff face in Morningside Park that Columbia was determined to remake as the gymnasium facility Butler had first promised forty years earlier (fig. 76). By the time the dust settled not only was Butler's original idea of putting the gym on South Field being taken seriously, but even the advice of the *Spectator*'s 1967 April Fool's headline – "New Gymnasium to Be Built under South Field" – no longer seemed so foolish. If nothing else the riots of April 1968 would change the future of Columbia's architecture and planning both on and off campus; ironically one of the results was to prompt a completely new evaluation of McKim's master plan.

I. M. Pei's master plan (1968–1970)

In the wake of publicly scrapping all previous plans for expansion, the announcement by Columbia's new president, Andrew Cordier, of architect I. M. Pei's appointment as consulting master planner at a carefully planned news conference on 7 November 1968 was heralded as "a new and brilliant epoch in the physical planning of the University."[238] A week after an administration spokesman declared that "the University is in a state of flux, and as such, has no definite physical plans," Pei's most pressing charge was to develop a process whereby the stalemate between Columbia and Morningside Heights might be broken. The relatively young Pei, who had first made his name with the Kip's Bay Plaza development (1959–1963), which revitalized an entire neighborhood in the east 20s and 30s, was a particularly astute choice. In 1968 his involvement in community redevelopment in Brooklyn's Bedford-Stuyvesant, a project launched by New York Senator Robert F. Kennedy, had garnered considerable attention and optimism for its innovative involvement of community residents in the planning process. In addition Pei had experience in large-scale campus planning, including the East-West campus at the University of Hawaii and the entire campus of SUNY at Fredonia, although both of these were for entirely new campuses. Consultations between Pei and President Grayson Kirk had begun in the immediate aftermath of the April riots and were resumed once Cordier had taken office and launched his program to open a dialogue with Morningside Heights community groups. By the time the press conference was held Cordier and Pei had worked out in considerable detail the premises for his firm's planning study, which would refocus attention on the campus itself, acknowledge that the competition for space between Columbia and the neighborhood demanded consideration of high-rise solutions, and study mixing both various university functions in new campus structures and university and community functions in the same building in the small handful of structures to be considered for off-campus sites.

Old dreams of a South Campus and of a West Campus remaking whole parts of the street grid in an institutional image were shelved in favor of a new catechism of "intensive use of the land," both on and off campus. "Where zoning permits, some buildings could be thirty stories or more," Cordier announced. Suspicions of social engineering toward gentrification were to be met head on, since Pei was charged with examining "prospects for structures that might contain both University and Community housing and service facilities and government sponsored rent subsidies that would make it possible to provide up-to-date housing for people with low and lower-middle incomes."[239] But the most important message Cordier had to convey was that "Mr. Pei and his associates will consult extensively with neighborhood groups, students and faculty to learn their needs and suggestions. Columbia will welcome from the neighborhood groups and residents constructive suggestions on how the University and its neighbors may plan together."[240] Although Pei's contract specified that "it is expected that the architect shall be engaged to design certain key buildings yet to be selected, which would be called for in the plan," these would be the subject of future agreements. For the time being Pei's talents as a community planner, even go-between, were more urgently needed by Columbia than his services as an architect.

In the spirit of "open communication" announced by Cordier, and later characterized by Pei as "reconciliation," the architect was in a difficult position. Three months into his study he drew up a list of nearly fifty groups he had met with, including government agencies, urban renewal agencies and study groups, community organizations, and student and faculty groups, many of which had been formed in reaction to the university's expansion plans in the 1960s. By the time his report was finally published in March 1970 the number had reached "literally hundreds." Many were openly suspicious of Pei's insistence that the university had granted him "total autonomy from the administration in making his study." One of the first testing grounds was the School of Architecture itself, a key flash point in the April riots and still imbued with both faculty and student commitment to forging a socially responsive profession. In a crowded evening meeting in December 1968 the students cut to the quick, asking the hard questions. They raised the issue of a conflict of interest. "How is your role and power defined by your contract? When can we receive a copy? How do you intend to reach and include people in the community who are normally excluded from the planning process in formulating future policy? Will you set up a field office?"[241] Pei was insistent that "it should not be interpreted that whatever the University tells us to do we will do." But pressed to take a public stand against the gym in Morningside Park—which the university did not formally renounce until the spring of 1969 once Cordier had canvassed nearly a hundred community groups and local leaders—Pei waffled. Reporting to the president, Architecture School Dean Kenneth Smith summed up the evening: "The attached list of questions was prepared by some of our more activist students aided by one SDS member, I am told, not one of the students. Pei did a fine job. He will be able to cope with this and other groups."[242]

Over the course of 1969 tensions and suspicions began to develop between Pei and Columbia as well. Pei and his associates, notably Henry Cobb, worked hard to tutor the administration, encouraging Cordier in private to drop charges against community residents arrested in Morningside Park and to abandon plans for a gym there. And they sought to define the scope of what was expected by the master plan that they were to develop. Should it be simply a matter of building design, as McKim had understood the master plan seventy years earlier, or should it be a question of land use, policies for decision making, and the range of procedure elements that were understood by modern urban planning? In February 1969 Pei met several times with Cordier, hoping to come to an agreement on several general concepts extracted from his meetings with community groups: Columbia should replace any housing destroyed with new housing for the same income level so as not to alter the social mix of the area; the university should coordinate with the urban renewal planner for the area; and facilities for combined public/university use should be considered. Finally, Pei encouraged Columbia to consider decentralization, moving some units of the university to other parts of the city "to permit growth of those which must remain on the Heights" without expansion into the adjacent neighborhood. Pei had already reached the conclusion that his new master plan must be an inward-looking document, one that not only concentrated on developing the historic campus but also involved a certain amount of soul-searching on the part of Columbia's administrators. Although Pei had Cordier's ear, the trustees seemed to drag their feet. Pei pressed that "unless some action is taken soon, momentum will be lost and all planning will grind to a halt."[243] At times it seemed they were even working at cross purposes. Among Pei's preliminary suggestions had been that the university consider using one of its properties elsewhere in the neighborhood or the city as a president's house–the Schinasi Mansion on Riverside Drive at 107th Street was suggested–leaving the valuable site on Morningside Drive for academic use or even for redevelopment with a taller building, since all of the campus was now to be squeezed for every inch of buildable space. (An added benefit of moving the president from the line of local fire was not mentioned.) But in December the Pei office caught wind of the university's plans to sell the Schinasi Mansion. "Planning for the Heights is a difficult task at best," Henry Cobb wrote to John Telfer, the university's planning coordinator, "and could be made impossible if property transactions are not coordinated with our planning efforts."[244]

By the time a draft of Pei's first public report was put in the hands of the administration, tensions had grown. Copies were circulated internally for comments and carefully studied for every nuance, since the final document would be vital to the university's efforts to rebuild the confidence of the community. Certain phrases and assumptions gave particular offense–"I do not consider the President's House an under-utilized site" and "the administration does represent an educational phase of the University"–but most alarming to many was the overall tone. "This report assumes a position adverse to that of the University. It almost cries out for an answer to the question 'Has Columbia done anything right in the last year and a half?'" one internal reader complained. Even after revisions one administrator in the Office of Public Affairs was skeptical:

> My high regard for Mr. Pei and his staff notwithstanding, I perceive no advantage for the University in having the Pei organization serve in a general political/community relations capacity as Columbia's agent or emissary. The sincere interest, energy and enthusiasm that Mr. Pei's staff has given to the Columbia project has been a benefit to us in many ways; I think, however, that the benefit begins to wane and threatens to become a burden when the Pei people lose sight of the fact that we are their principals and clients in this matter, and seem to act as though they are an independent third party–some sort of secu-

lar holy spirit—sent from on high to save us from our sins. I believe they have exhibited a tendency to do this.[245]

In March 1970 Columbia finally issued I. M. Pei & Partners' *Planning for Columbia University: An Interim Report* with its specific proposals for how Columbia should meet its needs for academic and administrative space for the next twenty years on its current campus and with suggested prototypes for off-campus development in which both university and community housing might be combined. Perhaps as startling as Pei's specific designs for office towers (plate 14 and fig. 77) framing South Field and for a huge horizontal slab for the Department of Chemistry (fig. 78) raised on stilts above the business library at the rear of Uris Hall was the framing of his overall planning philosophy for Columbia in terms borrowed from Seth Low and Charles McKim. Once again it was a matter of defining an image and a pattern for Columbia that had to do with its distinct character as "an urban university." While he did not cite McKim's insistence on "the metropolitan character of the situation," he did quote at length from Seth Low's famous speech at the dedication of the site in 1896 in which he had insisted that, as Columbia's administrators were only too aware after 1968, "a university that is set upon a hill cannot be hid." Although Pei asserted that McKim's plan "had become a victim of economic considerations and ad hoc planning" since the 1950s, he did not propose any literal return to it as a template; rather he celebrated the challenge of finding "20th-century means to make a 19th-century plan work." He promised a solution that would both fight the ad hoc disorder that had obscured the clarity and nobility of McKim's plan and at the same time would assess Columbia's space needs in such a way that the severe overcrowding in existing buildings could be relieved even as at least some of the projected expansion took place on the campus's vacant sites. "Columbia's present main campus is underbuilt, not only by today's norms of urban density but also by McKim, Mead & White's own master plan. . . . Specifically, the floor area ratio is very small—3 to 1. . . . That's about half the amount permitted by law. The Columbia campus is developed to about 50 percent of capacity."[246] Columbia, he concluded, should be planned not as a traditional campus but as a microcosm of the city itself:

> The physical hallmarks of a great urban university, like the city itself, are intensity of land use, variety of space, constant life and varied activity. By definition, physical facilities will be concentrated. But the activities they contain will not be limited to just one plane. Rather, some should be built high above the campus, others at ground level, and still others underground. A thriving central area which ties all parts together and forms the heart of the university is as vital to Columbia's health as downtown is to a city's.[247]

Only a few years earlier Pei had worked with William Zeckendorf on a series of proposals for the revitalization of downtown Montreal that combined a series of high-rise office towers and extensive planning of underground concourses both for commercial activity and for pedestrian travel between the subway and various points in the vertical city during the frigid winter months. The Columbia proposal was devel-

FIGURE 77 *I. M. Pei & Partners, View of South Field towers from the upper stories of John Jay Hall, 1970 (cat. 98)*

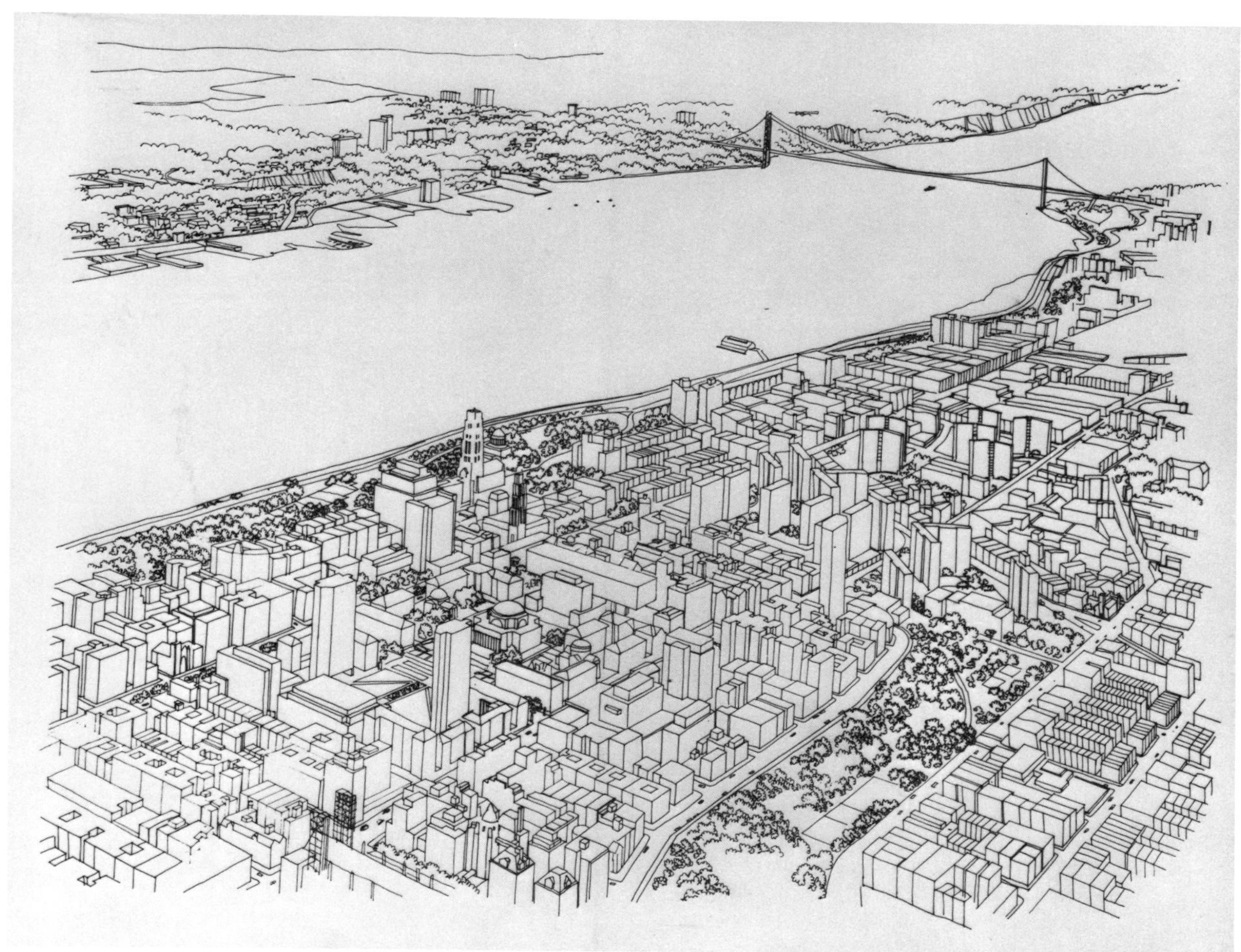

FIGURE 78 *I. M. Pei & Partners, Master plan for Columbia University: aerial view of campus and neighborhood with addition of towers on South Field and new science building behind Uris, 1970 (cat. 98)*

oped in parallel to his emerging approach to North America's ailing downtowns.

The most startling and controversial of Pei's proposals—and practically all that local lore has retained—were his ideas for the intensive development of South Field, which was to be flanked by two twenty-three-story towers connected underground by an extensive multilevel concourse. The towers would concentrate administrative and faculty offices, which had proliferated pell-mell throughout the campus, allowing the return of McKim's pavilions to the classroom use for which they were ideally suited. Pei compared the effect to musical chairs. South Field would be excavated for the creation of five underground levels, including a complete gymnasium and expansion of Butler Library to compensate for the projected undergraduate library lost with the cancellation of the South Campus extension below 114th Street. The uppermost level of the concourse, "within the long steel trusses of the roof structure"[248] would provide a student commons connecting all these services directly to the elevator banks of the two towers and provide space for lounges, meeting rooms, a branch post office, a "rathskeller," dining facilities, and shops. It might be possible even to make a connection

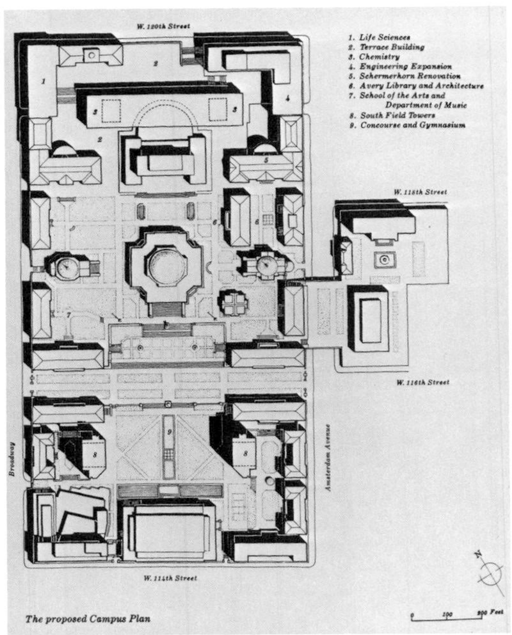

FIGURE 79 *I. M. Pei & Partners, Master plan showing proposed new buildings to be designed by Pei and others, 1970 (cat. 98)*

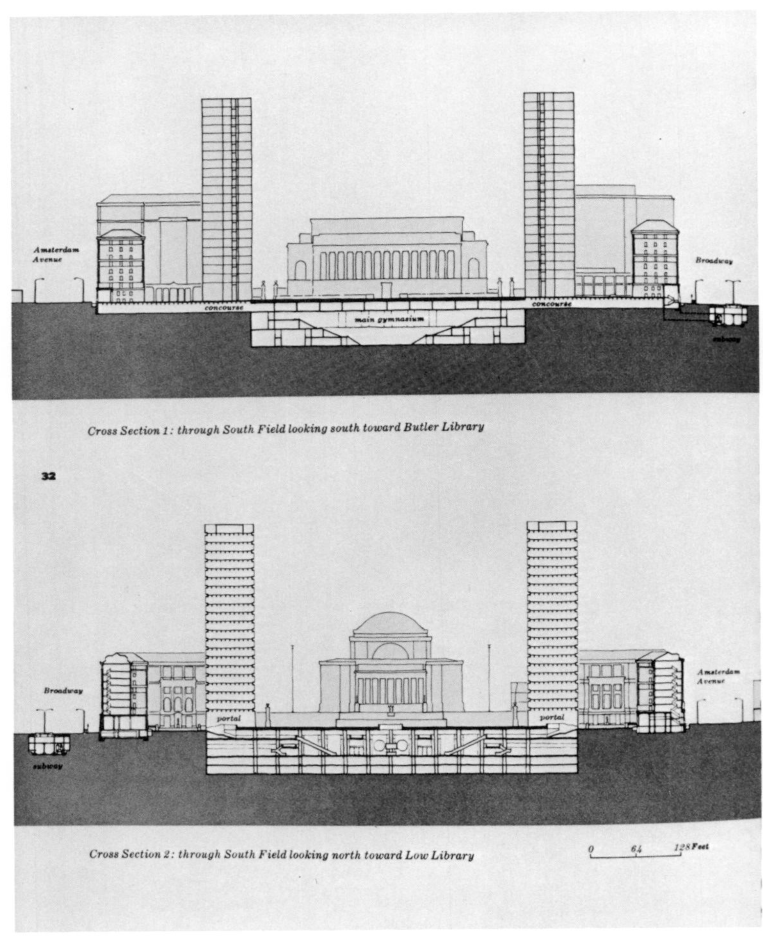

FIGURE 80 *I. M. Pei & Partners, East-west sections through South Field showing proposed towers and underground gymnasium/concourse project, 1970 (cat. 98)*

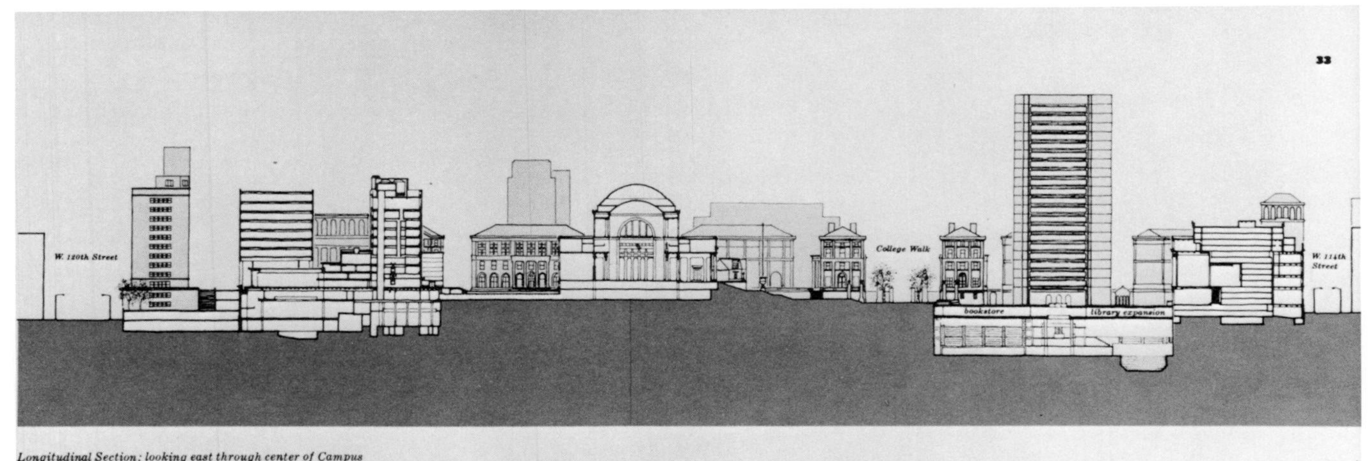

FIGURE 81 *I. M. Pei & Partners, Longitudinal (north-south) section through the Columbia campus showing proposed additions of a new science complex behind Uris and towers and concourse for South Field, 1970 (cat. 98)*

to the platforms of the 116th Street subway station (figs. 79–82).

Pei anticipated his critics by defending his proposal both in relation to McKim's master plan and in its creation of a protected zone of animation for students cut off from the local streets above. The towers, he pointed out, occupied the inner sites of McKim's incomplete residential quadrangles, thus reducing South Field to the dimensions originally called for in the 1903 master plan for South Field. South Field would be reconfigured as a bounded green space atop the roof of an invisible concourse while the bases of the towers would be opened up at their centers, both with broad stairwells descending to the concourse and leaving open pedestrian paths and views across campus, as his office demonstrated in a set of photocollages of pedestrians' experience of high-rise South Field. The neighborhood would not suffer by this inward focusing of student life, for Pei was confident that "the activities in the concourse might well spur the neighboring private sector to provide competitive services, shops, and theaters. Such a result would make upper Broadway a much more exciting place—at least as lively as Harvard Square in Cambridge, Massachusetts."[249] While Columbia may have taken Harvard as an appropriate rival, it is unlikely that most residents of Morningside Heights were yearning for greater Boston. Pei's proposals for Columbia, like his contemporary role in the development of underground Montreal, were descendants of the modernist functionalist approach to the city, which believed that the traditional city street might ultimately best be left to automobile traffic while protected pedestrian zones could be enclosed in protected and controlled environments. On the Columbia campus it expressed a continued uncertainty about the nature of student life in a dense city neighborhood.

Campus reaction focused almost immediately on Pei's stunning images for South Field. Pei insisted on every occasion that the twin towers were not mere products of necessity—how Columbia's ambition could be contained within its strictly delimited campus—but, in fact, were a means to clarify a blurred sense of order on a campus that "despite its excellent start, looks incoherent and incomplete. . . . The two towers, though higher, follow the original placement of buildings in the McKim, Mead & White master plan. That plan had great strength in symmetry, and our plan will try to restore some of that strength of the original plan. The space of South Field now is chaos. There is a varied collection of buildings there of dissimilar heights, scale and architecture."[250] Although anyone could plainly see on his drawings that his own buildings were likewise of dissimilar height, scale, and architecture, Pei insisted in a public presentation that "the two new towers will help to establish greater order in this scene."[251]

After the first publication of his vision of South Field, in late spring 1969, letters began to flow into the student newspaper. "When I. M. Pei's plans for the construction of two towers to flank Butler Library were published one would have thought that the *Spectator* was publishing another April Fool's issue," wrote sophomore Peter S. Title (CC 1972). He pointed out that in 1894

McKim had not envisioned the density that would develop outside Columbia's gates, so that the percentage of green space envisioned in McKim's plans needed to be reevaluated in contemporary terms. "The loss of South Field will undoubtedly be as harmful to Columbia's students as the gym would have been to the Harlem community."[252] The faculty was no less guarded in their reactions the following spring after Pei offered a slide presentation in the Law School and an exhibition of his drawings and a model of his new master plan in Avery Hall. Art History Professor Eugene Santomasso quipped, "I don't really see how those towers do what he says they will. I think they only confuse the south campus even more," while an assistant professor in the School of Architecture noted that "Pei has a fixation with those towers. They show up in every project he designs."[253] Several trustees had raised "financial and aesthetic objections" as well, the *Spectator* reported. The entire scheme for South Field was estimated at $35 million in February 1970, but precise studies of the costs of excavation and blasting for the underground gymnasium had not been undertaken. As late as April 1970 members of the University Senate, formed in the aftermath of the 1968 riots, were encouraging the administration to consider moving some of the university's facilities, perhaps even Columbia College, outside the city.[254]

Few of the other elements in Pei's carefully weighed proposals for the central campus (as he called the area of McKim's original plinth), the north campus, or even for such formerly controversial neighborhood sites as the so-called pharmacy site at Amsterdam Avenue and 122nd Street aroused much comment. Some aspects of the plan would eventually be implemented, albeit in a piecemeal way.

On the central campus Pei proposed to increase the density of classroom, library, and studio space. After nearly all administrative and academic offices had been removed to South Field, the McKim pavilions could be restructured within for classroom and seminar use. While Pei was eager to maintain, even restore, the grand spaces and tall ceilings on the lower floors, he proposed that "a modicum of upper-story space be double-decked and two new underground extensions be built."[255] Most of this work was involved in accommodating the departments and programs that Columbia had long sought to unite into an arts center, combining two existing schools–Architecture and the School of the Arts–and two academic departments–Art History and Music–with expanded facilities for theater and performing arts, which had long been felt lacking at Columbia. Pei concluded that an off-campus location was now ruled out since "no vacant size of sufficient size near the campus is available. . . . Every alternative site is occupied by a residential building [and] to demolish such a structure and then build the Arts Center is an expensive, time-consuming process that would further deplete the housing resources on the Heights for both the University and the Community." The arts center then would go underground. Dodge should be remodeled for the School of the Arts and for Music with modest extensions under the lawn

FIGURE 82 *I. M. Pei & Partners, Proposed underground concourse for South Field, 1970 (cat. 98)*

FIGURE 83 *I. M. Pei & Partners, Proposed renovation of the 800 level of Schermerhorn Hall for the Department of Art History and Archaeology, 1970 (cat. 98)*

between Dodge and Lewisohn to house extensions to the McMillin Theater. More ambitious proposals were made for Architecture and Art History, which sketched out essentially the plans for Avery Extension and the remodeling of Schermerhorn Hall that would be undertaken in stages over the next fifteen years. Beneath the only complete courtyard of McKim's original plan, Avery, Schermerhorn, and Fayerweather Halls were to be interconnected by a two-story extension that would accommodate major expansion of the Avery Library, merged now with the Art History Library moved from the eighth floor of Schermerhorn. The upper floors of Schermerhorn were to be extensively remodeled (fig. 83) for Art History and Archaeology, the department with "the most critical space problem of any school or department of the University."[256] Studies were already under way by Alexander Kouzmanoff–significantly a Columbia faculty member and chairman of the Architecture Division in the School of Architecture–for the highly particular solution realized between 1974 and 1977, that would encompass library, auditorium, and exhibition spaces for the School of Architecture in the underground space (plate 15).

I. M. Pei & Partners proposed a project for the renovation of the eighth floor of Schermerhorn Hall for Art History (fig. 83) "as a prototype of how to achieve more efficient use of existing space and how to enhance its amenity as well. . . . Whenever possible," they continued, "the University should preserve the double-height space of old buildings for teaching and exhibition. In the plans for the 800 level of Schermerhorn, however, we recommend creating two new mezzanine levels of faculty offices along most of the perimeter. These offices not only have windows that face out to the campus. They also look over a central exhibition space that is analogous to a town square. This arrangement, which meets all requirements of the New York City Building Code, will strengthen the sense of community between faculty and students in the Art History Department."[257] By the 1980s when the architect Susana Torre, working with Wank, Adams & Slavin, Associates, undertook the renovation of Schermerhorn Hall, a postmodern reappraisal of McKim's classicism led to a solution of much greater formality, even pretension,[258] while I. M. Pei's notion of a hybrid lobby/exhibition space seemed both dated and inadequate to meet the department's long-frustrated desire for gallery space equivalent to those in other top-ranking art history departments. Although Pei hoped to increase substantially the density of the main campus, he sought to preserve the status quo on the part of the campus he considered the most harmonious. He was, in fact, insistent that none of McKim's unrealized pavilions be added. Interestingly he did not argue that they could no longer accommodate university functions, but rather that McKim's plan was a finer achievement as it stood than as originally envisioned. Pei perhaps should be credited with the selective invocation of McKim's intentions that have prevailed on the Columbia campus ever since:

Only the Central campus . . . has been consistently well developed. There, the underlying order of McKim's original vision is maintained and even bettered. Low Library serves as a central focus within a complete frame of campus buildings along Broadway and Amsterdam Avenue. But a variation within this order—an asymmetry around Low created by the completion of only one of a pair of planned quadrangles to the east—actually improves on the spatial dynamics of the McKim plan. The counterpoint of the small Foreign Student Center [today's Buell Hall] against the larger surrounding buildings is perhaps the key to this successful arrangement.[259]

For the north campus Pei embraced the emerging emphasis on high-density science buildings. He proposed that in completing the 1950s vision of a terrace to bring the level of the old Grove up to the height of McKim's platform efforts be made to create new entrances to the campus that would break down the forbidding fortress wall Columbia presented to the community and to its sister institutions to the west and north, Barnard and Teachers College. Once again he fought the hodgepodge of solutions that had begun to appear in this part of the campus: "Unifying architectural elements must be sought in locating buildings, proportioning facades and selecting colors and materials to achieve a harmonious extension of the McKim plan."[260] The nearly 850,000 square feet needed for Chemistry, Life Sciences, and Physics as well as for the young Computer Center could be accommodated principally by three new structures, all of which were considered urgent, since the brain drain of Columbia's professors to less troubled campuses with greater resources and facilities had been noted as one of the gravest threats to the university's academic stature. Two of these new science buildings would occupy peripheral sites, more or less in accordance with Kendall's plans of the 1920s. Pei proposed not only that they respect the height of the existing buildings, to restore something of McKim's notion of consistency of cornice lines, but also that they incorporate new entrances to the campus. For the north campus, Pei likewise proposed increased density in a series of large structures specially configured for the needs of the experimental sciences. Thus he would propose revisions to the plans drawn up in October 1969 by the architectural firm of Warner Burns Toan and Lunde, which were already under review by the trustees, for a new life sciences tower at the corner of Broadway and 120th Street (fig. 84). His most noteworthy suggestion here was that the building include a new diagonally inflected entrance into the campus, a much needed link to this important intersection and to Barnard that had been lost with the cancellation of two successive buildings for this site. Similar conclusions were reached by Skidmore, Owings & Merrill, who were appointed in January 1969 to prepare a physical development plan for a major science complex on the north campus in collaboration with Pei's office. In 1996 his suggestion was reinvigorated by the new master plan study group.

The engineering building was to be extended to fill in the space between Mudd and Schermerhorn Extension along Amsterdam Avenue, leaving only the center of the 120th Street frontage undeveloped. Here Pei suggested that a lower terrace level be created, providing a sort of modernist equivalent of the gradual

FIGURE 84 *Warner, Burns, Toan, Lunde, Proposed science tower for the corner of Broadway and 120th Street, 1969 (cat. 103)*

transition from street level to campus level, with an asymmetrically placed monumental stair. From the top of this stair diagonal views would open into the heart of the campus, unobstructed by any new building, even though Pei proposed the largest single building of his scheme be raised here, carried above the terrace on piloti, or stilt-like piers.

Whereas the towers had provoked immediate and sustained controversy, the enormous horizontal bar that Pei proposed to bridge most of the dense north campus went all but unnoticed when his model was first unveiled.[261] This was to house the chemistry department, which would abandon Havemeyer Hall, and was clearly, along with the towers, the building that Pei envisioned being designed by his own firm: "The most important new structure of all will be a centrally located Chemistry Building. Elevated on pillars above the Uris Library and set across the major north-south axis, it will act as the centerpiece of the North Campus. This building will provide a uniform backdrop for Low Library, and its lobbies will be placed to provide natural terminations to the north-south pedestrian walkways." Indeed, since the 1950s McKim's failure to terminate these subsidiary axes of his plan had been criticized.[262]

While Pei insisted, all visual evidence in his model to the contrary, that "what is necessary is not a physical master plan so much as a new strategy for planning,"[263] he did detail a proposal for a new type of housing for the neighborhood "to demonstrate that the University and the neighborhood can not only survive together, but can effectively accomplish their respective goals through cooperative planning." He recommended that top priority be given to a new $8.5-million apartment complex and recommended that it be built on the vacant site at the corner of Amsterdam, Morningside, and 122nd Street, long slated for development as the School of Pharmacy, a gesture that he hinted would have enormous benefit for improving Columbia's relations with the community. This was to be realized with joint Columbia and federal funding and to include both faculty, graduate student, and community housing as well as street-level shops—which Columbia's East Campus superblock had nearly erased for a several-block stretch along Amsterdam Avenue. Not only the design but also the carefully staged proposals for relocating tenants during construction and renovation of the site was meant to provide "a prototypical housing program which can be applied elsewhere on Morningside Heights on a larger scale."[264] Although Pei recommended "early construction" of the new building, the complex combination of federal and university funds proved, unfortunately, difficult to assemble, and to this day the site is still vacant and the formula untried.[265]

The university remained under close public and media scrutiny, and the situation was rendered all the more difficult by the protracted search for a new president, which ended finally in late spring 1970 when William J. McGill accepted the helm in still turbulent waters. The university's financial position was weakening, but Cordier had assured Pei "that the University can make early and measurable progress in high-priority areas." Six weeks later, as Pei continued to meet with neighborhood groups, the situation was becoming untenable. "These meetings are becoming increasingly embarrassing," he complained to the university. "We desperately need some sign of progress if we are to maintain any communication with the community. Month by month, the goodwill you have built up is dissipating. Columbia's credulity is deteriorating."[266]

Shortly thereafter Pei resigned, effective 30 June 1970, saying that "Columbia must now weigh priorities," but offering "to provide additional services at appropriate times as decisions are made and new development opportunities appear."[267] Much to the university's annoyance the resignation made the evening news: "NBC has learned that both Pei and Columbia have decided that the university lacks the funds to go ahead with plans for high-rise towers . . . and for an underground gymnasium. Columbia's operating deficit last year of more than $15 million was the highest in the university's history."[268] The Office of Public Information drafted a statement noting that from the first I. M. Pei was to serve as a consultant, which he had begun to do on Kouzmanoff's Avery extension and the new life sciences building. "The only thing not anticipated was the severe financial position of the University at this time. The University expected to go into a construction program soon after the master plan was created, but funds are not immediately in sight for building projects. Therefore Mr. Pei may not be called upon for consultation quite as often as originally thought."[269] Pei would, in fact, not return to the campus again. In December 1970 President McGill officially scrapped the South Field gym project, estimated at $20 million without the towers, in favor of renovating the existing facility. "If we build that gymnasium now," he was quoted in the *Spectator*, "it would be evidence of a distorted value system." A year later, in December 1971, the life sciences tower project was also aborted. It seemed to many that even the public relations aspect of Pei's nearly two-year involvement with Columbia had not yielded impressive results.

A new attitude toward the campus context: projects of the 1970s

"Many many alumni," McGill told a *Times* reporter in 1971, "have said they will not give another dime to Columbia until we settle the gym question." Through the rising troubles alumni had continued to pledge funds—over $5 million by 1968—earmarked for improved sports facilities at Columbia, which had been an alumni preoccupation since the beginning of the century. "It has become a credibility question with the alumni. This is an essential step in trying to unblock funds with the university."[270] In June of 1971 Columbia released plans by R. Jackson Smith, a senior partner in the Eggers Partnership (as Eggers & Higgins was now known), the sixth building that the firm had designed for Columbia since the mid-1940s (see fig. 65). In an unusual moment of front-page irony the *Times* began its article about the resolution of the very public gym: "Columbia University has found a site for the new gymnasium it has been seeking amid many tribulations. . . . It will be on campus, connecting the old gym and extending west to Broadway, south of 120th Street." Indeed, it was almost the very site that Eggers & Higgins had first studied in the mid-1940s. The building would form the raised terrace that Harrison and Abramovitz and more recently Pei had proposed creating at the northeast corner of the campus as a continuation of the system began on the other side of the campus with the Engineering Center. The gym's roof would form a plaza leading to Pupin Hall, which would be remodeled to move its entrance up to the fourth floor, corresponding to the 150-foot grade of McKim's platform. Like Engineering Terrace, the new gym would be designed to provide foundations for a future tower, although for the time being it would be landscaped. Having been burned trying to build a gym in the park, the trustees decided to create a park on the gym, appeasing by anticipation any defenders of these fifty thousand square feet of the former Grove by promising that for every three trees felled two new ones would be planted. The building, moreover, was to be christened a Physical Fitness Center, for as McGill told the *Times* in a moment of prescient political correctness, "The word *gym* has an odorous quality in New York and we didn't want that term hanging around."[271] Even with the renovation of the old gymnasium, to which it was to be linked, the new gymnasium was smaller than the projected park and South Field facilities, but the university pledged to make it accessible at certain times of the day to the local community. While the new gym fell far short of what many had hoped for, the mere fact that Columbia could open it in 1974, only six years after the riots, signaled something of a comeback. In the same year the university pledged $250,000 for a restoration of the scarred site that it had left behind in Morningside Park. The innovative landscape designer Lawrence Halprin closely consulted with the West Harlem community in creating this design. "My position was I would not turn over a spade of dirt without agreement with the community," President McGill said.[272]

The sustained and severe criticism of Columbia's attitudes toward planning—culminating in architecture professor Romaldo Giurgola's renewed criticism of the university in the wake of its shelving Pei's work[273]—finally led to decisive steps. The university created the new post of campus architect, naming the young British architect Douglas Dean Telfer, who had studied at Columbia in the early 1960s and participated in the South Campus study of 1963 (see fig. 75). Telfer was now to concentrate on planning within the historic campus, which for the first time was to be celebrated as an important example of American Beaux-Arts design. Such appreciation was still considered novel two years later, when the Museum of Modern Art opened its exhibition of nineteenth-century Beaux-Arts designs (1975), greeted by many as a critique of modernism's sweeping rejection of the qualities of traditional spatial and urban values. Telfer's former teacher Alexander Kouzmanoff—himself involved just then with the Avery Library remodeling—described Telfer to the architectural press as "an architect and planner who is articulate in the sensitive adaptation of historical space to modern use,"[274] suggesting an openness to finding solutions that might adapt to the context of McKim's architecture.

By far the most decisive change came with the appointment of another young architect as dean of the School of Architecture in July 1972, James Stewart Polshek, who negotiated as a condition of his appointment a direct role in the selection of both designers and new designs for the campus. Polshek's own itinerary was a diverse one that had taken him across the spectrum of modernist practice and the emerging critiques of its hardcore assumptions. He had studied architecture at Yale in the exciting moment of the mid-1950s when Louis Kahn's impact led to a questioning of orthodox modernism, traveled widely looking at traditional architecture in Europe and Japan, worked for Ulrich Franzen, and taught at Cooper Union under John Hejduk. He made it his mission to bring to Columbia newly emerging points of view in architecture that critiqued modernism and were open to history and context.[275] Columbia would be invigorated by a new contextual and empirical philosophy that viewed each building as conditioned by the very specific conditions of its site and program, a reactive approach quite different from the late universal modernism of Pei's soon-forgotten master plan.[276] Reflecting on his fifteen years in the role of special advisor to the president, Polshek described the situation he found when he arrived at Columbia in 1972: "The quality of most of the modern architecture built after the Second World War was appalling, and the urban design of the classically inspired monumental McKim campus was being destroyed."[277]

By 1977, when the first of the buildings in which Polshek would play a critical role was complete, architectural critics were already talking of a complete turnaround. "Mr. Polshek's revolution is beginning to get Columbia back on the architectural map, from which it has been absent since early in the century, when its chief architects were the firm of McKim, Mead & White," wrote the recently appointed architectural critic of the *New York Times* Paul Goldberger.[278] Goldberger was a protégé of Vincent Scully, the Yale architectural historian who in the 1970s was championing a new approach to American modernism, one aligned with the theory and practice of accommodation championed since the mid-1960s by Robert Venturi and a number of Louis Kahn's followers in Philadelphia, including Giurgola. At Columbia this point of view was represented by Robert A. M. Stern (B.A. Columbia 1960; M. Arch. Yale 1965), who had been a controversial first-year studio critic in the School of Architecture, and by numerous visiting critics and lecturers, including Scully. But from the first Polshek sought to forge an ecumenical approach, represented by other key appointments, including that of Kenneth Frampton. For a moment it seemed as if Columbia might become the fulcrum of what critics had begun to call in the 1960s the Yale-Philadelphia axis.

At precisely this point Scully, among others, was spearheading a

FIGURE 85 *Romaldo Giurgola, Sketch for the south elevation of Sherman Fairchild Life Sciences Building, ca. 1972 (cat. 105)*

reappraisal of the work of McKim, Mead & White, celebrating their domestic work in the "Shingle Style" as a highly original and American contribution to the development of modernism's new spatial expressions and complexities, and attempting to restore something of the lost luster to their faith in the civic virtues of monumental Beaux-Arts design. Scully's widely read *American Architecture and Urbanism* (1969) was reprinted in 1972 just as Columbia, under Polshek's stewardship, began to look afresh at its McKim campus. In one of its most moving passages, directly paraphrased from his highly influential undergraduate lectures at Yale, Scully bemoaned the recent demolition of McKim's Pennsylvania Station in almost Spenglerian terms: "It was academic building at its best, rational and ordered according to a pattern of use and a blessed sense of civic excess. It seems odd that we could ever have been persuaded that it was no good and, finally, permitted its destruction."[279] Scully's rhetoric did not fall on deaf ears at Columbia, where Polshek was simultaneously seeking both to renew the design and history curricula of the School of Architecture and to guide the administration and the university's buildings and grounds and construction bureaucracies toward a reappraisal of the campus.

New talent in the years of Dean James Polshek

Polshek was the éminence grise of Columbia's architectural revolution. He not only turned to a group of young architects invigorated by the vibrant exchanges that renewed architectural theory and discourse in the 1970s but also set up guidelines for each site that defined a consistent and challenging approach to the legacy of the master plan, all the while avoiding stylistic dogmatism. "Lists of architects were assembled for each project and the locational parameters for the new buildings were predefined," he explained, "using their placement to repair, or at least to control, the damage already done to the campus."[280]

The first building fully planned under this new arrangement was the Sherman Fairchild Life Sciences Building (1973–1977), which fulfilled a promise that went back to the mid-1960s to improve and expand Columbia's biology department (fig. 85). The university had used its plans for the biology department to attract a number of leading scientists to campus and backed those claims with major building designs first by Skidmore, Owings & Merrill and then by Warner, Burns, Toan and Lunde (1969–1970). But when President McGill put a stop to all capital expenditures in 1971, many of the scientists accused the university of acting in bad faith. The decision to go ahead with the gym on a site earmarked for expansion of the sciences only intensified the "competition between gymnasium and sciences for precious real estate"[281] on campus, which plagued McGill in his early relations with the faculty. As the new term began in September 1972—Polshek's first on the campus—one associate professor of biology, Malcolm L. Gefter, announced he would leave Columbia because of the university's failure to make good on its promise for adequate space and facilities; and another, James Darnell, threatened to follow suit. McGill responded by promising a new biology building to rise above Engineering Terrace – intended since the 1950s as the site for a third building in the Engineering Center (see fig. 69) – but faculty and students alike were skeptical, even accusing Columbia of empty promises to stem defections from a department it had committed to expand by 60 percent even as retrenchment had become the theme of the day throughout departments and schools. Finally in October 1973, as two more star professors were threatening to join the exodus and insiders warned that the hemorrhage might also lead to the collapse of the chemistry department, the administration announced a major coup, a $6.5-million grant from the Sherman Fairchild Foundation for a new building for biology. Despite its troubles, the department was experiencing escalating enrollments and was receiving a broadening stream of federal research dollars.

Not only would the building play a major role in stemming the ebb tide in Columbia's prestige in biological research, but as a test case for Polshek's skills of architectural staging and casting, it also marked a dramatic watershed in the quality of Columbia's architecture and its commitment to responding creatively to the challenges of McKim's incomplete matrix. Even before a short list of three architectural firms – Ulrich Franzen and Stonehill & Lundquist in addition to Mitchell/Giurgola – had been drawn up following Polshek's advice, Polshek and Telfer had studied the campus site and proposed ways in which it could be developed to bring new coherence to the corner of the campus where insensitive modern design had first eroded the clarity of McKim's plan. Giurgola's building, as Polshek explains, "created a facade that ended the north-south campus axis east of Low Library and covered the banal Seeley W. Mudd Engineering Building." Some of the finest contextual features of the new building derived, in fact, from the various sketches of a spatial envelope drawn up before the architect was chosen. These would include masking Mudd but leaving open a view corridor to the neo-Gothic tower of Russell Hall at Teachers College (now severely compromised by the construction in 1989 of a bridge connecting the Schapiro Center for Engineering and Physical Science Research to Mudd) and the guiding precept that the building's overall volume be defined by the neo-Renaissance perspectival system of McKim's campus design (see fig. 85).

From the first the design was governed by its place as the culmination of the view along McKim's herringbone brick walkway as it extended beyond the Chapel and Avery Hall. In a memo to McGill, Telfer, who frequently peppered his feasibility studies with potted historical lessons, even suggested that the most fruitful analogy for the problem to be solved would be the famous architectural stage set by the Renaissance architect and theoretician Sebastiano Serlio. "The arrangement of these facades in relation to the pavement recalls a favorite exercise of architects since the first Renaissance ideal city, a varied but unified street of palaces along a brick paved path." [282] That Giurgola, whose course in Renaissance architectural history was a mainstay of his teaching in the Columbia Architecture School, was in sympathy with Polshek's advocacy of a design that could tie together the disparate elements of a confused scene was underscored by his own letter accepting his appointment in March 1973: "The problem, as I see it, besides one of developing proper efficiency within the new building, is one of creating an architectural transition between the various elements which now constitute the northeast end of the campus, and thus establishing the proper connection of the spaces of these new laboratories with the campus as a whole."[283]

Giurgola had received national attention for his urban contextual approach in a series of acclaimed competition entries–including Boston City Hall (1962) and the AIA Headquarters in Washington (1965–1968)–and in several prominent commercial and campus buildings in and around Philadelphia (where he had set up a partnership with Ehrman Mitchell in 1958). His name was much on the lips of architecture critics in the early 1970s, as the East Coast architectural scene was enlivened by debates between the inclusivist attitude of a series of "gray" architects–Giurgola, Robert Venturi, and Charles Moore–and the neo-purist approach of the "whites," most prominently the New York Five centered around Peter Eisenman, Richard Meier, and Charles Gwathmey. In opposition to the whites, who maintained that architecture must seek an autonomous language of form, the grays maintained that without necessarily abandoning the language and techniques of twentieth-century architectural modernism each building should be "inflected" in relation to the specific conditions of its program and of its site. However complex and confused an environment, whether in an impacted and layered urban context or on a college campus that bore the traces of time and changing tastes, a new building should at once relate to and even clarify the diverse forces in its environment.

Giurgola was ideally positioned for Columbia's needs because his work commanded both critical respect and the confidence of commercial and institutional builders. While the administration was reassured by his exposition of a fast-track approach to design and construction, which could calm the state of alarm in the biology department, his attitude toward the campus would underscore the viability of the new architectural criteria that Polshek was working to establish.

While the geometrical and organizational clarity of the plan of the Sherman Fairchild Center for the Life Sciences with its core of laboratories wrapped by the "servant" spaces of circulation and meeting rooms attests to the continued influence of Kahn in Giurgola's approach to design, the facades are clear testimony to the theory of an architecture inflected to its environment, which he developed in parallel to Venturi's notions of "complexity and contradiction." The dialogue between a core of white-enameled panels and floating screens of red-tiled panels reflects Giurgola's commitment that the building must at once speak of its program and construction and defer, or be inflected to, as he would say, its immediate context in all its variety. The lightweight screens bear testimony to the cantilevered construction of this building which seems almost suspended above the campus and connected to it only by a thin bridge (perhaps the least successful aspect of the design). Each of the facades, moreover, is different, reflecting not only differences of the internal program—the large cut for the conference room that dominates the fragment of the south or campus facade, for instance—but Giurgola's determination that each facade should serve to mediate its immediate environment. While some critics would bemoan the particular shade of red chosen, the tiled facades were intended as a modern sunscreen, or *brise-soleil*, that would both be expressive of steel-frame construction and serve as a reference to the brick facades and floor of McKim's campus. Using a nearly biological metaphor, Giurgola spoke often of his approach as "splicing a building into its environment," and he managed even to take up elements from his much maligned neighbors, Uris and Mudd—notably window types—at once weaving together elements from the fragmented context and demonstrating how modernism could respond to, even heighten, the coherence and richness of historical context without literally imitating it.

For the first time since the turn of the century, when the press had heralded each of McKim's new designs, a Columbia building was covered extensively by the professional architectural press. *Progressive Architecture* editor and Columbia alumnus Martin Filler praised Fairchild as a "great building" and noted proudly, "Columbia now has a building that surpasses many of the highly vaunted monuments of the 1960s that were built at Yale, Harvard, and Penn, while their Ivy League cousin languished in architectural limbo."[284] Robert A. M. Stern, also an alumnus, told *Columbia College Today* that for the first time in decades Columbia had commissioned a design by an architect "who is still making an important statement with each building he does. . . . Romaldo Giurgola helped lead the profession out of the cul-de-sac that the International Style had become,"[285] an assessment made all the more poignant by the juxtaposition of the Fairchild building with some of the International Style's least-loved bastard children on the north end of Columbia's McKim campus.

Until he resigned as dean in 1987, Polshek pursued for fifteen years a two-pronged strategy for making Columbia a nondoctrinaire showcase of new architectural talent and for fostering a critical and creative engagement with the legacy of McKim's incomplete master plan. At the same time he adeptly steered clear of the return to a literal classicism that had gained force among certain postmodernist designers after 1980 and might have found a natural home on the Columbia campus. While interior renovations were given to promising young designers, many of them also teaching at the Architecture School—Jerome Greene Hall and later Ferris Booth Hall by Robert A. M. Stern, Lewisohn Hall by Mostoller & Wood, and Schermerhorn Hall by Susana Torre among them—new commissions were directed to some of the most challenging and prominent postmodern architects. Just as Polshek encouraged dialogue and diversity in the lecture program and in the choice of studio critics

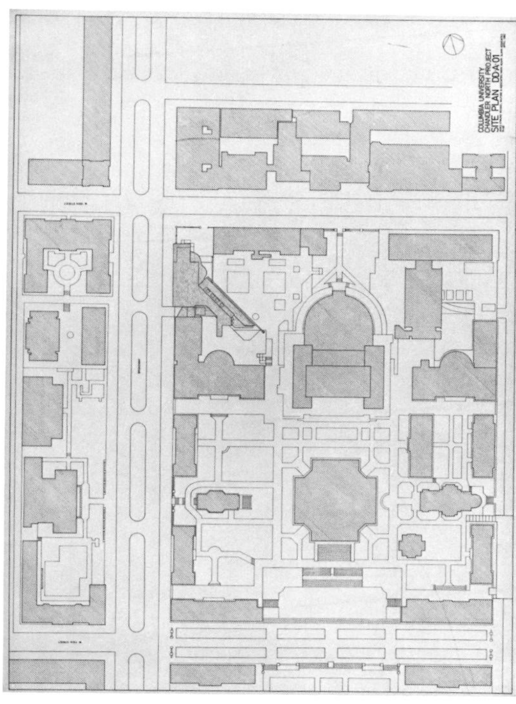

FIGURE 86 *James Stirling, Michael Wilford & Associates, Chandler North project: site plan, April 1982 (cat. 106)*

within the school, he also directed the administration to a group of talented architects who in highly individual ways were exploring a critical reappraisal of modernism in design. By 1980 the university had commissioned two major projects for key campus sites, both of which were followed with considerable excitement by the profession, the press, and the campus. Both were at once responses to the existing campus context and explorations of new urban attitudes, opening up to critical debate Columbia's interface with the surrounding neighborhood. Neither, unfortunately, came to a happy conclusion.

James Stirling and Michael Wilford's design (1979–1982) for an extension to the chemistry department, the Chandler North project, (fig. 86) was ultimately canceled when its budget far exceeded original estimates. The building was to rise above the terrace of the Dodge Physical Fitness Center, behind the existing chemistry department in Havemeyer and Chandler Halls, roughly the pendant to Giurgola's Sherman Fairchild Center. Like the biology building, the chemistry extension had its origins in demands first formulated in the 1960s for expansion of Columbia's scientific laboratories; it, too, was an unfulfilled promise of the canceled Pei master plan. Again the challenge was to develop a design that could weave together a diverse group of neighboring structures while confronting the difficulty of designing a building that would of necessity be engineered in midair. Like the biology building, the new chemistry building was to take its footings on preexisting structural supports, in this case four heavy engineering columns embedded in the gym for future development of its air-rights potential.

Stirling and Wilford's design would have provided a stimulating pendant to Giurgola's, for they too proposed radically different architectural expressions for facades facing different contexts. They were eager to prove a good neighbor to McKim on both his south elevation and especially along Broadway. Their building would rise atop the plinth of the gym, a highly original interpretation of Kendall's high-rise vocabulary for Columbia's science buildings, and it would feature a huge flaring cornice, pioneered a few years earlier in their startling museum design for the Staatsgalerie in Stuttgart. But its most memorable image was the bold exterior expression of a huge truss – reminiscent of Stirling's earlier celebration of technology in such acclaimed English university buildings as the Engineering Building at Leicester – that revealed the way in which the building's diagonal extension into the campus had been engineered as a bridge (plate 16). As Stirling himself explained, this was not simply a celebration of the building's exploitation of modern structural techniques to solve a difficult problem – the diagonal extension was held aloft by dropping an additional structural pylon into the service yard behind Havemeyer Hall – but a strong statement of his philosophy of the building's urban responsibility to both campus and neighborhood: "To have merely extended the chemistry department with the large amount of accommodation required could have resulted in a new building extending and connecting with Pupin, thus producing a continuous wall of building around the north-west corner of the campus which would have been untypical and perhaps hostile to the neighborhood."[286] Instead Stirling and Wilford created a dramatic corner to the campus, where a transparent S-curved glass lobby would serve as a hinge between the tall slab on Broadway and the diagonal bridge-truss building. For the first time an architectural expression was found for the structural gymnastics long at play in the buildings engineered to transform McKim's Grove into an integral part of his raised plinth campus, answering belatedly faculty complaints that Columbia's engineering buildings were so traditional in expression even as modern architecture was being transformed by new construction technologies in the 1950s and 1960s.[287]

Perhaps the most suggestive new attitude in this design was the determination of both architect and Columbia administrators that the new building preserve a view of the neighborhood from the campus. For Stirling's introduction of a dramatic diagonal into the campus plan was no mere architectural gesture; rather he sought to preserve the view, which had come to be treasured, of the towers of the Union Theological Seminary and the Riverside Church. The sinewy wall of the glass elevator lobby on the Broadway facade, which Stirling referred to as a "window" (and which he subsequently made a signature feature of his Stuttgart gallery), was to provide similar views out to the campus and the neighborhood for users of the building. As in the case of Giurgola's project here was a design that had achieved an extraordinary and subtle dialogue with McKim, Mead & White.

Stirling and Wilford's project, redesigned in 1982, was ultimately killed by its own ambitions. Their truss raised not only the building to the level of McKim's campus but also elevated the cost far beyond the university's budget and its fund-raising capacities. In its stead in 1986 a much more modest extension to Havemeyer Hall, on a slightly different site, was commissioned from the New York firm of Davis Brody and Associates, under project architect Belmont Freeman. This established a model of contextual restraint and good manners in its reinterpretation of McKim, Mead & White's original pavilions, with a refined attention to materials worthy of McKim's original concern for details. Ironically enough the addition to Havemeyer Hall rose not on the piers embedded within the new gym but on two columns spanning the service drive at almost precisely the point that Stirling and Wilford had designated for trusses of their more ambitious and daring design.

The first new dormitory building constructed on the Columbia campus since the 1920s—the East Campus complex commissioned from Gwathmey/Siegel & Associates in 1979—has no less checkered a history. In 1975 a specially appointed board of visitors was named to examine quality of life issues at Columbia, and in the college in particular. They homed in immediately on the dilapidated state of campus housing, leading to a program of rehabilitation of the original McKim dormitories during the next two decades as well as a commitment to new construction.

With its apartment-style suites with kitchens and common rooms, designed to enhance a sense of community on the model of Harvard houses or Yale colleges, the East Campus complex was to set the standard for the retrofitting of Columbia's older dorms. But it was also given the tall order of both housing an unprecedented number of students, 750 in the original brief, and resolving the complex planning issues on Columbia's eastern edge where the plinth of the 1960s abruptly met McKim and Kendall's earlier ground-level planes. Polshek's preliminary analysis of the site set the stakes high. Any design should create a focus for the strong east-west axis introduced by Harrison & Abramovitz's pedestrian bridge and raised platform, which came to a sudden stop behind two apartment buildings on Morningside Drive, as well as mediate between the enormous scale of the freestanding "object" buildings raised above that plaza and the dense adjacent urban fabric. Polshek's promotion of Gwathmey/Siegel & Associates, a firm that had come to prominence under the neomodernist banner of the "whites," or the New York Five, was both indicative of his ecumenical approach and a calculated gamble that the evidence of the firm's work up to that point, almost all small scale and residential, promised both a high-quality contribution to East Campus's modernist context and an adept solution that could bring order to one of the campus's most confused and blurred edges.

Gwathmey/Siegel played with the elements of the multipurpose program, recomposing them as a series of building blocks to create both high-rise and village scales. The path leading from the main campus was terminated by a large triumphal arch and a sentinel cylindrical stair tower opening to a set of low-rise houses around a courtyard. The bulk of the student housing was accommodated in a high-rise slab set hard on Morningside Drive whose scale could only be related to surrounding buildings by a play of different-colored tiled facings. A five-story datum of red-tile panels was to relate the lower scale to Columbia's historic buildings, and in particular to the neighboring blocks of the Faculty House and President's House, while the upper stories, faced in light gray panels, were to be read as a monumental apartment house. Even the enthusiastic architectural press admitted that the sheer size of the building could not be explained away: "In terms of urban design, the East Campus Complex follows the established New York tradition of treating high-rise buildings as 'edge', both to parks and to north-south avenues," *Architectural Record* noted, "although the 23-story slab is considerably more of an edge than Morningside Drive is accustomed to."[288]

Although the building was critically acclaimed, its fast-track construction led to serious problems. In February 1988 a large chunk of the campus facade fell into the courtyard, a building failure all too reminiscent of the problems that had resulted from the delayed maintenance on Columbia's institutional real estate during the 1970s, when a piece of the apartment house at Broadway and 115th Street had fallen and killed a passing Barnard student. This was something scarcely expected, however, from a new building meant to mark a turnaround in Columbia's residential life. The university filed suite immediately against both the contractor and the architect and awarded a contract for refacing the building to Gruzen Samton Partners (architects also of the Schapiro Residence Hall then being designed for a site on West 115th Street off Broadway), whose new color palette and composition made no reference to the original design.[289] This was not the only compromise: the plan to soften the blow of East Campus's bulking presence in neighborhood by inserting shops in the ground story along Morningside Drive was never implemented, and the security fencing the university installed in their place has in recent years been repeatedly bemoaned by neighborhood groups as evidence of Columbia's continued development of its campus as a fortress.

If these ambitious undertakings of the early 1980s were monumental disappointments, two more modest, but highly successful and acclaimed, interventions emerged from Polshek's close working with university officials and younger designers that have proven lasting testaments to his personal philosophy of an architecture of "context and responsibility." Kliment & Halsband's Computer Science Building of 1981–1983 and Peter Gluck's extension to the Business School of 1983–1985 were additions to two of the most vilified of Columbia's postwar buildings, the Engineering Center (Seeley W. Mudd and the Engineering Terrace) and Uris Hall respectively. Both new designs were conceived to give a dignified demeanor to highly respected professional programs and to restore some of the lost architectural harmony and spatial definition at the northern end of McKim's original campus. After studying three possible strategies for adding to Uris, including that favored by the university's planners, who hoped to add two symmetrical additions on the roofs of Uris's east and west wings, Gluck and Polshek advocated, despite enormous structural challenges, building in front of the existing building. In this way a modest addition would not only change the physiognomy of the looming building but also restructure the courtyard space behind Low Library, a major focus of the central campus. Gluck developed a system of large-scale fenestration deliberately divorced from the interior division of floors and rooms, thus creating a four-story facade responding to the rear elevation of Low in materials, rhythms, and overall mass. Gluck's new front for Uris effectively distracts attention from the banal slab behind and provides, with its strong and dignified entrance, an appropriate culmination of McKim's grand ceremonial axis. Gluck resolutely steered clear of a literal classicism in his final design, although developmental sketches reveal that he played with a triangular, pediment-like crown over the open center of his composition and at the same time developed a vocabulary outside the canons of modernism.[290] Not the least of his accomplishments is to have turned the slab of Uris Hall into something of the background building administrators had disingenuously claimed it to be in the 1960s.

An even more complex problem and arguably a more subtle solution was offered by R. M. Kliment and

Frances Halsband in their design for the Computer Science Building, one of a series of campus projects that established their practice firmly in public view in the 1980s.[291] This young firm–established in 1972–was no stranger to the Columbia campus. Kliment had worked with Giurgola, taught in the School of Architecture, and together with his wife and partner, Frances Halsband, had renovated the nursing home on Broadway at West 114th Street to form dormitories and offices (Hogan Hall, 1974–1977). From Giurgola they had formed their ethos of an architecture that "makes more of what's there." In the Computer Science Building they extended the logic of his Fairchild Center, refacing the inherited plinth of the Engineering Terrace Building and inserting a one-story limestone-and-glass rotunda both to terminate the north-south axis of McKim's walkway along the east side of Low and to announce the entrance to a building that develops in the difficult interstices left after three generations of construction. Their solution achieved with deft sleight of hand the magical act of squeezing thirty-nine thousand square feet into a midair site, while creating such a graceful sense of place and community that the atrium–the focal point of the complex–could be seen as an original lost courtyard of McKim's urbane plan (fig. 153).

New master plans for the 1990s

By the time these buildings were under construction it seemed likely that Columbia's future growth would require not simply a case-by-case reactive approach to the master plan as opportunities arose but a new master plan to guide the university's future growth and ability to adapt to both changes in disciplines and new patterns of federal and state funding of private universities. The sweeping charge of the Commission on the Future of the University set up by President Michael Sovern in the early 1980s yielded among other things a perceptive report, issued in January 1986 but never publicly released, on the physical resources of the university, in which both Polshek and the recently appointed director of project development and coordination Bernhard Haeckel participated. The report provided the following appraisal of McKim's master plan:

> While McKim's creation was original . . . it also was "an impossible act to follow," particularly outside of the narrow confines of the upper platform. Indeed, McKim's plan created a very difficult setting for the design of the more than 80 percent of today's total campus building area which was added after his time, including designs by other members of his firm. Whether the later buildings repeated the vocabulary of his architecture or whether they were designed to relate by contrast, whether they reflect a decision to ignore the context of his original campus or whether (as currently preferred) they were designed to pay homage to that context, their general inferiority to his masterwork demonstrates that McKim's contribution was a mixed blessing. It excelled in creating an impressive and lasting image for the University, right at its inception, but it failed to provide a sufficiently open-ended framework for the development of space for a dynamic institution of higher learning.[292]

The report's conclusions were modest: the urgent need for more undergraduate housing on or near the campus was identified and a strategy of moving "space consuming services which do not have to be

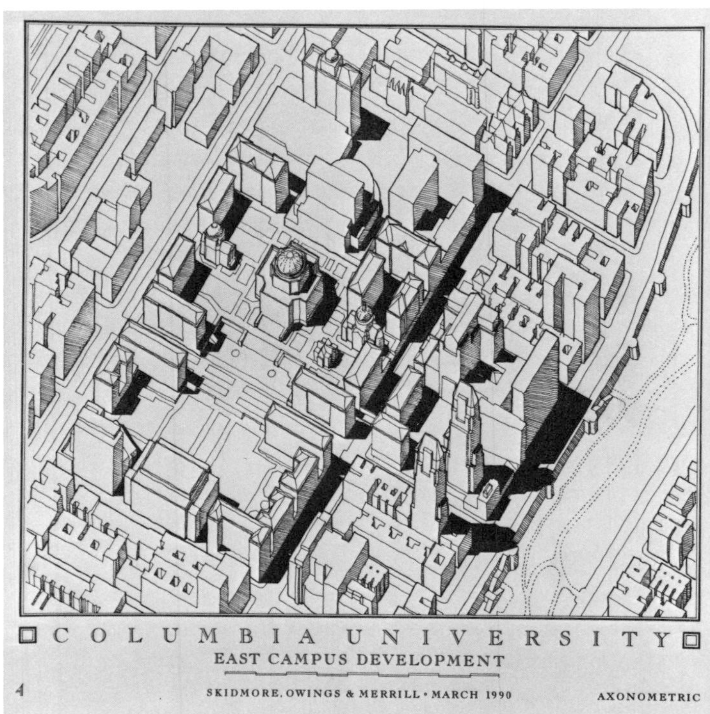

FIGURE 87 *Skidmore, Owings & Merrill, Axonometric view of proposed East Campus development, March 1990 (cat. 112)*

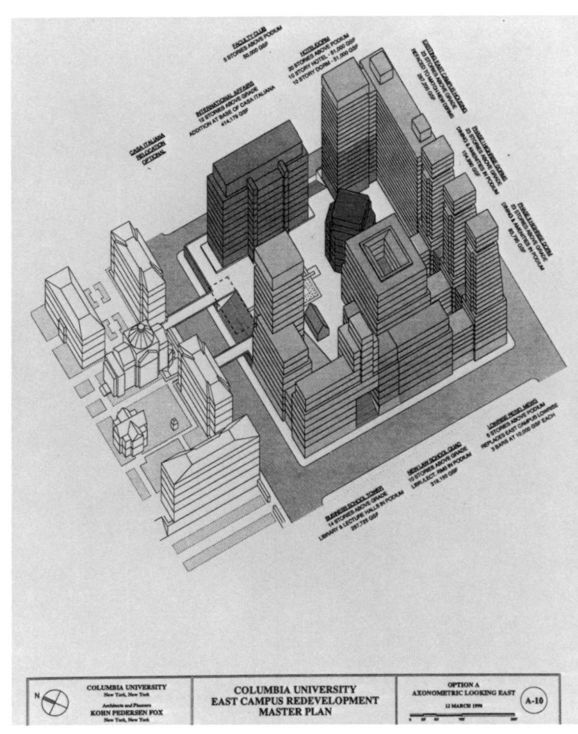

FIGURE 88 *Kohn Pedersen Fox, Axonometric view of proposed East Campus development, March 1990 (cat. 113)*

on the campus (such as printing and storage, including library storage) to off campus locations" was recommended. It led shortly thereafter to major studies of university expansion and campus master planning.

In 1990 Columbia commissioned two comprehensive studies, from the New York architectural firms of Skidmore, Owings & Merrill (SOM)–which had already been involved in campus planning in the 1960s–and Kohn Pedersen Fox (KPF) (figs. 87 & 88). From the outset it was clear that development would be more or less frozen on the McKim campus; each firm was to focus attention on East Campus, where comprehensive planning had been abandoned since the mid-1960s superblock project. Even Gwathmey/Siegel's effort to instill some order to this area, where the juxtaposition of McKim, Mead & White with Harrison & Abramovitz had left a legacy of radical disjunctions of scale, level, and urbanistic attitudes, was but another piecemeal intervention. Despite East Campus's courtyards and heroic pedestrian bridges and plazas, the raised plinth had become more of an obstacle than an amenity, and daily users were more likely to follow a series of labyrinthine pathways and shortcuts through corridors and service stairs. Skidmore's report summed up the challenge:

> The East Campus was not part of the original campus. Its development, in contrast to the Main Campus, occurred parcel by parcel over an extended period without a coherent master plan for the block or for its relationship to the Main Campus. Each building is the center of its own composition with little relationship to adjacent buildings. With the exception of Wien Hall, Casa Italiana, the Faculty House and the President's

House, the massing, proportion, material and architectural language for each building are not related to each other or to the Main Campus. The east/west axis across the center of the campus through 116th Street is not effectively used to clearly connect the East Campus back to the Main Campus.[293]

The university asked both SOM and KPF to propose at least three schemes, each of them phased for long-term implementation, representing minimal, intermediate, and radical restructuring of the East Campus. At the very least the schemes were to provide for major expansion of the facilities of the Law School; at their most ambitious they could provide new buildings for the School of Business, the School of International Affairs, graduate and undergraduate residence halls, a hundred-room hotel for university guests, and other amenities such as new dining halls and parking. Such a radical restructuring would double the usable square footage on the two city blocks. Both SOM and KPF offered to provide Columbia with a series of high-rise buildings of the type they were currently designing in quantity for the office tower boom that had changed the face of many American cities in the mid-1980s. But each firm studied this type as an element in a larger urban strategy in which campus design and high-rise development might coexist at once to give focus and coherence to East Campus and to lend Columbia a new profile in the Upper Manhattan skyline.

In their most ambitious scheme (see fig. 87) SOM, under the direction of designer David Childs, proposed twin twenty-eight-story towers near the corner of 116th Street and Morningside Drive, one set immediately behind the President's House, the other as a pendant on the south side of the block on the site of the old King's Crown Hotel (today's Deutsches Haus). These would create a major "gateway" to the campus, marking Columbia in the skyline above the cliff of Morningside Park with distinctive pitched-roof towers, reminiscent of the great skyscraper crowns of the 1920s and similar in picturesque intent to SOM's restructuring of the skyline of Midtown Manhattan with the enormous World Wide Plaza development on West 50th Street. As in their commercial work of the late 1980s, SOM proposed to juxtapose these bulky towers with lower, pedestrian-scale courtyards on adjacent sites. The existing Law School and Wien Hall were to be replaced with four lower buildings emulating McKim's pavilions, which would create a new courtyard; the densely redeveloped superblock would be stripped of most of its 1960s elevated pedestrian plazas. In an alternative project they concentrated development in a single tower set within the site. But what was salient in all their proposals was their combination of distinctive high-rise development, which might for the first time give Columbia a symbol rivaling Low Library, with a scheme of courtyards and axial processional routes through East Campus that could lend it something of the sense of place, focus, and hierarchy that were increasingly valued as the legacy of McKim's master plan.

Kohn Pedersen Fox likewise offered a variety of approaches, all of them involving high-rise development and a major increase–at least twofold–in the density of the

East Campus. What distinguishes their attitude is a resolute commitment to developing East Campus on its own terms, as a coherent modern campus in sharp contrast to McKim's campus on the other side of Amsterdam Avenue. Whereas SOM sought to bring all building entrances back down to street level, KPF proposed to extend the raised pedestrian plaza in order to unify the site. While the new site would have important public outdoor spaces, the composition was to center on a new monumental building, a centrally planned octagonal faculty club–practically a post-modern academic baptistery–as a pendant to Low Library in the East Campus high-rise precinct (fig. 88). KPF even proposed that the older buildings of East Campus entered on street grade be either demolished or, as in the case of the landmarked Casa Italiana and the much admired President's House, relocated to the main campus. Casa Italiana, they felt, would make a fine pendant for Avery Hall, the building either to be dismantled and reassembled or moved on rollers to the site facing Mathematics. The idea of a pendant here is a perennially favorite studio problem in the Architecture School. The President's House would be placed to the west of Low Library as a pendant to Buell Hall, a scheme that they argued "would complete the original McKim, Mead and White plan and simultaneously improve the organization of open space and built form on the East Campus."[294]

While neither scheme was ever seriously considered by the trustees, both raised for the first time the possibility that Columbia's future planning on its dense urban site might involve replacing existing campus buildings. For with a handful of minor exceptions–notably the short-lived Branders Matthews Hall and more recently Ferris Booth Hall–Columbia had not yet demolished any of its buildings on Morningside Heights. Equally important, both master plans articulated the view that the McKim campus required a different kind of planning than the university's later expansions to the east or to scattered neighborhood sites.

An unfinished narrative

In autumn 1997, as Columbia celebrates its first century on Morningside Heights, the local landscape has been transformed in ways that Seth Low and Charles McKim could never have imagined, yet the framework that they laid over four sparsely populated city blocks on the heights above the Hudson remains both the image of Columbia and the center point of designs and debates on Columbia's future growth and change. Since the arrival in 1993 of President George Rupp (fresh from Rice University which itself had reinvigorated its master plan in the 1980s), Columbia has launched its most ambitious program of capital construction ever, currently estimated at $650 million in projects. Most prominent among these are two major new buildings that will represent Columbia's attitudes to both the historic campus and the neighborhood as it enters a second century on Morningside Heights. A new student center, Lerner Hall, designed by Bernard Tschumi, dean of the School of Architecture since 1988, together with associate architect Gruzen Samton, is currently under construction to replace Ferris Booth Hall (demolished in the summer of 1996) and is scheduled to open in 1999. At the same time the university plans to open the first of the new dormitories required to accommodate the controversial policy of the "expansion and enhancement" of Columbia College, which was announced shortly after Rupp took office. A fourteen-story residence hall designed by Robert A. M. Stern will rise on the corner of 113th Street and Broadway. Connected to Hogan Hall and entered from within the block, it will be linked to the main campus via a pedestrian path to 114th Street opposite the Carman gates (fig. 154).

These two new buildings, but a city block apart, are situated in radically different contexts – one at a vital corner of McKim's master plan, the other on the commercial thoroughfare of Broadway – and have been awarded to designers with almost diametrically opposed architectural philosophies. Ironically enough Stern, a firm believer in McKim's world as a lost golden age and an increasingly literal designer in a contextual neo-historicism (as witnessed by his recent neo-Jeffersonian Business School at the University of Virginia) has been given the task of building amid the fallen grace of upper Broadway.

Tschumi, whose notion of an architecture determined by the vitality of urban events and whose pioneering role in the theory of architectural deconstruction made Columbia a "hot" school of architecture in the early 1990s, has the task of taking up some of the archaeological traces of McKim's unfulfilled master plan to temper his exploration of an architecture of high technological expression and instability. The Lerner Hall design takes on with gusto the challenge of amalgamating a fairly literal re-creation of one of the never constructed pavilions of McKim's 1903 master plan, extending the cornice lines of Furnald Hall to the south, and creating a dramatic four-story glass atrium, crisscrossed with long-span glass pedestrian gangways angled to dramatize the half-story difference in level between Broadway and the campus (plate 17). The Hub, as this glass embodiment of one of McKim's never realized open courtyard spaces is called by its designers, is both a void and a dramatically staged set of routes. "During the day," Gruzen Samton wrote in his master plan for the building, "light filters through the suspended glass ramps. At night, as light glows from the inside of the building, figures in movement along this route will appear as in a silent shadow theater."[295] The stakes are high and the project is being followed with guarded anticipation by the architectural world, many of whom could scarcely have imagined ten years ago, as Tschumi was fine-tuning the final designs of his follies for Paris's Parc de la Villette, that the next major geometric matrix he would be in dialogue with would be that of McKim's American Beaux-Arts campus.

While these major buildings are transforming one corner of the campus, a major study, based on the most thoroughgoing historical appraisal ever undertaken of Columbia's architectural, landscaping, and planning heritage, has been commissioned from Beyer Blinder Belle, working with faculty and community consultants and aimed at creating a framework for future decisions and development. Along with Tschumi's and Stern's projects, as well as the recently completed additions to the Law School by Polshek and projected new Law/Business Building at 115th and Amsterdam, these plans have occasioned vibrant, even heated, debate over McKim's plan and its proper interpretation as the usages, population, and density of the campus continue to change. Revised repeatedly, and in some ways fundamentally altered with the addition of South Field, McKim's master plan can only be understood as a framework that has been continually negotiated and interpreted rather than as a simple diagram awaiting completion. The banality of Columbia's architecture of the 1950s and 1960s only eroded rather than negated the underlying order and spatial hierarchy of McKim's plan during this period when the values of the City Beautiful movement were generally held in low esteem. In more recent years it might be said that the challenges of repairing and respecting the plan gave Columbia some extremely sophisticated architecture in a period when other campuses oversubscribed to post-modern imagery.

It is perhaps telling that at the same time the working group—convened in 1996 to consult with Beyer Blinder Belle on how Columbia might develop planning guidelines without drawing up yet another master plan—could not in fact agree on just which of McKim's many plans constituted *the* master plan. Through a process of continual rethinking and redefining Columbia's plan has been in constant evolution, negotiation, and adaptation. Yet the group recognizes that even in that process certain enduring values of architecture and open space are inherent in McKim's plan and need to be articulated and preserved. Stopping short of recommending landmark designation for the core of McKim's campus, as many local preservation advocates have done in recent years, the working group acknowledges that the campus between 114th and 118th Streets has "a compact and harmonious plan with symmetrically ordered Beaux-Arts buildings . . . as monumental and memorable as any campus in America, and represents the highest achievement of urban design by McKim, Mead & White."[296] They offer a critical reappraisal of both the northern end of the original campus, precisely the area left blank on McKim's 1897 plans which has been subject to intensive superimposition and impacted development due to the unresolved problems of grade and level, and of the East Campus, already identified in 1990 as the greatest challenge facing the university. Though developed in counterpoint, McKim's master plan and Manhattan's grid plan have transformed the topography of Morningside Heights so fundamentally that both will continue to provide the framework in which the university seeks to develop its physical environment and architectural image, as well as its responsibilities to both campus and community.

NOTES

Many of the materials referred to in the following notes are in the Columbiana Collection (CC) and in the Columbia University Archives (CUA). Avery Library is used as a shortened form of the Avery Architectural and Fine Arts Library.

1. *Educational Exhibit of the State of New York: Handbook no. 20, Columbia College in the City of New York* (Chicago, 1893), 44 (CC). For a survey of the reaction in the local press to the new site, see the collection of news clippings, mainly from 1892, that fill the two thick volumes *Reports and Papers on the New Site of Columbia College 1892,* collected by George L. Rives, arranged by John McMullan (CC).

2. See "The New York Exhibition of 1892," *Scientific American* (4 January 1890): 8.

3. *Educational Exhibit* (see note 1), 44.

4. "The Morningside Acropolis" (editorial), *Columbia University Quarterly* 2 (1900): 149.

5. *Educational Exhibit* (see note 1).

6. Preliminary findings compiled in *Morningside Heights Planning Framework. Submitted to Columbia University, Prepared by Beyer Blinder Belle, Architects & Planners LLP, April 1997*; final report to be published in Fall 1997.

7. Quoted in *A History of Columbia University, 1754–1904* (New York, 1904) 26.

8. Ibid., 103.

9. See Adolf Placzek, "Design for Columbia College 1813," *Journal of the Society of Architectural Historians* 11 (1952): 22–23; and Paul Venable Turner, *Campus: An American Planning Tradition* (New York, 1984) 110–11. On Ramée's design for Union College, see P. V. Turner, *Joseph Ramée, International Architect of the Revolutionary Era* (Cambridge, 1996) 189–216.

10. Cited in *Columbia University Quarterly* (June 1904): 232.

11. William F. Russell, ed., *The Rise of a University I: The Later Days of Old Columbia College, From the Annual Reports of Frederick A. P. Barnard, President of Columbia College, 1864–1889* (New York, 1937) 339.

12. Frederick Law Olmsted and James R. Croes, "Preliminary Report of the Landscape Architect and the Civil and Topographical Engineer, upon the Laying Out of the Twenty-Third and Twenty-Fourth Wards" (1877), reprinted as "The Misfortunes of New York," in Frederick Law Olmsted, *Civilizing American Cities, Writing on City Landscapes*, ed. S. B. Sutton (Cambridge, Mass., 1971; reprint New York, 1997) 46–47.

13. Ibid., 46.

14. "Columbia College," *Harper's New Monthly Magazine* (November 1884), reprinted in James C. Stone and Donald P. DeNevi, eds., *Portraits of the American University 1890–1910* (San Francisco, 1971) 68–69.

15. See Harold S. Wechsler, *The Qualified Student: Selective College Admission in America, 1870–1970* (New York, 1977).

16. Minutes of the Board of Trustees, vol. 7 (1874): 61 (CUA).

17. "College Edifices and Their Relation to Education," *American Literary Magazine* 1 (1847): 271.

18. Minutes of the Board of Trustees, vol. 7 (1874): 55 (CUA).

19. This was discovered by one of my students in a seminar on American campus design, fall 1994: Hideki Yamamoto, "The Development of Columbia College's Midtown Campus, 1857–1884," M.A. paper, Art History Department, Columbia University, 1997. C. C. Haight entered Columbia in 1857 as a member of the first class accepted on the Midtown campus, received the A.B. in 1861, after a year's military service attended the Law School without graduating in 1863, and earned the A.M. in 1864. His father, Benjamin Haight, served as a trustee from 1843 until his death in 1879.

20. Montgomery Schuyler, "A Review of the Work of Charles C. Haight," *The Architectural Record*, Supplement (July 1899): 8.

21. Plans survive in the Drawings and Archives Collection of Avery Library.

22. William C. Shopsin, *The Villard Houses: Life Story of a Landmark* (New York, 1980) 24.

23. *King's Handbook of New York* (New York, 1893) I:272.

24. Brander Matthews, "Twenty Years of Change at Columbia College," *Harper's Weekly* 6 (February 1892): 136.

25. *Annual Report of Columbia College,* 1882, quoted in W. F. Russell, ed., *Rise of a University*, 348 (see note 11).

26. Thomas Bender, *New York Intellectual* (Baltimore, 1987) 270. The issue of the trustees' greater interest in matters of real estate than curriculum was also argued by Robert McCaughey, who is currently engaged in a history of Columbia for the 250th anniversary of the university, in an illuminating presentation to the University Seminar on the Morningside Centennial in spring 1996.

27. Ibid.

28. Gerald Kurland, *Seth Low, The Reformer in an Urban and Industrial Age* (New York, 1971) 42–43.

29. *Kansas City Times* (13 October 1889) (CC).

30. See Seth Low, "An American View of Municipal Government in the United States" (1888), reprinted in James Bryce, *The American Commonwealth* (New York, 1973) II:303. An excellent analysis of this parallelism was provided in a senior thesis done under my direction by Zachary Levy, "'A University on a Hill': Columbia under Seth Low," spring 1996.

31. *Brooklyn Eagle* (27 October 1889).

32. *New York Times* (4 February 1890): 4.

33. James Martin Keating, "Seth Low and the Development of Columbia University 1889–1901" (Ed.D. diss., Columbia University Teachers College, 1973) 98.

34. "President Low's Inaugural Address," in *Columbia College, Installation of President Low, February 3, 1890*, 52, 56 (CC).

35. Columbia College in the City of New York, *Annual Report of the President, 1891* (CC).

36. Columbia College in the City of New York, *Report of the Committee on Site, 7th December 1891*, 1 (CC).

37. Andrew Scott Dolkart's research into the real estate development of the area was presented to the University Seminar on the Morningside Centennial, spring 1996, and forms part of his forthcoming book *Morningside Heights: Architecture and Development on the Acropolis of New York, 1887–1934*, to be published by the Columbia University Press in 1998.

38. The hospital had acquired an act of the state legislature in 1838 closing the streets through their property.

39. "The Removal of Columbia," *New York Times* (28 February 1892).

40. *Report of the Committee on Site, 7th December 1891*, 13–14 (see note 36).

41. Minutes of the Board of Trustees, vol. 12 (1 February 1892) (CUA).

42. "A Great Opportunity," *Christian Union* (30 January 1892).

43. "The Removal of Columbia College," *Evening Post* (20 January 1892).

44. Bender, 280–81 (see note 26).

45. Quoted in Thomas Hines, *Burnham of Chicago, Architect and Planner* (Chicago, 1974) 401.

46. Letter from McKim to Low, 5 June 1893 (CUA, Central Files).

47. Statement of the Committee on Site, January 1892, in the Minutes of the Board of Trustees, vol. 12 (1 February 1892): 7 (CUA). The tenfold increase might seem odd when one considers that Columbia moved from a one-block site to a four-block site, but it must be remembered that the new blocks were nearly twice the size of the old ones, since Madison Avenue was inserted after the original grid had been drawn up.

48. Ibid.

49. Minutes of the Board of Trustees, vol. 12 (2 May 1892) (CUA).

50. Seth Low, Inaugural Address, 59–60 (see note 34).

51. Letter from Pine to Low, 4 May 1892 (CUA, Central Files).

52. *Correspondence etc. in relation to buildings on the new site, May 1892–April 1893*, in the Minutes of the Board of Trustees, vol. 14 (1892–1893) (CUA).

53. Letter to Olmsted of April 1893, now in the Library of Congress, cited in Charles Moore, *The Life and Times of Charles Follen McKim* (New York, 1929) 264.

54. On the Sorbonne design by Paul-Henri Nénot, see Philippe Rivé, ed., *La Sorbonne et sa reconstruction* (Paris, 1987).

55. Letter from McKim to Low, 18 April 1893 (CUA, Central Files).

56. Letter from McKim to Olmsted, 18 April 1893, quoted in Moore, 265 (see note 53).

57. *Report of the Committee on Buildings and Grounds*, in the Minutes of the Board of Trustees, vol. 13 (June 1893) (CUA).

58. Quoted in Moore, 265 (see note 53).

59. Seth Low, "The World's Columbian Exposition," *Columbia Literary Magazine* 11 (October 1893): 1–5.

60. This is first mentioned in Seth Low's letter to the trustees of 8 January 1894 (in the Minutes of the Board of Trustees, vol. 14 [1893–1894]) (CUA). These volumes were later deposited in Avery Library, where a special folio case was made for them; they have since disappeared, and although they are listed in Columbia's records of major gifts no reference to them in the library catalogue can be found.

61. *Report of the Committee on Buildings and Grounds in Relation to the New Site*, printed report bound with the Minutes of the Board of Trustees, vol. 14 (11 November 1893): 10–11 (CUA).

62. Although John William Robson (*A Guide to Columbia Univeristy, with Some Account of Its History and Traditions*, New York, 1937, 37) said that this was penned by Nicholas Murray Butler, it was clearly written by Low who claimed authorship and quoted it in correspondence with John B. Pine, notably in Low to Pine, 27 March 1896 (CUA, Central Files). The inscriptions were discussed by the trustees on 5 October 1896 and approved on 4 January 1897 (Minutes of the Board of Trustees, vol. 17 [1896–1897] [CUA]).

63. Letter from Low to Pine, 27 March 1896 (CUA, Central Files).

64. Minutes of the Board of Trustees, vol. 14 (November 1893) (CUA).

65. Benjamin R. C. Low, *Seth Low* (New York, 1925) 64.

66. Leland Roth, *McKim, Mead and White, Architects* (New York, 1983) 182.

67. This is currently the subject of research by Professor Mary Woods of Cornell University, aspects of which were presented in a session of the University Seminar on the Morningside Centennial, 25 April 1997.

68. See Richard Krautheimer, "The Panels in Urbino, Baltimore and Berlin Reconsidered," in Henry A. Millon and Vittorio Magnago Lampugnani, eds., *The Renaissance from Brunelleschi to Michelangelo: The Representation of Architecture* (New York, 1994) 233–58.

69. Minutes of the Board of Trustees, vol. 15 (4 October 1894) (CUA).

70. See Roth, 185ff. (see note 66).

71. In a letter of 2 March 1894 to Low, John B. Pine wrote: "When the design of the Library was first submitted with the statement that it would cost a million dollars, you at once expressed the opinion that its cost put it out of the question, and I entirely agreed with you. If you will calculate the probable cost of the Library as now proposed, including the portico and the peristyle, and including all the costs of fitting up the Library with shelves, etc., I think you will find that it is likely to amount to nearly a million dollars. This will serve merely as an illustration of the risk we run of being led into expenditures much greater than we anticipate or approve" (CUA, Central Files).

72. Francesco Passanti ("The Design of Columbia in the 1890s: McKim and His Client," *Journal of the Society of Architectural Historians* 34 [1977]: 69–84) relates it to Low's bid for the mayor's office.

73. Letter from Low to McKim, Mead & White, 3 November 1893 (CUA, Central Files).

74. Letter from Pine to Low, 26 April 1894 (CUA, Central Files).

75. Letter from Pine to Low, 17 April 1894 (CUA, Central Files).

76. Letter from Low to McKim, 16 April 1894 (CUA, Central Files).

77. *Report on New Buildings from Committee of Buildings & Grounds*, in the Minutes of the Board of Trustees, vol. 14 (7 May 1894) (CUA).

78. Quoted in Moore, 266 (see note 53).

79. Letter from Low to Pine, 19 September 1894 (CUA, Central Files).

80. Letter from McKim to Mead, date unknown, McKim, Mead & White Papers, Library of Congress, quoted in Passanti, 76, n. 18 (see note 72).

81. Letter from McKim to White, 24 July 1894, Stanford White Papers, Avery Library, Drawings and Archives Collection.

82. Letter from Low to Pine, 18 April, 1894 (CUA, Central Files).

83. Talbot Hamlin, *Forms and Functions of Twentieth Century Architecture II: The Principles of Composition* (New York, 1952) 561.

84. Minutes of the Board of Trustees, vol. 14 (4 December 1893) (CUA).

85. Letter from McKim to Low, 7 December 1894 (CUA, Central Files).

86. "Letter of the President to the trustees as to the measures to be taken for the immediate improvement of the new site. Presented 5 November 1894," in the Minutes of the Board of Trustees, vol. 15 (1894–1895) (CUA).

87. Letter from Low to McKim, 27 October 1895 (CUA, Central Files).

88. *New York Sun* (12 May 1895) (CC).

89. Letter from McKim to Low, handwritten, London, 6 April 1896 (CUA, Central Files).

90. Letter from McKim to Low, 8 September 1894 (CUA, Central Files).

91. Letter from Low to McKim, 13 October 1894 (CUA, Central Files).

92. Letter from McKim to Low, 16 October 1894 (CUA, Central Files).

93. Letter from Low to Pine, 19 September 1894 (CUA, Central Files).

94. Letter from McKim to Low, 16 October 1894 (CUA, Central Files).

95. *Report of the Olmsted firm, 1 January 1895*, in Minutes of the Board of Trustees, vol. 15 (1894–1895) (CUA).

96. Letter from Ware to Low, 28 December 1895 (CUA, Central Files).

97. *Report of the Committee on Buildings and Grounds on Schermerhorn Hall and the Physics Building, 18 November 1895*, in Minutes of the Board of Trustees, vol. 16 (1895–1896) (CUA).

98. *Dedication of the New Site, Morningside Heights, Saturday, the Second of May* (New York, 1986) 29 (CC).

99. Letter from Ware to Low, 28 December 1895 (CUA, Central Files).

100. William H. Goodyear ("Horizontal Curves in Columbia University," *Architectural Record* 9, no. 1 [July–September 1899]: 82–93) notes that "in their designs for the Columbia University Library and University Hall, Messrs. McKim, Mead and White are probably the first among modern architects to make the experiment of using the Greek horizontal curves on an extended scale" (82).

101. As the Olmsted firm pointed out (letter to Low, 1 January 1895 [CUA, Central Files]), this would also "relieve the glare which is so disagreeable, especially in summer. . . . With proper selection of brick, and good workmanship in laying, such a sidewalk would be not only perfectly smooth and neat, but also durable and appropriate." These have all been removed in recent years.

102. *Report of the Faculty of Mines to the Committee of the Trustees on Buildings and Grounds, 15 November 1892*, in the Minutes of the Board of Trustees, vol. 13 (1892–1893) (CUA).

103. On the teaching role of the seminar rooms included in the library's innovative plan, see B. Bergdoll, "Laying the Cornerstone of the New Columbia University (Library), December 7, 1895," *Columbia Library Columns* 44, no. 2 (Autumn 1995): 13–24.

104. *Report of the Committee on Buildings and Grounds in Relation to the Development of the New Site, 11 November 1893*, in the Minutes of the Board of Trustees, vol. 14 (1893–1894) (CUA).

105. *Annual Report of the President, 1 October 1894*, in the Minutes of the Board of Trustees, vol. 15 (1894–1895) (CUA).

106. Montgomery Schuyler, "Architecture of American Colleges IV: New York City Colleges," *Architectural Record* 27 (1910): 446.

107. Ibid., 447.

108. Ibid.

109. Ibid.

110. Ibid., 448–49.

111. Minutes of the Board of Trustees, vol. 18 (3 January 1898) (CUA).

112. *Annual Report of the President for 1899*, in the Minutes of the Board of Trustees, vol. 20 (1899–1900): 66 (CUA).

113. Low, *Seth Low*, 64 (see note 65).

114. Both would eventually give more.

115. Letter from Dodge, in *Columbia University Quarterly* (Sept. 1900): 367.

116. See Janet Parks and Alan G. Neumann, *The Old World Builds the New: The Guastavino Company and the Technology of the Catalan Vault, 1885–1962* (New York, 1996) 26–27.

117. *Annual Report of the President for 1899* (see note 112).

118. J. H. Van Amringe, "What the College Buildings Should Be," *Columbia University Quarterly* (June 1899): 272.

119. Ibid., 273.

120. Letter from Low to McKim, 12 March 1901 (CUA, Central Files).

121. The asylum building on that site, moreover, was much smaller than the one serving as the temporary College Hall, which stood near the corner of Amsterdam Avenue and 116th Street until it was moved in 1905 to its current site and renamed East Hall.

122. Minutes of the Board of Trustees, vol. 20 (1 April 1901) (CUA).

123. *Annual Report of the President for 1898*, in the Minutes of the Board of Trustees, vol. 19 (1898–1899): 60 (CUA).

124. Undated memorandum in Pine's papers from 1895 (CUA, Central Files).

125. Letter from Ware to Low, 18 December 1896 (CUA, Central Files).

126. Letter from Pine to Low, 2 January 1897 (CUA, Central Files).

127. Letter from Pine to Low, 9 December 1894 (CUA, Central Files).

128. See Turner, 163 passim (see note 9).

129. Letter from Pine to Low, 30 November 1896 (CUA, Central Files).

130. *Annual Report 1898*, 62 (see note 123).

131. Letter from Low to Pine, 12 April 1897 (CUA, Central Files).

132. *Annual Report 1898*, 65 (see note 123).

133. Letter from Pine to Low, 10 June 1898: "This morning I had a conference with Mr. McKim and Mr. Mead as to a dormitory, and found that Mr. Mead had prepared a perspective drawing of proposed dormitory. This drawing will be ready for submission next week, and I told Mr. McKim that I thought it would be possible for you and me to meet him at his office some day next week, when we could discuss the whole dormitory question. I left him with a copy of my letter to the Finance Committee on the subject, and asked him to give his advice upon all the questions involved, as to the situation and style of the building, and as to the relative advantages of placing dormitories upon the upper or lower level. Mr. McKim is to let me know when he is ready to meet" (CUA, Central Files).

134. Undated memorandum in John Pine's papers for 1895 (CUA, Central Files).

135. See the articles on the proposed dormitories in *Columbia University Quarterly* (December 1898): 60–63, and (March 1899): 149–52, the latter signed by Pine.

136. Letter from Low to Pine, 12 April 1897 (CUA, Central Files).

137. Letter from Low to Pine, 17 January 1898 (CUA, Central Files).

138. Letter from the Olmsted firm to Columbia University, 1 January 1895 (CUA, Central Files).

139. "The Morningside Acropolis," *Columbia University Quarterly* (March 1900): 150.

140. Minutes of the Board of Trustees, vol. 22 (4 November 1901) (CUA).

141. *Annual Report of the President for 1902*, in the Minutes of the Board of Trustees, vol. 23 (1902–1903): 9–10 (CUA).

142. Letter from Butler to Hamlin, 25 July 1902 (CUA, Central Files). On the reorganization of the Architecture School in these years and Hamlin's role, see Richard Oliver, ed., *The Making of an Architect, 1881–1981* (New York, 1981) 38 ff.

143. Ibid.

144. *Annual Report 1902*, 29 (see note 141).

145. *Columbia University Quarterly* (1904): 234.

146. Minutes of the Board of Trustees, vol.29 (5 April 1909): 249 (CUA).

147. On these key years see Steven M. Bedford and Susan M. Strauss, "History II: 1881–1912," in Oliver, 23–48 (see note 142).

148. See, for instance, the numerous McKim plans analyzed and upheld as models in a series of articles "The Group Plan," published by Alfred Morton Githens in *The Brickbuilder* (July 1906–December 1907).

149. Letter from Hamlin to Butler, 28 July 1902 (CUA, Central Files).

150. J. B. Pine, "South Field: Its Possible Uses," *Columbia University Quarterly* 5 (June 1903): 256.

151. Ibid., 253.

152. For both of these schemes, see Robert A. M. Stern, Gregory Gilmartin, and John Montague Massengale, *New York 1900: Metropolitan Architecture and Urbanism, 1890–1915* (New York, 1983) 414–15.

153. *Report of the Trustees Committee on Buildings and Grounds, 13 October 1910* in the Minutes of the Board of Trustees, vol. 31 (1910–1911): 14 (CUA).

154. Bender, 284 (see note 26). This theme is also explored in Bender's introduction to the volume that he edited *The University and the City From Medieval Origins to the Present* (New York, 1988).

155. Quoted in *Columbia University Quarterly*, Hamilton Hall Supplement, March 1907: 267–68.

156. *Report of the Trustees Committee on Buildings and Grounds, December 1916*, in the Minutes of the Board of Trustees, vol. 37 (1916–1917): 109 (CUA).

157. In the Minutes of the Board of Trustees, vol. 42 (1920–1921): 198 (CUA).

158. See Michael Rosenthal, "Nicholas Murray Butler: Captain of Erudition," *Columbia Library Columns* 44, no. 2 (Autumn 1995): 5–12. Professor Rosenthal is currently completing a full-length intellectual biography of Butler.

159. *Annual Report of the President for 1911*, in the Minutes of the Board of Trustees, vol. 32 (1910–1911) (CUA).

160. *Annual Report of the President for 1921*, in the Minutes of the Board of Trustees, vol. 43 (1921–1922): 51 (CUA).

161. Ibid. The state universities are those cited by Butler in his 3 January 1921 speech to the trustees on Columbia's future (see note 157).

162. Upton Sinclair in *The Goose-Step* (1922), quoted in Horace Coon, *Columbia: Colossus on the Hudson* (New York, 1947) 25.

163. *Annual Report of the President for 1919*, in the Minutes of the Board of Trustees, vol. 41 (1919–1920): 32 (CUA).

164. Rogers's work at the Medical Center has been most recently summarized by Aaron Betsky, *James Gamble Rogers and the Architecture of Pragmatism* (New York, 1994): 213–26.

165. On Bard College's connection to Columbia after 1929, see Robson, 169–74 (see note 62).

166. Bender (288–92, see note 26) has argued persuasively that a strong element in this was an unspoken policy of reducing the high percentage of Jewish students that Columbia had attracted in its early years on Morningside Heights.

167. *Annual Report of the President for 1916*, in the Minutes of the Board of Trustees, vol. 38 (1916–17): 3 (CUA).

168. *Annual Report of the President for 1919*, 32–36 (see note 163).

169. On the sundial, see Robson, 87–88 (see note 62).

170. Ibid., 73.

171. Letter from William Kendall to Henry Lee Norris, 21 April 1925 (CUA, Central Files).

172. Letter from Kendall of McKim, Mead & White to Butler, 10 December 1926 (CUA, Central Files).

173. *Report of the Committee on Buildings and Grounds, 3 December 1928*, in the Minutes of the Board of Trustees, vol. 50 (1928–29) (CUA).

174. *Annual Report of the President for 1921* (see note 160).

175. *Annual Report of the President for 1922*, in the Minutes of the Board of Trustees, vol. 44 (1922–23) (CUA).

176. Letter from Gildersleeve to Butler, 2 April 1925 (CUA, Central Files).

177. This commission is documented in the correspondence between J. G. Rogers and N. M. Butler (CUA, Central Files).

178. Minutes of the Board of Trustees, vol. 46 (7 December 1925) (CUA).

179. June 1929 resolution, cited in the Minutes of the Board of Trustees, vol. 50 (7 October 1929) (CUA).

180. This is a paraphrase of the famous inscription to Sir Christopher Wren in the floor of St. Paul's Cathedral, London.

181. Michael Stoller, "Columbia's Library for the Twentieth Century: The Rise of South Hall," *Columbia Library Columns* 45, no. 2 (Autumn 1996): 8. See also Betsky (see note 164).

182. Letter from Butler to Harkness's secretary Malcolm Aldrich, 9 December 1930 (CUA, Central Files).

183. Letter from Butler to Aldrich, 4 May 1931 (CUA, Central Files).

184. Letter from Williamson to Butler, 16 August 1927, in the Rare Book and Manuscript Library, Columbia University, quoted in Stoller: 6 (note 181).

185. Betsky, 203 (see note 164).

186. Letter from Butler to Aldrich, 4 May 1931 (see note 183).

187. Betsky, 60 (see note 164).

188. Letter from Rogers to Henry Lee Norris, 1 October 1930 (CUA, Central Files).

189. Letter from Rogers to Butler, 9 October 1930 (CUA, Central Files). It is interesting to note that these types of arguments have been used almost verbatim in recent architectural theory, notably by Bernard Tschumi and Rem Koolhaas, to justify new hybrid building programs.

190. Letter from Rogers to Butler, 13 February 1931 (in Butler's correspondence from Rogers) (CUA, Central Files).

191. Letter from Rogers to Kendall, 13 February 1931 (copy) (CUA, Central Files).

192. Letter from Rogers to Butler, 13 February 1931 (see note 190).

193. Letter from Rogers to Butler, 9 April 1931 (CUA, Central Files).

194. Federal Writer's Project, *WPA Guide to New York* (New York, 1939) 387.

195. Letter from Butler to Rogers, 2 June 1931 (CUA, Central Files).

196. See, for instance, Judith Oberlander, "History IV, 1933–1935," in Richard Oliver, 119–26 (see note 142).

197. Ms. attached to a letter from Joseph Hudnut to Frank D. Fackenthal, 7 June 1935, 1 (UCA, Central Files).

198. Ibid., 2.

199. Blueprints for this project are among the McKim, Mead & White office files at the New-York Historical Society.

200. Letter from Boring to President Butler's office, 18 February 1932 (CUA, Central Files).

201. Letter from Butler to Harkness, 3 February 1930 (CUA, Central Files).

202. Letter from Henry Lee Norris (director of the Department of Buildings and Grounds) to Butler, 26 February 1941 (CUA, Central Files). The idea was briefly revived under Acting President Fackenthal in January 1947; see the letters from Fackenthal to the trustee Douglas Black, 11 January 1947, and from Black to Fackenthal, 16 January 1947 (CUA, Central Files).

203. "The Development Program of Columbia University, An Address by Douglas M. Black, Chairman of the Board of Trustees' Committee on Development before the Officers of the Alumni Federation on January 22, 1948," typescript, Black's papers (CUA, Central Files).

204. John A. Kouwenhoven, *Made in America, The Arts in Modern Civilization* (Garden City, NY, 1948) 95.

205. *WPA Guide*, 387 (see note 194).

206. Coon, 1 (see note 162).

207. Ibid., 362.

208. Letter from Butler to Black, 21 September 1945 (CUA, Central Files).

209. Robert A. M. Stern, Thomas Mellins, and David Fishman, *New York 1960: Architecture and Urbanism between the Second World War and the Bicentennial* (New York: 1995) 734.

210. Elliot Sclar of the School of the Architecture is currently completing a manuscript on the history of urban redevelopment on Manhattan's Upper West Side.

211. Joseph Hudnut, "On Form in Universities," *Architectural Forum* (December 1947): 88–93.

212. Search for an off-campus site had since the 1930s led Columbia to commission studies of sites upstate and in the Bronx that were conveniently located near either river or rail transport. Voorhees, Walker, Smith, Smith & Haines's studies for the sites of today's Prentis Hall and 560 Riverside Drive, the latter to cost $22.1 million and to be financed from a fund-raising drive leading up to the bicentennial of the university in 1954, are in the photographic collection of Columbiana (fig. 147).

213. See the reprint from the *Congressional Record* 100, no. 62 (5 April 1954) contained among the papers of Joseph Coffee, head of the Fund for Columbia College in the 1950s (CUA, Central Files).

214. See Voorhees, Walker, Smith, Smith & Haines, Architects, *Laboratories* (March 1961), pamphlet among the collection of brochures on the firm's work presented by their architectural render Charles B. Price to the Avery Library.

215. See Victoria Newhouse, *Wallace K. Harrison, Architect* (New York, 1989).

216. As these proposals were paraphrased in Adams & Woodbridge, "A Report on General Development of the Campus, Columbia University," sent to William J. Whiteside, director of buildings and grounds, 19 July 1955 (CUA, Central Files).

217. Ibid.

218. Ibid., 6.

219. "Plans for New East Campus Are Born," *Columbia Alumni News* (May 1956): 12–13.

220. Stern et al., 763 (see note 209).

221. Letter from Abramovitz to Kirk, 23 January 1963 (CUA, Central Files).

222. Stern et al., 738 (see note 209).

223. *New York Times* (29 April 1962).

224. See the special issue of *Columbia College Today* 9, no. 1 (Fall 1963) for extensive background history on sites, negotiations, and fund-raising for the Columbia gym between 1947 and 1963.

225. Ada Louise Huxtable, "Expansion at Columbia: A Restricted Vision and Bureaucracy Seen as Obstacles to Its Development," *New York Times* (5 November 1966): 33.

226. Quoted in *New York Times* (29 April 1962).

227. Ibid.

228. *New York Times* (19 April 1962).

229. Quoted in Stern et al., 739 (see note 209).

230. Quoted in *New York Times* (19 April 1962).

231. James T. Burns Jr., "Uris Hall: An Opportunity Missed," *Columbia Spectator* (8 May 1964).

232. "Morningside Heights Is Having Growing Pains and Strain Shows on Area's Residents," *New York Times* (18 January 1964): 26.

233. Steven V. Roberts, "Columbia's Expansion to Uproot Area Residents," *New York Times* (2 November 1966): 47.

234. Huxtable, 33 (see note 225).

235. Quoted in *Columbia Spectator* (18 March 1968) as a comment made the previous year.

236. Robert E. Price (CC, 1965), letter to the editor, *Columbia Spectactor* (10 October 1967).

237. In addition to the report of the Cox Commission, *Crisis at Columbia: Report of the Fact Finding Commission Appointed to Investigate the Disturbances at Columbia University in April and May 1968* (New York, 1968), see Roger Kahn, *The Battle for Morningside Heights* (New York, 1968). An excellent summary relating especially to issues of architecture is Marta Gutman and Richard Plunz, "Anatomy of Insurrection," in Oliver, ed., 183–210 (see note 142). The late Professor George R. Collins and his wife, Christiane, took a particularly active role in fighting the gymnasium project and compiled a voluminous archive of clippings now in the Schomburg Center for Research in Black Culture of the New York Public Library. Known as the Christiane C. Collins Collection/ West Harlem Coalition for Morningside Park and Urban Problems of the Contiguous Communities, it has recently been inventoried and provided with an excellent finding aid by Janice Quinter. Permission to consult Ms. Collins's unpublished account of the events surrounding the gymnasium, also on deposit at the library, was not granted.

238. *Columbia University Newsletter* 10, no. 8 (18 November 1968): 1.

239. Ibid.

240. Ibid.

241. *Columbia Spectator* (12 December 1968).

242. Letter from Kenneth Smith to Andrew Cordier, 12 December 1968 (CUA, Central Files).

243. Pei, as paraphrased in an internal memo from the vice president of administration Warren F. Goodell, to Andrew Cordier, 5 June 1969 (CUA, Central Files).

244. Letter from Henry Cobb to John D. Telfer, 19 December 1969 (CUA, Central File).

245. Memo from Martin J. Gleason to John D. Telfer, 14 April 1970 (CUA, Central Files).

246. "The I. M. Pei Master Plan for Columbia, Notes on Pei's presentation Thursday, June 12, 1969," typescript, 1 (CC).

247. I. M. Pei & Associates, *Planning for Columbia University: An Interim Report* (New York, 1970).

248. Ibid., 26.

249. Ibid., 27.

250. Ibid., 16.

251. "I. M. Pei Master Plan for Columbia," 2 (see note 246).

252. *Columbia Spectator* (12 May 1969).

253. "Planner Discloses Dissent on Towers," *Columbia Spectator* (13 February 1970).

254. See *Columbia Spectator* (16 April 1970).

255. Pei, *Interim Report*, 35 (see note 247).

256. Ibid., 41.

257. Ibid., 44. In addition to Pei's own project, included in his report, a project for alterations was drawn up in January 1970 by Philip Brotherton Associates, Architects and Planners, and revised in March 1970. Copies of the blueprints are among the Columbia papers in the archives of the I. M. Pei firm.

258. Daralice D. Boles, "Teaching Architecture, " *Progressive Architecture* (September 1986): 128–31.

259. Pei, *Interim Report*, 8 (see note 247).

260. Ibid., 53.

261. Although the model was discarded in the 1980s, photographs of it survive in the archives of the Pei office.

262. Hamlin, 561 (see note 83).

263. Pei, *Interim Report*, 9 (see note 247).

264. Ibid., 82.

265. See also Ada Louise Huxtable, "Columbia Plan Includes Underground Expansion," *New York Times* (18 February 1970): 1.

266. Letter from I. M. Pei to John D. Taylor, 24 April 1970 (CUA, Central Files).

267. Letter from I. M. Pei to Andrew Cordier, 21 May 1970 (CUA, Central Files).

268. Transcript of the 15 June 1970 newscast, President's papers, I. M. Pei file (CUA, Central Files).

269. Notes obtained by Fred Knubel from Warren F. Goodell "on the I. M. Pei matter," 17 June 1970, President's papers, I. M. Pei file (CUA, Central Files).

270. *New York Times* (7 June 1971).

271. *New York Times* (23 September 1974).

272. Ibid.

273. Romaldo Giurgola, "Planning at CU," *Columbia Spectator* (5 February 1970).

274. "Columbia University Appoints a Campus Architect," *Interiors* 132 (January 1973): 14.

275. For an account of Polshek's years as dean, see Oliver, ed., 243–63 (see note 142).

276. Polshek had briefly worked side by side with Pei in 1955, see the autobiographical account of his work in *James Stewart Polshek: Context and Responsibility, Buildings and Projects, 1957–1987* (New York, 1987) 23.

277. Ibid., 34. In addition this section is based on an interview of Polshek by the author, 29 May 1997.

278. Paul Goldberger, "Science Building Marks New Day for Architecture at Columbia U.," *New York Times* (25 October 1977).

279. Vincent Scully, *American Architecture and Urbanism* (New York, 1969) 142–43.

280. Polshek, 35 (see note 276).

281. Memo from Telfer to McGill, 23 February 1971 (CUA, Central Files).

282. Memo from Telfer to McGill, 6 December 1972 (CUA, Central Files).

283. Letter from Romaldo Giurgola to Provost James Young, 22 March 1973 (CUA, Central Files).

284. Martin Filler, "Hail Columbia," *Progressive Architecture* 59 (March 1978): 59.

285. Quoted in Jamie Katz, "New Life for Columbia's Life Sciences: The Sherman Fairchild Center," *Columbia College Today* (Winter 1973–1974): 6.

286. "1980 Chandler North: The Extension of the Chemistry Department, Columbia University, New York," *Architectural Design* (London) 53, nos. 3/4 (1983): 11. See also the comments by Michael Wilford, "Responding to Context," *International Architect* 5 (1984): 29.

287. For instance, in the manuscript of an apparently unpublished article by the late professor of art history George R. Collins on the occasion of the inauguration of Seeley W. Mudd in 1961, he notes: "It is, however, especially poignant that our Engineering building should be so miserable an effort, because it is precisely among the ranks of the structural engineers that the most rationally satisfying and emotionally exciting buildings of our day have been created." Collins collection, Schomburg Center for Research in Black Culture of the New York Public Library (see note 237).

288. "Expanding Horizons: The East Campus Complex by Gwathmey Siegel & Associates," *Architectural Record* 170 (February 1982): 68.

289. Norman Coplan, "Law: Substantial Completion," *Progressive Architecture* (January 1993): 33.

290. See Roger Kimball, "Business as More than Usual," *Architectural Record* 174 (April 1986): 120–25; "Uris Hall Addition at Columbia University," *Building Stone Magazine* 1/2 (1986): 41–43; "Manhattan Job Fights Tight City Site," *Engineering News Record* (25 April 1985); and R. Douglas Hamilton, "A New Facade for Modernism," *Columbia Art Review* (Spring 1985): 10–12.

291. Barry Bergdoll, "Back to the Campus: Five University Building Designs by R. M. Kliment & Frances Halsband Architects," *Five Campus Buildings 1981–1989*, exh. pamphlet, Roger Williams College, Bristol, R.I., 1990; Sharon Lee Ryder, "Building Threaded Between Neighbors," *Architecture* (May 1987).

292. Columbia University. Commission on the Future of the University. Draft Report, Part III. Physical Resources of the University. A. Morningside Heights Campus. 1. Campus. (May 1985) 10–11.

293. Skidmore, Owings & Merrill, *Columbia University: East Campus Development* (March 1990).

294. Kohn Pedersen Fox Associates, *Columbia University: East Campus Redevelopment Master Plan,* vol. 2, sec. 6.3 (12 March 1990).

295. Quoted in *New York Construction News* (28 April 1997): 4.

296. Beyer Blinder Belle, Architects & Planners LLP, Morningside Heights Planning Framework. Draft report, April 1997, 2.2.

HOLLEE HASWELL

CONSTRUCTING LOW MEMORIAL LIBRARY

A CHRONICLE OF A MONUMENTAL ENTERPRISE

SILENT as a majestic sailing ship our days pass, the pace seemingly regulated by us. As we race to the end of a century, it is fitting that we pause to reflect upon the work of previous generations and to celebrate their enduring gifts. Without reflection our current decade might easily pass with no notice of cause for celebration.

In 1891, since Columbia College had already outgrown the Forty-ninth Street campus, the trustees of Columbia College agreed to purchase the property of the Bloomingdale Asylum, which extended from 116th to 120th Street, between Broadway and Amsterdam. The trustees wisely decided against taking the monies for this purchase from the college's already encumbered funds. Two million dollars were raised, not with great ease, from wealthy benefactors, citizens of New York, and alumni. Once the property was secured, a plan for using the asylum buildings was proposed but never executed. New buildings were needed.

On 6 May 1895, at a regular trustees' meeting, President Seth Low made the following announcement:

> It was a favorite saying with my father, the late Abiel Abbot Low, that "commerce is the handmaid of civilization." As a memorial of him, a merchant who taught his son to value the things for which Columbia College stands, I propose, if the Trustees consent, to cooperate with the College in the construction of the new University Library. . . . I will undertake to give to the College . . . a sum equal to the cost of the Library, up to but not exceeding $1,000,000.

Newspaper accounts of the day called Columbia lucky and the gift noble, magnificent, princely. Seth Low, then age forty-five, was commended and thanked for the wisdom of his choice no less heartily than for his munificence.

We pause, now, to reflect on the ideals brought forth, maintained, cherished, and given to generations by this place; we commemorate the technical skill, craftsmanship, artistry, and labor which in two short years, from 1895 to 1897, brought forth the first buildings on the Morningside campus. A decade of centennial celebrations has begun.

These photographs are from the Columbiana Collection. This special collection, devoted to the history of Columbia University from the King's College era to the present, is a vital part of the Columbia University Libraries as well as the University Archives.

For convenience, the captions for the photographs use the commonly accepted cardinal orientation rather than the strict compass point. For example, although the cornerstone of Low Memorial Library is actually at the east corner of the building (according to the compass), its location is commonly referred to as the northeast corner of the building.

The group of photographs from which the following images were selected are proof prints; their height ranges from $6\frac{15}{16}$ *to* $9\frac{5}{8}$ *inches and their width from* $7\frac{1}{8}$ *to* $9\frac{7}{8}$ *inches. The exhibition features enlargements made from the original prints. Thirty of these images are in the catalogue.*

A number of these original photographs are stamped "Philip S. Lacy" on the verso. Documents in Columbiana suggest that this was Philip Sawyer Lacy, born in New Jersey in 1893. The Lacy family moved to New York City within one month of Philip Lacy's birth. Educated in the public schools, Lacy entered the Columbia University School of Architecture in 1911. His studies were interrupted by service in World War I; in 1920 he received a Certificate of Architecture. A member of the American Institute of Architects, during the span of his career he was employed by the firms of McKim, Mead & White and Carrère & Hastings. His pastimes were sports, especially sailing; over the years, as a volunteer, he photographed various sports events of Columbia teams. He gave generously of his time and eventually also donated his collection of photographs to the college.

Although Lacy was much too young in 1895 to 1897 to have taken these photographs, one can imagine that, as a child, he might have seen the actual construction of this campus and been inspired to become an architect. The photographs of the construction were later included in his files at McKim, Mead & White. We are deeply indebted to Philip S. Lacy for donating these photographs to the university.

6 OCTOBER 1895

For the library project, McKim secured the Norcross Brothers, Contractors and Builders, from Worcester, Massachusetts. As the Norcross Brothers' masonry building projects–Trinity Church, Boston (1877); Albany City Hall (1881–83); and Allegheny County Courthouse and Jail, Pittsburgh (1884–88), among others–demonstrated, a more innovative, practical, and precise company could not have been chosen. The foundation for the ten columns of the portico appears just above ground level in this view looking south.

27 OCTOBER 1895

The vertical boom cranes, fixed in place and steadied by guy wires, will rise with the building and eventually tower over the trees of the Grove (on the left).

16 NOVEMBER 1895

From the east, an apartment building (a Teachers College residence), along with the greenhouse and Macy Villa of the Bloomingdale Asylum, watches over the work site. Wooden scaffolding now covers Low Memorial Library's brick foundation.

16 NOVEMBER 1895

Yard after yard of brick, each one meticulously placed, form the internal structure of this massive building. Iron beams span the distance between the load-bearing walls to create the floors. The cupola of Main Hall at Teachers College (1894) is visible through the Grove (or the Green).

7 DECEMBER 1895

Out of respect for Seth Low's father, who had recently died, the laying of the cornerstone was a solemn occasion with no fanfare. The Reverend A. Van De Water, chaplain of the university, read a short service and prayed that the Lord "Give patience, skill and courage to all whose hands are busy with this work. . . . Mercifully protect from harm the workmen here employed, and keep them in all their ways" (*Proceedings upon the Laying of the Corner-Stone of the Library*). As President Low laid the cornerstone, he said: "This cornerstone is now to be set in its place. I hope that this stone will remain where it is set for centuries, bearing impressive witness so long as it shall stand to the skill and faithfulness of the men who construct this building, and to the genius of the architect who has designed it. I hope that the building to be placed upon this cornerstone will be at all times a centre of illumination and power for study and thought, both near and far, and to be a memorial of Abiel Abbot Low, in loving memory of whom this building is being raised. On behalf of the Trustees of Columbia College and in their name I declare that this cornerstone is now laid" (*New York Times, 8 December 1895*).

28 DECEMBER 1895

The cornerstone, with its face still protected by wooden packing, is in place, perpendicular to the east facade of the building. The numbered limestone blocks, with clevis attached, were transported by railroad and canal boat from a quarry in Indiana. They sit in the foreground with the mechanically powered crane, ropes, and pulley blocks. As Norcross informed McKim, the "mortar of the backing of the limestone and granite work [is] to be made up of La Farge Cement and lime mortar," to avoid staining the stone (*Norcross Brothers to McKim, Mead & White; New York, 5 January 1896, t.l.s., 1p., Columbia University Archives, Central Files*). According to all the known sources, the bridge crane in the on-site limestone storage shed (not shown) was the sole piece of electrically powered equipment used on this project.

18 JANUARY 1896

The equal-length arms of the Greek-cross floor plan become distinct here. The Macy Villa of the Bloomingdale Asylum, known today as Buell Hall, is to the right, on its original site with its porches still intact.

28 APRIL 1896

The first level above ground was completed by 4 April; this was no small accomplishment, considering the thirty inches of snow that fell on New York City in March of 1896. In order to complete the second level above ground, tile block of various shapes and sizes will be hoisted up, over, and into the structure. The square, four-part blocks in the foreground will become part of the flooring. The other, oddly shaped blocks (to the right) will probably serve as conduit and ductwork.

2 MAY 1896

This depicts the dedication of the Morningside site, a typical nineteenth-century celebration. Note Low construction to the right, the uniformed reviewing regiment, and the tent. "A university that is set upon a hill cannot be hid. I count it a matter of no little moment that here, in its new home, Columbia cannot escape the observation of the city, nor can the city escape from it. In the desire to be of service to the city, the university must ever find a potent inspiration. The university cannot be indifferent to the great city of which it is a part, and neither can the city forget, as it looks toward that hill, that there is in its midst, in the university, a life the great watchword of which is truth" (*Seth Low, President of Columbia University, at the Dedication of the Morningside Campus, 2 May 1896*).

8 JUNE 1896

The darkened bays along the south face suggest classical ruins, from which a gladiator or a lion might appear; the bays in fact form part of the brick foundation for the massive columns of the portico.

27 JUNE 1896

St. Luke's Hospital (newly opened, as of January 1896) presides over this monumental enterprise. The boom cranes and central scaffolding for the dome grow taller.

29 JUNE 1896

Three weeks have passed since the last photograph of this scene (p. 163); the third story is now complete.

3 JULY 1896

July of 1896 was hot, humid, and wet. This did not, however, hinder construction. Pausing briefly for this early morning photograph, the workmen put their stamp on what was to become one of the most photographed vistas on campus.

18 JULY 1896

The brick interior will be faced with stucco in preparation for the finished walls. The main vestibule is at the left, opposite the scaffolding for the dome. The southwest pier, one of the four massive limestone supports for the dome, now measures half of its final height. These piers also accommodate part of the original heating and ventilation systems.

23 JULY 1896

The workmen, some seventy feet above ground, seem unaffected by the potential danger of their elevation. Neither the names of these workmen, nor those of the Norcross brothers, are recorded on this structure. The Hudson River is in the distance.

26 JULY 1896

On a quiet Sunday morning, the new building seems foreshortened by the rough stone wall and the absence of the grand staircase. Low Memorial Library waits for the workmen to return.

29 AUGUST 1896

The portico appears complete. The fluted Ionic limestone columns rest on circular white marble bases, which are hidden and protected by wooden planks.

21 SEPTEMBER 1896

An aproned stonemason poses, with the pride of a great chef, next to a column capital, some thirty-five feet above the floor of the portico.

1 OCTOBER 1896

The next marble drum is ready to be lifted into place. Veined dark-green marble from Connemara, Ireland, forms the columns of the vestibule.

1 OCTOBER 1896

With the keystone in place, no small achievement, this photograph records the communal pride in the accomplishment. The massive vault, similar to the arches of ancient bridges and aqueducts, spans the distance between the supporting piers. In their intended places, the square tile blocks sit on joists to form the floor.

24 OCTOBER 1896

The cornerstone now seems dwarfed by the piers and vaults stretching to the baseline of the dome.

23 NOVEMBER 1896

The huge timbers of the central scaffolding are silhouetted against the sky. With plans in hand, the workmen prepare the wooden frame for the massive masonry dome. The "Danger Beware of Elevator" sign stands sentry. Notice the tools these men are holding: hods and shovels. Orlando W. Norcross, master builder, had planned a continuous-pour concrete dome for Low Memorial Library. Employing this technology on such a massive structure was a daring innovation for the time. In the lengthy debates over this proposal, Seth Low immediately voiced his approval. The New York City Building Department, however, did not give Norcross final authorization to proceed with the pour until late in November of 1896. As Norcross was unwilling to risk a concrete pour in cold weather, he chose instead to create a genuine vault of brick masonry.

21 DECEMBER 1896

Grant's Tomb is framed by the arch of the west vault. The open spaces stand ready to hold the clerestory windows that will light the main reading room in the Rotunda.

FEBRUARY 1897

Despite the snowy winter of 1896–1897, work continued. Stonemasons carved the inscription on the south face and the exterior ornamental laurel wreaths. The brick and limestone of the Engineering Building and the mansard roof of the West Hall, a remnant of the Bloomingdale Asylum, are to the left.

19 MAY 1896

An iron beam from the Pennsylvania Steel Company supports the top of a vertical crane used to raise a drum of green granite from Ascutney Quarry in Vermont. Each piece of the sixteen Rotunda columns was positioned in this manner. A piece of the entablature lies in the foreground.

14 JUNE 1897

As the final stone is placed, the highest masonry dome in North America is completed. Less than four months after this photograph was taken, Low Memorial Library would be ready for opening day.

17 JUNE 1897

Sophocles, Demosthenes, Euripides, and Augustus Caesar, as two-dimensional cartoons, pose where the heroic-size sculptures will be placed. In all, sixteen statues were planned. Only these four were placed and have stood guard over the Rotunda for the century. Sophocles and Euripides exchanged places when the sculptures were installed.

22 JUNE 1897

The newly carved exterior details gleam above the roughed-out grand staircase. Stone rubble piled here will be used as support fill for the granite stairs. Queen Victoria celebrated her Diamond Jubilee on this day; the two workmen on the right appear to be celebrating as well.

22 JUNE 1897

Gaslights dot the curb along the south side of 116th Street. On the north side, beyond the work shed, the mansard roof of a building from the Bloomingdale Asylum is visible through the trees. The willing hands of a local youth (left) steady the brake as the workmen prepare to move the massive pink granite slab into place on the plaza before the library. This slab is the signature stone of the architect Charles Follen McKim; it is the only place on campus where his name appears. It lies, centrally located, in the midst of the structures and campus he designed.

12 AUGUST 1897

Engineering, West Hall, and Havemeyer Hall peer over the workmen's shoulders as they place the top step.

4 OCTOBER 1897

Skill, dedication, and hard work brought forth this magnificent building in a little more than two years; on 4 October 1897, the Rotunda of Low Memorial Library was the setting for the opening ceremonies, and Columbia University began holding classes on the Morningside campus. As Seth Low said at the ceremonies: "This library is at the centre of the university. It is the hub of the wheel. If there is anything peculiar about this building in its adaptation to the work to be carried on here it is that this building has been developed not simply as a storehouse for books, but as a laboratory for those who use books. . . . The founders of this university looked upon God as the source of all wisdom, and they placed upon the college seal as its motto for all time 'In thy light we shall see light' [Psalms 36:9]. A century and a half of years almost have rolled around since then, and the authorities of Columbia still believe that that is the spirit in which all study should be carried on. The seal of the college is set in the pavement of the corridor just outside the entrance to this room. I can hardly imagine a better motto for a library or for a university" (*New York Times, 5 October 1897*).

CATALOGUE OF THE EXHIBITION

FIGURE 89 *William Rutherford Mead, Charles Follen McKim, and Stanford White (left to right), ca. 1905 (Avery Library)*

JANET PARKS & BARRY BERGDOLL

CATALOGUE OF THE EXHIBITION

Unless otherwise indicated, all works are from the Drawings and Archives Collection of the Avery Architectural and Fine Arts Library. Dimensions are in inches, height before width.

I. COLUMBIA'S NEW SITE

1

View of Morningside Park looking west

ca. 1890
Photograph mounted on board, 10¼ x 13 15/16 in.
Columbiana Collection
Fig. 1

The third of Frederick Law Olmsted's major Manhattan parks, Morningside Park opened in 1887 several years before the construction of St. John the Divine, St. Luke's Hospital, and the new Columbia campus. This photograph shows the park in a raw state, without planting, where both Olmsted's interventions in the topography and the natural characteristics of the landscape are plainly visible. Traversing this rocky, irregular terrain are wide pathways punctuated by stairs and terraces constructed to negotiate the various grades in the park and to allow access to the upper esplanade on Morningside Drive. The high, rustic retaining wall emphasizes the difference in elevation and the separation of Morningside Heights from nearby Harlem. The buildings of the Bloomingdale Asylum are visible through the group of trees on the Heights. [JP]

2

HENRY C. THOMPSON,
WILLIAM H. STUART

Topographical survey of a part of the grounds of the Bloomingdale Asylum in the City of New York

22 January 1892
Watercolor on paper, 39¼ x 32½ in.
The New-York Historical Society
Plate 1

In 1891, when Columbia College was located at Forty-ninth Street and Madison Avenue, the trustees' Committee on Site studied the question of the future of the college and decided that it needed to look for a property large enough to "permit the university to retain its essential character as a university in the heart of the City of New York." At this time, the New York Hospital, owner of much of Morningside Heights, decided to sell off the land of the Bloomingdale Asylum in anticipation of a move to Westchester County.

This topographical map, which records the diverse grade levels of the property, was drawn in response to President Low's inquiry in November 1891 about the land from 116th to 120th Street. It survives in many copies and was probably used by Low and the trustees in discussion and fund-raising for the site. For one of the last undeveloped sections in Manhattan, the asking price was a steep $2 million; and although the trustees debated whether to buy still more land, an agreement for this parcel was reached in late spring of 1892. [JP]

3

Bloomingdale Asylum: north from 114th Street

1892
Photograph mounted on board, 13½ x 10¾ in.
Columbiana Collection
Fig. 90

Operated by the New York Hospital, the Bloomingdale Asylum occupied a group of Second Empire buildings on the crest of the site running from 116th to 120th Street. The asylum buildings, seen here through a group of trees, were situated in a parklike setting, which was thought to be a therapeutic retreat for its inmates. The approach to the buildings followed the natural terrain, winding around trees until the main building finally came into view. [JP]

4

View from near 114th Street looking north to Low Library

1 October 1897
Photograph, 7³/16 x 9½ in.
Columbiana Collection
Fig. 91

Taken three days before the first day of classes at the new campus, this photograph shows Low Library rising high above neighboring fields on the newly created platform of the Columbia University campus. McKim and the trustees had oriented the campus to the south, looking toward the dense development of the city. While there is a continuing assumption that Columbia moved to Morningside Heights to go to the country, there is in fact little reality to it. A main attraction of the Bloomingdale Asylum site was that the east-west streets of the city grid had not yet been laid out, as can be seen in this photograph, although Amsterdam and Broadway were already major avenues. Ironically, the arrival of the university and the other institutions led to the development of this area so that the monumental presence planned by McKim was soon obscured by later buildings. [JP]

FIGURE 90

FIGURE 91

FIGURE 92

5

C. GRAHAM

View of Morningside (Cathedral) Heights, Hudson River, and New Jersey Palisades

1898

Print on paper (laminated), 9⅞ x 23½ in.

Columbiana Collection

Fig. 92

This commercial print of the new Morningside Heights was one of many available to the public through publications such as *Harper's Weekly* and commercial postcards, photographs, and prints. Having first come to national attention as the site of New York City's losing bid to host the World's Columbian Exposition, the area retained its cachet when several cultural, civic, and religious institutions purchased land and began construction of major buildings. The artist has mixed fact and fancy in this print of bustling urban life in a monumental, City Beautiful landscape. St. John the Divine is shown as complete in accordance with the design of its original architects, but, in fact, only the apse and the crossing without the dome were finished by this date. [JP]

6

HARRY FENN

Bird's-eye view of the projected campus

1904; copyright 1903 by M. R. Harder

Watercolor on paper, 29¼ x 49¼ in.

Columbiana Collection, Gift of Isaac Seligman

By 1903, the new campus had six completed buildings and the partially finished University Hall. Parts of the Bloomingdale Asylum remained in use: Macy Villa (now Buell Hall), West Hall (to the north of Earl Hall), and the Headmaster's House (on the site of Dodge Hall). Harry Fenn was a well-known English illustrator who also produced a line drawing of this view (fig. 115) which became the basis for an engraving.

At this point, the trustees had not yet purchased the land between 116th Street and 114th Street. This property, however, was already being used as athletic fields by the students through an agreement with the New York Hospital. Athletics were deemed an essential component in fostering the community of college life, but finding the space required was a daunting challenge in the tight real estate market of the Manhattan grid. During the next eighty years, the search for appropriate recreational facilities would lead the trustees to consider Riverside and Morningside Parks, and eventually to acquire Baker Field at the uppermost part of Manhattan. [JP]

7

McKIM, MEAD & WHITE

Suggestion for the development of South Field

14 August 1903
Ink on linen, 23½ x 34⅞ in.
The New-York Historical Society
Fig. 93

Working with the undulating grade of the natural terrain, McKim's master plan transformed the site into stepped platforms that integrated this multiblock property into a cohesive unit. Many surviving drawings record the original conditions and document the careful working out of the spatial and topographical relationships of the new campus. This drawing, like the others, presents a coherent and hierarchical relationship between the buildings and the terraces.

The natural topography is subsumed into McKim's rational plan, with Low Library resting at the crest of the site, 150 feet above sea level. The grade at 120th Street is 110 feet at its lowest point. The only excavation done on campus was for the south court in front of Low, and the earth removed there was later deposited around the buildings on the upper terrace. The landfill measured anywhere from 3 to 18 feet, depending on the area. [JP]

8

View of Columbia University and Teachers College from the top of Grant's Tomb

ca. 1900
Photograph mounted on board, 10⅜ x 13 11/16 in.
Columbiana Collection
Fig. 94

As seen from the vantage point of the dome of Grant's Tomb, completed in 1897, the property north of the Morningside Heights campus appears as an area in transition. Columbia and Teachers College form a cluster of large-scale buildings on the southern edge. Above that the rocky landscape is dotted with a mixture of elegant, isolated townhouses on Riverside Drive and ramshackle frame constructions. At the foot of Grant's Tomb a photographer's tent offers souvenirs for visitors to the newly opened monument. [JP]

FIGURE 94

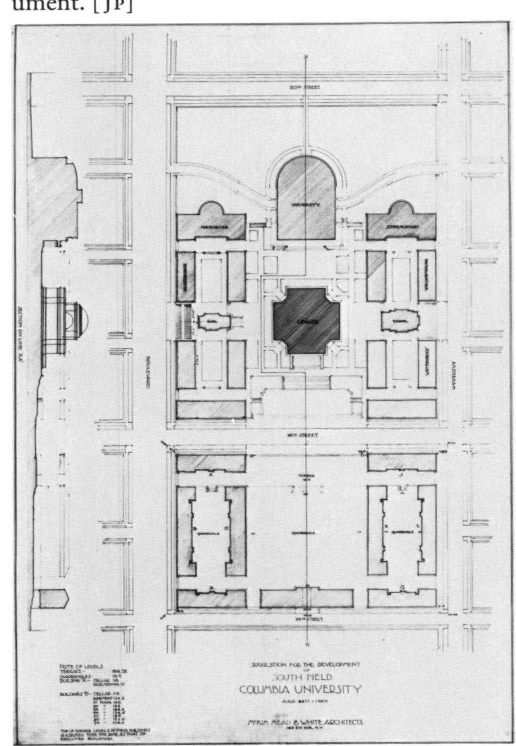

FIGURE 93

II. THE "COMPETITION" OF 1893

CHRONOLOGY OF THE MASTER PLAN

While the trustees were clear that a move to Morningside Heights was desirable, they knew also that it could not be done without considerable expense and planning. Prior to the purchase of the site in 1892, William Robert Ware and William Petit Trowbridge of the School of Architecture and Edward A. Darling, head of buildings and grounds, surveyed the property and structures of the Bloomingdale Asylum. They concluded that the asylum buildings, worth about $900,000, could continue to be used as the university began its own construction. The university did not take title of the property until 1 January 1895, thus allowing time to evaluate and plan for the move.

Realizing the tremendous financial burden and the precious commodity of this rare open site in Manhattan, President Low asked each part of the college to prepare a report on its needs. He noted that "it may be one hundred years or longer before the block will be developed to its utmost capacity. On the other hand the first building which is placed there will condition everything that is to follow, both by its location and its architecture." Ware, Trowbridge, and Darling had estimated that the two essential new buildings, the library and a law school, would cost about $700,000, double the cost of the same two buildings at the Forty-ninth Street campus. Clearly the university was preparing a move upward, both geographically and financially.

The trustees then asked three architectural firms to prepare a preliminary study of the site: Charles Coolidge Haight; Richard Morris Hunt; and McKim, Mead & White. By March 1893, all three firms had each submitted several plans for the new campus. Professor Ware and Frederick Law Olmsted were asked either to critique them and formulate a proposal incorporating the best features of each or to create an altogether new design. These composite schemes, in turn, were submitted to the trustees in May 1893, and the three architects were asked to collaborate on a definitive plan for September or October 1893. Unwilling to work together, they also refused to submit competitive designs, stating that Ware and Olmsted's ideas were defective and nothing good could be built from them. In the ensuing months, McKim, Mead & White were appointed architects for the new campus. May 1894 marks the date of McKim's first scheme for the campus, followed by a revised plan in November. [JP]

9

RICHARD MORRIS HUNT

Plan for Scheme A

10 February 1893

Black and red ink with pencil on linen, 15⅞ x 19⅛ in.

Fig. 17

Richard Morris Hunt, the oldest of the architects invited to participate in the Columbia planning, had just finished Biltmore, the vast mansion for the Vanderbilt family in North Carolina. He submitted two variants of a scheme in which the university would face the Boulevard, as Broadway was then known, with an entrance on 118th Street in the center of the property. Faced with a natural grade that varied about 40 feet, Hunt proposed a series of three courts, each on a different grade, with arcades connecting the buildings as a means of unifying the site. Hunt felt that this system would require the least amount of grading and thus save a considerable amount of money, especially if the construction were to hit rock. Hunt, in part because of his failing health, was ultimately not selected for the position. [JP]

10

CHARLES COOLIDGE HAIGHT

Plan for Scheme A

February–March 1893

Black and red ink with red wash on linen, 18¼ x 22⅜ in.

Fig. 15

The son of a Columbia trustee, Haight was the architect of the Forty-ninth Street campus during the 1880s and was later known for his work at Yale University. He eschewed the Boulevard/Broadway frontage as his entrance to the campus, stating that the westerly winds coming off the Hudson during the winter made that approach particularly undesirable. Additionally, he felt that transportation on Amsterdam Avenue, then running a cable line, was more reliable. The Boulevard/Broadway entrance would be accessible only to carriages, and thus beyond the reach of those who would be attending the college.

Like Hunt, Haight proposed distributing his buildings at three different grades to avoid unnecessary expense. The great variation of street grades, Haight wrote, does not lend itself to the successful development of continuous facades, a problem that he thought could be dealt with by breaking up the block fronts and organizing the buildings around small courtyards. Haight also pleaded for the use of Collegiate Gothic, a style that would adapt itself easily to the irregular site as well as to the variations of plan within. To Haight, the regularity of facade demanded by a classical language of architecture would necessarily compromise the program of an academic building on an uneven site. The trustees, however, did not agree, stating that the Gothic was not a style in which most architects were then comfortable nor would it allow sufficient light and ventilation for the needs of the classroom buildings. [JP]

11

WARE AND OLMSTED

Composite scheme

May 1893

Colored wash, red and black ink, and pencil on tracing paper, 23 x 19¼ in.

Plate 2

After Professor Ware of the School of Architecture and Frederick Law Olmsted reviewed the designs of the three architects, they submitted a report and numerous alternative plans to the trustees. While McKim's original plan has been lost, his report to the trustees remains, and it is clear that Ware and Olmsted drew heavily upon his vision of the Columbia campus for some of their major recommendations.

McKim proposed that the campus be oriented to the south and that only the southern portion of the campus be constructed at the start. Ware and Olmsted initially concurred with the recommendations to leave the northern portion unbuilt at that time. They did not turn their backs on Haight and Hunt's ideas, however, as they endorsed a system of courtyards and connected buildings. The red outlines on this drawing indicate the position of the asylum buildings. [JP]

12

WARE AND OLMSTED

Composite scheme

May 1893

Colored wash with black ink and pencil on brownline print, 24¾ x 18⅜ in.

Plate 3

This scheme shares some of the characteristics of the final plan of the campus as developed by McKim. A main centrally placed building faces a forecourt, similar to the arrangement of Low Library and South Court. There is also a notation in pencil on the land below 116th Street, indicating the continuation of the court, as would become reality when the extended master plan was completed after the purchase of South Field in 1903. [JP]

13

McKIM, MEAD & WHITE

Plan showing arrangement of proposed buildings

May 1894

Lithograph with red ink on paper, 18½ x 14 1/16 in.

Fig. 18

This is the earliest visual record of McKim's idea for the Columbia campus, but the written descriptions of his three initial proposals show that he, too, had considered using a courtyard system with connecting arcades between the buildings. Using a plaster model to study the topography, McKim initially proposed limiting development to the lower two-thirds of the property. He also favored the "pure Classic style" as being the simplest and most monumental expression of the purpose of the buildings.

The radical change in the plan, from connected courtyards to freestanding pavilion buildings, is difficult to explain. After receiving Hunt's, Haight's, and McKim, Mead & White's refusal to submit further designs based on Ware and Olmsted's critique of their initial proposals, the trustees' Commission on the Site stated that there should be a central axis of buildings consisting of the library, chapel, offices of administration, theater, and gymnasium. All the other buildings should be laid out in a system of pavilions and treated as separate but harmonious structures, since it would be a considerable time before they could be completed.

This proposal by McKim reflects the new definition of the campus, with a strong central axis running north-south (with a forecourt at the south end) and an east-west axis containing the library, chapel, and theater. A second plan was developed by McKim by November that year, and the major change then was a clarification of the centrality of the plan. Instead of being a long rectangle as in this drawing, the library building became a centralized Greek-cross plan. [JP]

III. COLUMBIA'S NEW DOMED SKYLINE: THE MAJOR MONUMENTS

14

CHARLES FOLLEN McKIM

Low Library: elevation and plan

24 July 1894

Pencil on paper (verso of letter from McKim to Stanford White), 8 x 10½ in.

Fig. 23

In McKim's first plan for the campus presented to the trustees in May 1894, the library was a long rectangle occupying the center of the southern edge of the property. There was a discussion at that meeting about the plan of the library, and by the beginning of October it was resolved that the plan be changed to a Greek cross, as it appears on the revised master plan of November 1894.

This sketch, the earliest known drawing of Low Library in its present form, dates from a period when McKim would have been considering the plan and elevation of his first Columbia building. It is found on the back of a copy of a letter from McKim to his partner Stanford White, explaining that he was unable to meet White in Europe for a planned golfing trip because President Low, before leaving for vacation himself, had given him so much work to do that he could not leave town. It is interesting to note that at this time White was at work on the master plan for the new Bronx campus of New York University, the central feature of which was also a domed library.

The letter presents an interesting conundrum. Although the letter, incomplete and amended in McKim's handwriting, is found in White's files for 1894, the drawing is in McKim's hand. The letter itself was folded at one time, with the drawing on the outside, and that panel is discolored. Perhaps the letter, which was never mailed, was used as scrap paper and subsequently misfiled with White's correspondence. [JP]

15

Columbia University exhibition at Trans-Mississippi Exposition and Indian Congress, Omaha, Nebraska

1898

Photograph mounted on board, 10 x 12 in.

F. A. Rinehart, photographer

Columbiana Collection

Fig. 28

Columbia participated in many expositions and world's fairs at the turn of the century. In Chicago, the university had an exhibit in the New York State Pavilion, a building also designed by McKim, Mead & White. Subsequently the marble floor of that pavilion, with the signs of the zodiac, was reinstalled in the entrance of Low Library. By the time of the Omaha exposition in 1898, the university had commissioned this model, which was later shown at the Louisiana Purchase Exposition in 1904 in St. Louis. Many photographs documenting the buildings and classrooms used in that exposition survive. The model was exhibited for many years on campus in a small structure near Low Library. [JP]

FIGURE 95

FIGURE 96

16

MᶜKIM, MEAD & WHITE

Earl Hall showing corner of West Hall

ca. 1903

Photograph mounted on board, 21 x 18⅜ in.

F. E. Parshley, photographer

Fig. 95

Earl Hall terminated the transverse axis of the campus to the west of Low Library and served as a pendant to the projected chapel to the east. These domed structures were to be of a character that would set them off from the classroom or pavilion buildings. Earl Hall is constructed of brick and limestone like the classroom buildings. Its dome and Greek temple portico, however, relate it to Low Library, although the building accepts a more modest place in the architectural hierarchy of the campus. To the north of Earl is West Hall, a portion of the main asylum building used for dormitories, which would shortly be demolished. [JP]

17

View of Columbia University from the Hudson River

1903; copyright by Detroit Publishing Company

Color photograph mounted on board, 7 x 16⅞ in.

Fig. 24

Meant not only to be seen from the city, the new domed skyline of Morningside Heights was also highly visible from the Hudson River. The white wooden building on the riverfront was Columbia's boathouse. A more permanent boathouse, designed by Palmer and Hornbostel, would be considered for this site in 1906. [JP]

18–21

HOWELLS AND STOKES

Alternative projects for St. Paul's Chapel

ca. 1904–5

18

Floor plan

Pencil and ink on tracing paper, 18 x 14¼ in.

Fig. 96

19

West elevation

Pencil on tracing paper, 11⅜ x 12¼ in. (irreg.)

Fig. 97

20

East elevation with campanile

Pencil with crayon on tracing paper, 15¼ x 15½ in.

Fig. 98

21

West elevation with large dome

Pencil with crayon on tracing paper, 14 13/16 x 9⅜ in.

Fig. 99

While the trustees and the architects knew that more than one architectural firm would eventually build on campus, they had probably thought that day would not come as early as 1904. The donors, the Misses Olivia Egleston Phelps Stokes and Caroline Phelps Stokes, stated that their nephew, I. N. Phelps Stokes, should be the architect of the new chapel to rise just east of Low Library.

Well regarded by McKim, Stokes

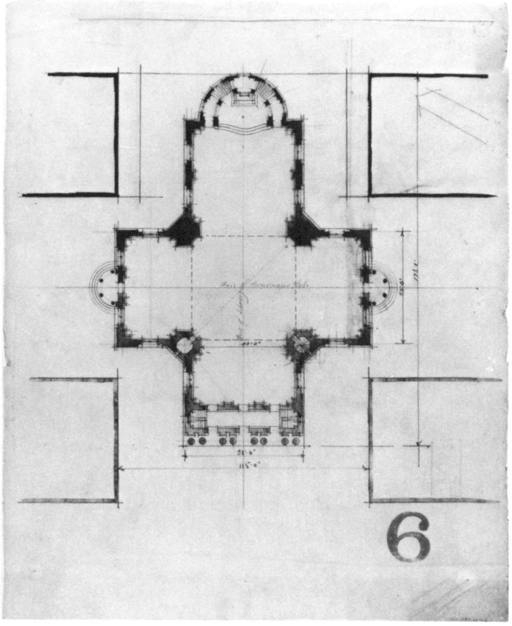

designed a building that obeyed the ground rules of the master plan. The plan (fig. 96) shows four surrounding pavilion buildings, although at the time, only Fayerweather, the building on the upper left, was actually standing. Although the axis is incorrectly labeled (it should read Schermerhorn), the lines position the chapel directly to the east of Low and Earl and in the center of the two side courtyards. The transepts and apse of the chapel were eventually shortened, allowing broader circulation areas around the buildings.

The positioning of the chapel relative to the pavilion buildings is also studied in the other drawings. One shows the chapel connected to the pavilions on either side by an arcade. In other drawings, the chapel abuts the roof lines of the neighboring buildings or is seen in the context of the courtyard. Well aware that the chapel had to have a dome compatible with those of Low and Earl Hall, Stokes tried out several variations—one design even included a campanile—before deciding that a shallow dome on a raised drum was the best solution. Stokes chose an Italian Romanesque style compatible with the Greek details of Earl and the Roman model of Low Library. [JP]

FIGURE 97

FIGURE 98

FIGURE 99

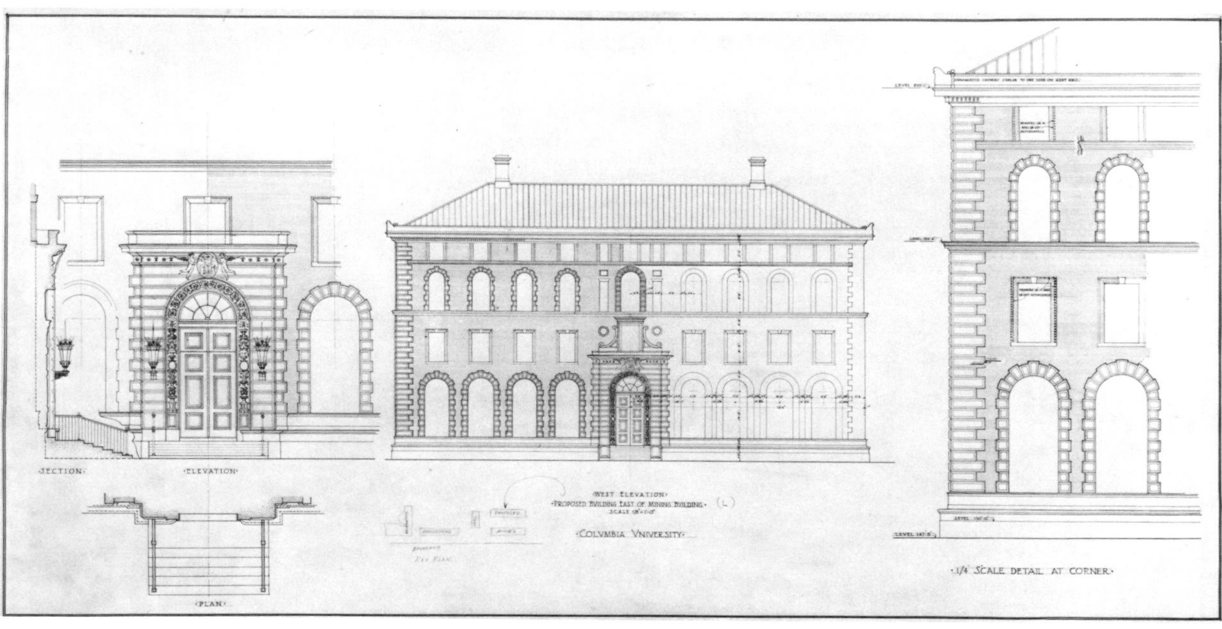

FIGURE 100

IV. CREATING AN ARCHITECTURAL LANGUAGE FOR COLUMBIA: McKIM'S PAVILIONS

22

McKIM, MEAD & WHITE

Proposed building east of Mining building: west elevation

N.d.

Ink with pencil on linen, 27 x 50¼ in.

Fig. 100

The Italian Renaissance style of architecture was a language that many architects of that era, trained at the Ecole des Beaux-Arts in Paris, were most skilled in. McKim, Mead & White nonetheless had to translate that into a working vocabulary for the specific needs of the Columbia campus. Written on this drawing and many other working drawings are inscriptions indicating the repetition of details from one building to the next. Not only would this save money, but it would also give an external cohesiveness to the campus.

The program demands on McKim were quite precise, coming in the form of departmental reports requested by Low in 1892. The science departments were very practical in describing the physical setting needed for their classrooms and laboratories. They stated that a "modern university is composed of laboratories and workshops and not of cloisters" and demanded that the functionality of the rooms not be sacrificed for external architectural effect. Most of all, they wanted large windows and high ceilings, at least 14 feet or higher, to allow for abundant light and ventilation. Areas in the basement would provide much-needed storage and laboratory space at what was imagined to be a reduced cost. These requirements prevailed over the interests of the Faculty of Philosophy and determined the general appearance of the pavilion buildings. [JP]

23

McKIM, MEAD & WHITE

Building at northeast corner of 116th Street and Broadway: elevation on court

8 November 1907
Ink with pencil on linen, 26⅛ x 47½ in.
J. C. McGowan, delineator
Fig. 101

Another consideration for the pavilion buildings was the materials and the level of detail of the facades. There was much discussion as to what would be an appropriate counterpoint to the splendor of Low Library at the center of the campus, which cost more than $1 million to construct. The pavilion buildings could not have all-limestone exteriors, not only for reasons of cost but also in order not to compete with the prominence of Low. A combination of limestone and brick was sought whose relative proportions would be ornamental enough to create a compatible environment for the library. There was also the question of the color of the brick. A buff, yellow brick was originally considered but rejected in favor of a deeper red brick called Harvard red.

The pavilion buildings running east-west are fifty feet longer than the ones oriented north-south, but it is a testimony to their coherent style that this size differential is not immediately noticeable. This early version of Dodge Hall has twelve equal windows and one door across its facade; its neighbor had only eight windows and one door, all on the same scale.

By the time this drawing was done, the design of the facade had already been stripped of much of its detail, due to cost constraints. The early buildings—Havemeyer, Fayerweather, and Schermerhorn—were by comparison more ornamented. As construction and material costs and the number of buildings needed rose, however, it was difficult to

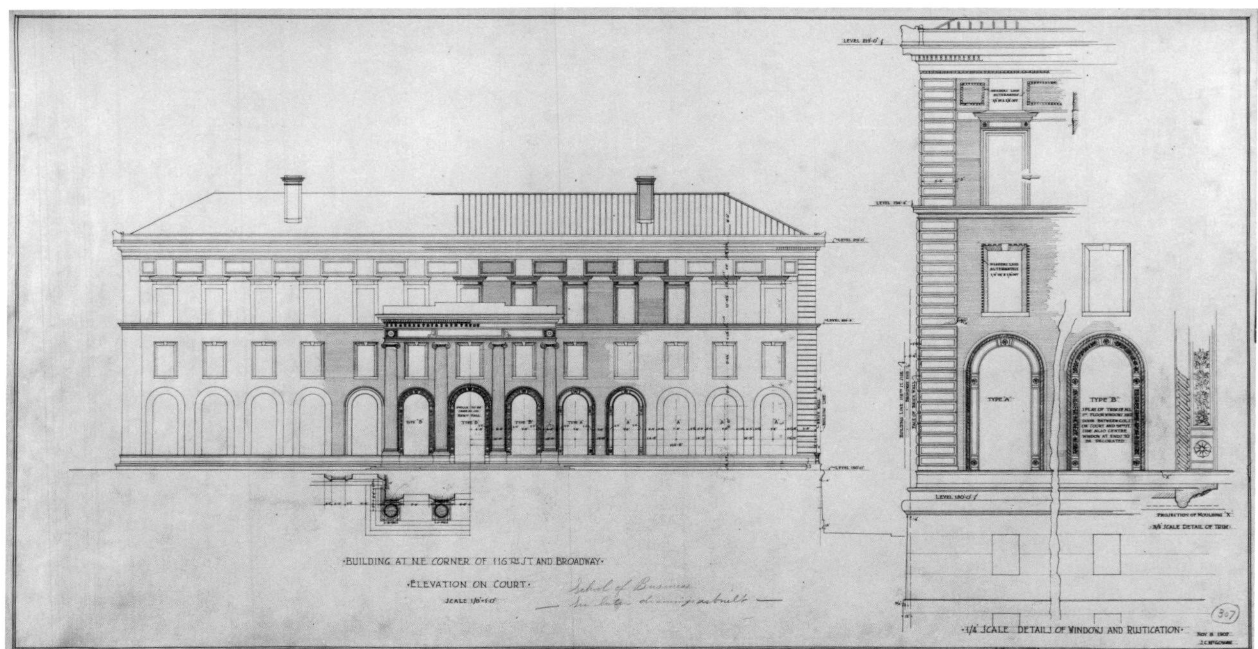

FIGURE 101

FIGURE 102

FIGURE 103

maintain that level of ornamentation. The taller buildings presented both an aesthetic problem as well as an economic one: how to articulate them with sufficient detail so that they would appear to be part of the ensemble. [JP]

24

MCKIM, MEAD & WHITE

Detail of entrance on small court: elevation and plan

N.d.

Ink with pencil on linen, 28 x 18⅛ in.

Fig. 102

This design for a building that was never constructed is typical of the thousands prepared by McKim, Mead & White's office in that it indicates the reuse of details from other buildings. Nonetheless, subtle variations individualize this door; the window surround above the doorway is different from the others on this floor, thus giving a vertical accent to the entrance. [JP]

25

MCKIM, MEAD & WHITE

Avery Hall: front elevation

ca. 1910

Watercolor on paper, 20½ x 30¾ in.

The New-York Historical Society

Fig. 103

Completing the first and only inner pavilion, Avery Hall was built to house Avery Library and to provide studios for the School of Architecture until the library needed the extra space. The library had been founded in 1890 with a gift from Samuel Putnam Avery in memory of his son Henry, an architect, when the college was at Forty-ninth Street. When the university moved to Morningside Heights, the Avery Library at first occupied the room in Low Library that is now the home of the Columbiana Collection. In 1906, Samuel Putnam Avery Jr. gave money for a separate building to accommodate the library's collections, which were growing at an unexpectedly rapid rate.

In accordance with instructions from the science faculty, the windows of the upper stories extend from floor to ceiling in order to give maximum light to the drafting tables. Like the other north-south buildings, this one has nine equal bays across the front. This watercolor is one of the few surviving renderings of one of the early buildings. [JP]

26

MCKIM, MEAD & WHITE

Pierce Hall: first floor plan

1927–28

Pencil on tracing paper, 17 x 28¼ in.

Fig. 104

The John B. Pierce Foundation had been set up with the aim of creating a permanent institution devoted to "the promotion of . . . research, education, technical or scientific work in the general field of heating, ventilation, and sanitation for the increase of knowledge to the end that general hygiene and comfort of human beings and their habitations may be advanced." This purpose was defined in the minutes of a meeting of Charles E. Lucke of the Department of Mechanical Engineering, William A. Boring of the School of Architecture, Teunis Van Der Bent of McKim, Mead & White, and others, held on 12 March 1928 (CUA). Thinking to establish itself in close proximity to the educational and research institutions on Morningside Heights, the foundation had acquired a site on Morningside Drive between 117th and 118th Streets on which to erect a building.

In late 1927 President N. M. Butler opened protracted negotiations with the Pierce Foundation, proposing that in exchange for its site—which stood in the way of the university's projected eastward expansion—Columbia would construct and operate a building for the foundation on campus. Columbia's lawyers and administrators set to work interpreting Pierce's will, while McKim, Mead & White set to work drafting designs of how an innovative new university department could be housed in one of the as yet unbuilt pavilions called for by the master plan. The conclusion of the lawyers, that Pierce's will "obviously means any sort of engineering process, appliance or structure, that will increase comfort or healthfulness of occupancy of buildings," placed the new activities, as yet only vaguely defined, somewhere between architecture and engineering.

Over the course of the next year Butler worked with deans and faculty members in the Schools of Engineering and of Architecture to devise a program for the foundation, while Van Der Bent of McKim, Mead & White studied the design for a pendant to Avery Hall—where the School of Architecture was located—as the home to the new foundation. In addition to offices, lecture halls, and classrooms to be housed on the upper floors of Pierce Hall, the ground floor was to be developed as a memorial hall and museum devoted to hygienic and comfort issues in building, from air conditioning to rationalized kitchen layout to fireproofing. The project seems to have died with the stock market crash of 1929. [BB]

27

MCKIM, MEAD & WHITE

Pierce Hall: perspective

ca. 1927–28

Colored pencil on paper mounted on board, $12^{3}/_{16}$ x $17^{9}/_{16}$ in.; $16^{3}/_{16}$ x $21^{1}/_{2}$ in. (board)

Fritz Steffens, delineator

Plate 8

The last pavilion building designed for McKim's master plan, Pierce Hall—together with Mathematics, Havemeyer, and Earl Halls—would have completed the quadrangle on the west side of campus. The floor plan of Pierce Hall shows that the building was capable of having different functions and layouts while still maintaining an exterior similar to the other McKim pavilions. The exterior is an exact replica of Avery Hall on the opposite side. [JP]

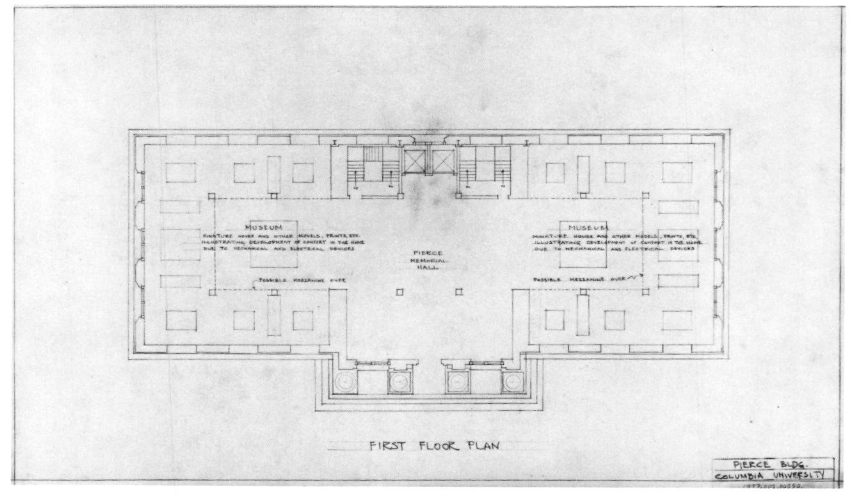

FIGURE 104

V. THE FIRST PAVILION: NATURAL HISTORY (SCHERMERHORN HALL)

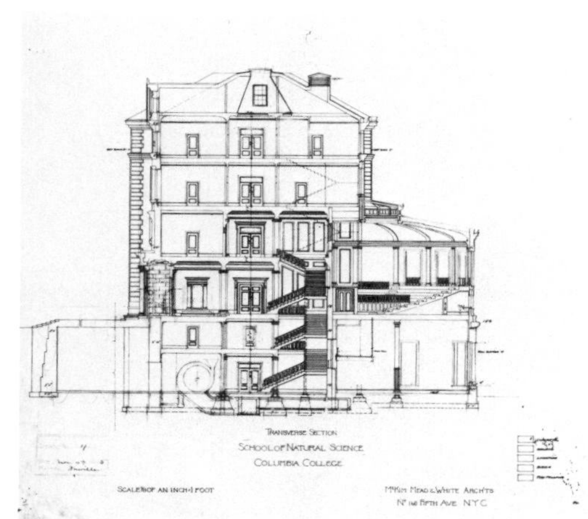

FIGURE 105

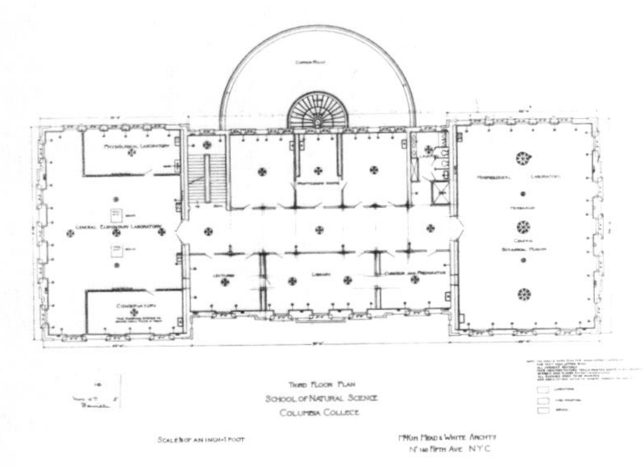

FIGURE 106

28

McKIM, MEAD & WHITE

School of Natural Science/ Columbia College: transverse section

4 November 1895
Ink on linen, 23¾ x 34¼ in.
William B. Faville, delineator
The New-York Historical Society
Fig. 105

Among the faculties, the science and engineering departments made perhaps the greatest demands on the physical plant of the new campus. The old classrooms at Forty-ninth Street had been adjacent to the railroad tracks going into Grand Central Terminal, and the vibrations and dirt from the trains were disruptive to the students' laboratory assignments and professors' research. The Morningside Heights campus would afford a much quieter and cleaner environment for their work.

Schermerhorn Hall, built for the natural science departments, followed closely the requirements of the science faculty. There were large windows for light and ventilation, two underground floors for laboratories and storage, and a large lecture hall set in a rotunda at the back. Originally the building had a central two-story staircase on the entrance level, with one flight going up and the other descending to the lowest level. On the second level above grade, the staircase was located on the west side of the building in order to maximize the space for classrooms, laboratories, and offices. Around 1926, the central staircase was removed, an elevator installed, and the offices rearranged on the upper floors. Given the heights of the ceilings, two additional floors could be inserted and the floor of the lecture hall raised. [JP]

29

McKIM, MEAD & WHITE

School of Natural Science/ Columbia College: third floor plan showing general elementary laboratory and conservatory and morphological laboratory, herbarium, and general botanical museum

4 November 1895
Ink on linen, 23⅞ x 34 in.
William B. Faville, delineator
The New-York Historical Society
Fig. 106

One of the desiderata for the classroom buildings on campus was that the interiors be constructed so as to permit changes in their layout that would accommodate new developments and requirements. While the exterior masonry walls are load-bearing, the floors are carried on steel beams and girders that allowed for significant restructuring of interior walls.

The original third floor of Schermerhorn became the eighth floor after the installation of the elevator and the insertion of intermediary stories. The central hallway, the offices, the Wallach Art Gallery, and the Slide and Photograph Collection all occupy spaces shown on this original plan. The gallery occupies the space of the original General Elementary Laboratory, which in

FIGURE 107

FIGURE 108

FIGURE 109

FIGURE 110

FIGURE 111

turn became the Fine Arts Library. The layout is the result of a major renovation in the mid-1980s, designed by Susana Torre.

William B. Faville, the delineator of these two drawings, worked for McKim, Mead & White from June 1895 until 9 March 1898, more or less the period during which Schermerhorn was planned and constructed. [JP]

30–36

McKIM, MEAD & WHITE

Schermerhorn and Fayerweather Halls: construction progress

Photographs

Columbiana Collection

30

Schermerhorn

29 June 1896

7 5/16 x 9 5/8 in.

Fig. 107

31

Schermerhorn and Fayerweather: looking west toward the river from Amsterdam Avenue

[July 1896]

7 1/4 x 9 1/8 in.

Fig. 108

32

Schermerhorn and Fayerweather

8 August 1996

7 1/4 x 9 5/8 in.

Fig. 109

33

Schermerhorn

12 September 1896

6 3/4 x 9 5/16 in.

Fig. 110

34

Schermerhorn and Fayerweather

1 October 1896

7 1/4 x 9 11/16 in.

Fig. 111

35

Schermerhorn: entrance

12 September 1896

9 x 6 15/16 in.

Fig. 112

36

Schermerhorn: interior construction of stairs

ca. 1898

7 3/8 x 9 1/2 in.

Fig. 113

Construction of both Schermerhorn and Fayerweather Halls, the latter originally the Physics Building, began in 1896. These photographs reveal many details of the construction as well as the topography of the campus before the interventions of McKim. Harlem, seen in the background of several photographs, was a thriving community, its development spurred by the mass transportation provided by the Eighth Avenue El, which had bypassed the Morningside Heights area. The trees directly behind the Schermerhorn site were part of the Grove, or the Green, which existed on a grade level about 40 feet below that of the upper campus. The edge of the terrace above the Grove and the exterior walls of the floors below the upper campus can be seen at the northwest corner of the building.

FIGURE 112

FIGURE 113

FIGURE 114

The mixed structural system of the building is apparent in the photographs. The exterior walls are load-bearing masonry, as is evident by the rising of the walls independent of the inner floor beams. The limestone components—the corner rustication and the window frames—were built first, and then the brickwork was laid to fill the spaces in between. The curved wall at the back of the building, seen through the door in the views of 8 August and 12 September, is the foundation of the apse, which contains the lecture hall. [JP]

37

Schermerhorn Hall: laboratory of stratigraphical geology and palaeontology, Department of Geology

ca. 1904

Photograph mounted on board, 10⅛ x 13 13/16 in.

Columbiana Collection

Fig. 49

This photograph was exhibited at Columbia's display at the Louisiana Purchase Exposition in St. Louis in 1904. The space, with high ceilings and only one, very large supporting column in the middle of the room, exemplifies the flexible, open classrooms that the sciences departments wanted. [JP]

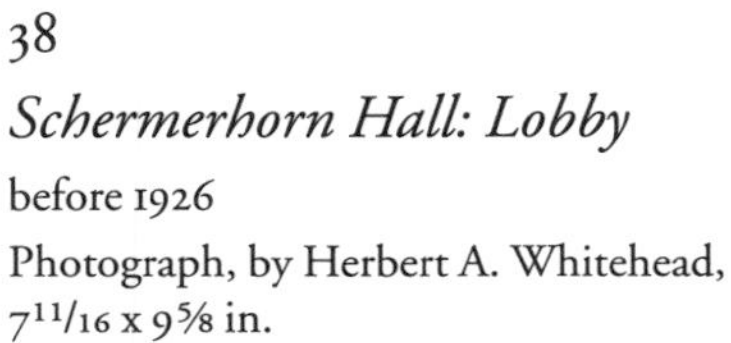

38

Schermerhorn Hall: Lobby

before 1926

Photograph, by Herbert A. Whitehead, 7 11/16 x 9⅝ in.

Fig. 114

All of the faculties wanted their own display and exhibition areas in the new buildings. This is the lobby of Schermerhorn before the elevator was installed. The whereabouts of the caribou skeleton are not known, but the large rock in the glass case is still in the lobby of this building. [JP]

VI. CREATING A LANDSCAPE LANGUAGE FOR COLUMBIA: THE SCHERMERHORN/ FAYERWEATHER COURTYARD

39

HARRY FENN

Bird's-eye view of Columbia University

Ink on tracing paper, 16 3/16 x 23 11/16 in.
1903; copyright 1903 by M. R. Harder
Fig. 115

Because McKim's architectural ideas dominate the campus so completely, it is easy to assume that landscape played little or no part in the conception of the design. There was, in fact, a great deal of interest in and debate over the planting. The Fenn drawing shows the Morningside Heights property in a period of transition from its more natural setting to the highly planned urban campus.

Both Frederick Law Olmsteds, senior and then junior, were the landscape architects advising the university. Olmsted Sr. had collaborated with Ware on critiquing the first submissions for the campus plan and then with McKim on the master plan itself. In 1903, the younger Olmsted was called in to consult and wrote a lengthy report to the trustees. He described with sensitivity and in detail the difficulties of designing natural surroundings for the Columbia campus. The strong urban and classical character of the architectural language implied, according to the design sensibilities he and McKim shared, a more formal approach, such as low, clipped hedges and few floral plantings. Trees were to be kept at a minimum because they would cut down light to the classrooms and library spaces. The hedges surrounding the buildings were meant in part to

FIGURE 115

keep the students from cutting corners and wearing dirt paths into the grass. Flowers, they thought, would look too small in relation to the monumental architecture.

McKim and Olmsted's ideas did not have the unanimous support of the trustees, John B. Pine being the most vocal critic. With good reason, he complained that in winter the campus was quite stark and desolate. He suggested evergreen trees as appropriate, but he met with opposition from both McKim, for aesthetic reasons, and Olmsted, for horticultural reasons. [JP]

40–41

Grove seen from the upper campus

1907
Photographs, by A. Fowler, 10⅝ x 13⁹⁄₁₆ in.; 10½ x 13½ in.
Columbiana Collection
Figs. 116 & 117

McKim's master plan called for leaving about a block and a half at the north end of the original property as a parklike setting. Because the new buildings sat on a platform approximately 40 feet higher in grade than the Grove, a rusticated retaining wall and flights of stairs were constructed to connect the upper to the lower level. This wall can still be seen in the lowest floors at the back of Uris and Schermerhorn Halls.

Olmsted was the landscape designer for this area, and the connections to his work in Central, Riverside, and Morningside Parks are clear. Contained within the university's campus were both the urban architectural vocabulary of the upper campus and the pastoral setting of the Grove. Once the Grove became the site for the expansion of the science departments, these complementary ambiences were lost, and the intelligence and balance of McKim's master plan compromised. [JP]

42

McKIM, MEAD & WHITE

Schermerhorn Hall: plan of pavement and terrace

1 January [1896]
Ink on linen, 25 x 34 in.
The New-York Historical Society
Fig. 118

McKim, Mead & White designed both architectural and landscape treatments for the pavilion courtyards in the master plan. This working drawing for Schermerhorn shows both floors below grade, the patterns of the pavement in front of the building, and the architectural components that would define the courtyard. Envisioned as a sunken court about 2½ feet below the 150-foot grade of the upper campus, the green space in front of Schermerhorn would be separated from the pavement by a balustrade. The balustrade abuts Fayerweather, seen in section on the right, and extends to the left as well. This plan was never carried out. [JP]

43

McKIM, MEAD & WHITE

Statue with fountain and steps with railing on terrace at front of Schermerhorn

2 June 1930
Pencil on tracing paper, 14¼ x 26⅛ in.
JCM, delineator (John C. McGowan?)
Fig. 119

FIGURE 116

FIGURE 117

FIGURE 118

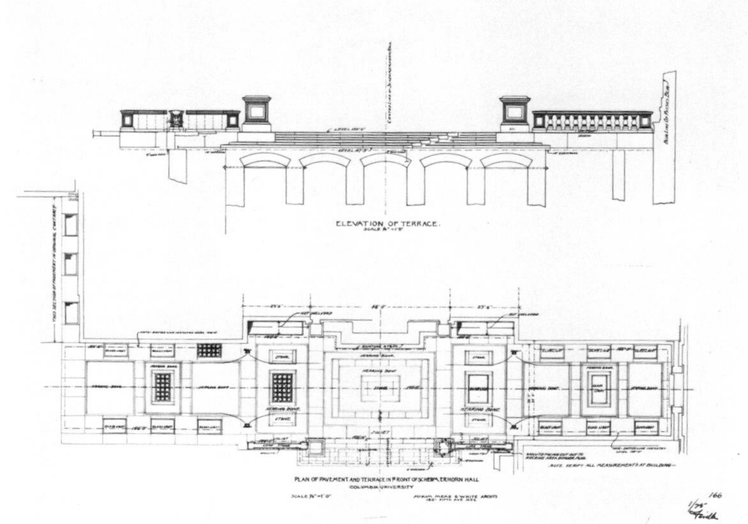

FIGURE 119

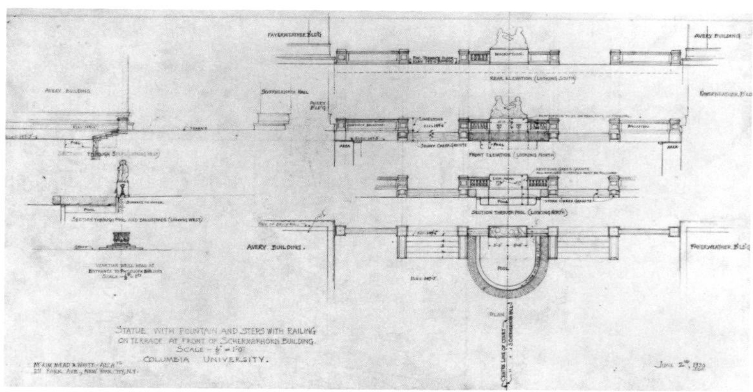

FIGURE 120

The original Schermerhorn courtyard plan was never executed, but the general concept was resurrected in 1930 when the university considered moving the *Great God Pan* by George Gray Barnard to this location. The style and design of the garden were still appropriate to the McKim buildings and the sculpture would fit in reasonably well here as it would in several other locations on campus. The draftsman in this case was a model of longevity: J. C. McGowan initialed working drawings in 1906 and was still on the job at McKim, Mead & White in the 1930s. [JP]

44

McKIM, MEAD & WHITE

Schermerhorn courtyard as sculpture garden

ca. 1930

Photograph of rendering by Fritz Steffens, 9¾ x 7½ in.

The New-York Historical Society

Fig. 120

This rendering shows the Schermerhorn courtyard as a small sculpture garden, an idea never fully realized. Only the central fountain was moved there and it was re-installed on this site after the renovation of the plaza during the construction of Avery Extension. [JP]

45

McKIM, MEAD & WHITE

Bird's-eye view of projected campus built to full density

1903

Watercolor on paper, 25½ x 40¼ in.

Jules Crow, delineator

The New-York Historical Society

Plate 6

In 1902, the negotiation and purchase of the area known as South Field spurred a flurry of activity to develop this two-block extension of the campus. The acquisition of this property was one of the first major acts of the university's new president, Nicholas Murray Butler, who succeeded Seth Low in 1901 when the latter became mayor of New York. Butler had been associated with Columbia before its move to Morningside Heights and thus had witnessed its transition from college to university and from Midtown to Morningside Heights. During his more than forty years as Columbia's president, Butler would oversee vast development and expansion of the campus.

At the time of the purchase, there was no immediate need for additional space, only seven of the projected sixteen buildings having been erected on the upper campus. But the trustees and administration had been surprised by the unprecedented growth in academic departments and in demands on the university's resources. Thus, in anticipation of a continued boom in the Morningside Heights real estate market, the university purchased the new land as a guarantee that it could continue to grow.

The inherent logic of the master plan as well as the allegiance of the trustees to its concept was so strong that the firm of McKim, Mead & White was asked to draw up these plans. Indeed, by orienting Low Library to the south, McKim predicated a view from that direction, implicitly advocating such an extension from the start. [JP]

46

McKIM, MEAD & WHITE

Campus from library platform, grade 150, looking south

1903

Watercolor on paper mounted on board, 15 1/16 x 20½ in.

Plate 7

Seen under an intense, almost Mediterranean sunlight, the south campus stretches out like an enormous plaza in an ideal urban setting. The height of the platform of the upper campus, crucial in its transformation of the undulations of the natural terrain to an urban monumental setting, is continued in the line of the base of the buildings around the interior. [JP]

47

McKIM, MEAD & WHITE

Columbia campus: from Amsterdam Avenue and 114th Street looking north

1903

Watercolor with pencil on paper mounted on board, 13⅜ x 18 in.

Fig. 121

Like Low Library and South Court before it, the southern edge of the expanded campus opens up to the

FIGURE 121

surrounding neighborhood with a courtyard. While the proposed corner buildings are solid and impenetrable, the central building is set back from the street and has an arcade through which pedestrians can enter or exit the campus. In the final version of the new master plan, this building has been moved out to the lot line and turned inward, thus completing the continuous perimeter of the campus. [JP]

48

McKIM, MEAD & WHITE

East entrance: looking west

1903

Watercolor with pencil on paper mounted on board, 14¾ x 18¾ in.

Fig. 122

Until 1954, 116th Street was an open thoroughfare. This rendering indicates that the junction of the campus and the urban street was an important part of the master plan. [JP]

FIGURE 122

49

McKIM, MEAD & WHITE, ATTRIB.

Plan for extension on South Field, with obelisk and two towers: perspective view

1903

Watercolor and pencil on paper, 16½ x 29 in.

Fig. 123

Given the similarities of John Jay Hall and Butler Library to the projects shown here, this drawing would appear to be of a later date than the other 1903 master plan drawings. But the window details and wall treatment on Hamilton Hall and Journalism do not correspond to the buildings as they were completed in 1908 and 1913 respectively. The drawing also refers to the quadrangles on both sides proposed by McKim. The footprints of the interior pavilions are represented by a dotted line, thus allowing a clear view of the dominant corner buildings.

This plan also uses the height established by the terracing of the upper campus as an organizing principle for the new facades. The base of each building on 114th Street turns from stone to brick at 152'2" (see pencil notes on left side), the level of the terrace around Low Library. [JP]

50

MᶜKIM, MEAD & WHITE, ATTRIB.

Twilight view of South Field with two domed buildings

1903

Watercolor on paper, 11 x 17 7/16 in. (irreg.)

Fig. 124

This unusual twilight view of South Field presents an alternative suggestion perhaps made by a faculty member, probably of the School of Architecture, some of whom were occasionally asked for ideas on campus development. The vision is a mixture of respect and divergence from the master plan. The perimeter buildings on the avenues retain the character of the pavilion buildings of the upper campus. Yet the north-south orientation of University Hall and Low Library is not carried through to a dominant central building on 114th Street. Instead the enormous cupolas—rivaling the domes of Low Library, Earl Hall, and the Chapel—shift the focus of the campus to the corners. [JP]

FIGURE 123

FIGURE 124

51

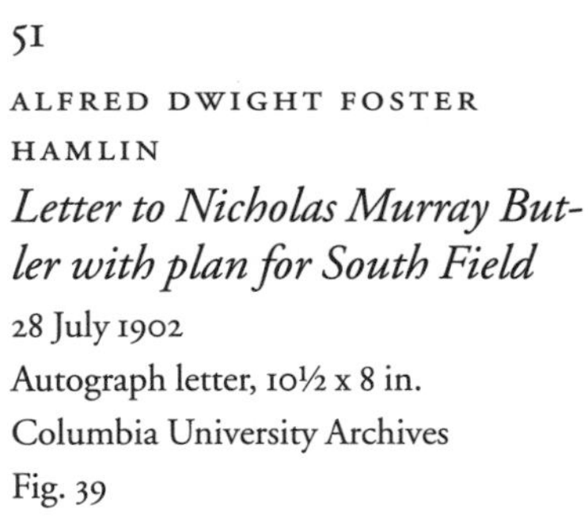

ALFRED DWIGHT FOSTER HAMLIN

Letter to Nicholas Murray Butler with plan for South Field

28 July 1902

Autograph letter, 10½ x 8 in.

Columbia University Archives

Fig. 39

In 1902, Professor A. D. F. Hamlin was appointed acting dean of the architecture school while Butler courted McKim, unsuccessfully, to take over on a permanent basis. Butler asked Hamlin to see what

FIGURE 125

the students of the school would do with the newly acquired site of South Field. Hamlin immediately replied with his own ideas on the development of the property as sketched in this letter. [JP]

52

MᶜKIM, MEAD & WHITE

Extended master plan of 1903

1915

Lithograph from *A Monograph of the Work of McKim Mead & White, 1879–1915*, 20 x 14 in.
Frontispiece

Published as a compendium of the best examples of McKim, Mead & White's architecture, this multivolume work included the master plans of Columbia University, New York University in the Bronx, and the University of Virginia. The Columbia buildings were documented extensively in this portfolio of plates. [JP]

53

H. M. PETTIT

View of expanded campus

1905

Black, gray, and white wash on paper mounted on board, 20 x 28⅛ in.
Fig. 125

Commissioned for the very popular illustrated book *King's Views of New York, 1906*, this drawing shows the continuing interest of the press in the development of the Columbia campus. The gracefully proportioned and sunny spaces of the architects' renderings contrast with the gray palette used by Pettit, undoubtedly chosen for its reproducibility. In Pettit's hands, the density of the campus is accentuated, perhaps in order to fit all the buildings into an illustration of limited size. The true feeling of the projected campus would probably have been somewhere between McKim's idealized scheme and Pettit's journalistic view. In either case, this cannot be tested because only one courtyard, that formed by Avery, Schermerhorn, Fayerweather, and the Chapel, was ever completed and thus the succession of closed and open spaces in quadrangles envisioned by McKim cannot be experienced. [JP]

54

MᶜKIM, MEAD & WHITE

Hamilton Hall and Hartley Hall

1907

Photograph, by A. Fowler, 9¾ x 13½ in.
Columbiana Collection
Fig. 126

When Columbia decided to move to Morningside Heights, the faculty outlined many requirements for the classroom buildings. Several trustees wanted to include dormitories in the master plan as well. It was not until the actual move took place, however, that it became clear that the university had to provide housing for its students if they were to come that far uptown. This photograph of Hamilton, a classroom building, and Hartley, a dormitory, shows clearly the major similarities and differences between the building types. Both structures share the same roof line and plinth height and a similar architectural style. The major difference is the greater number of windows in the dormitory, obviously reflecting the number of small rooms needed to house many students. [JP]

55

McKIM, MEAD & WHITE

Proposed building for South Field opposite Hartley Hall

12 April 1906

Ink with pencil on linen, 23¾ x 46⅞ in.

J. C. McGowan, delineator

Fig. 127

While South Field was purchased to preserve the future growth of the university, it had not been done with any pressing need at hand. Nonetheless, once the master plan was extended to include the property, there was no reason not to build on it. Hartley and Livingston Halls—built as a response to a continued need for student dormitories—and then Hamilton Hall, as the new home for the college, followed in quick succession from 1904 to 1907. The building in this drawing was planned to enclose the Hamilton and Hartley courtyard, and, if constructed, would have become the first of the inner pavilion buildings on campus.

The details on the drawing show how the lower campus was designed to relate to the platform of the upper campus, whose grade of 150 feet is continued as the top of the granite base of the building. The building would have been directly connected to Hamilton by a passageway similar to that between Hartley and Livingston. The wall treatment is detailed throughout with elements used in Hamilton Hall. [JP]

FIGURE 126

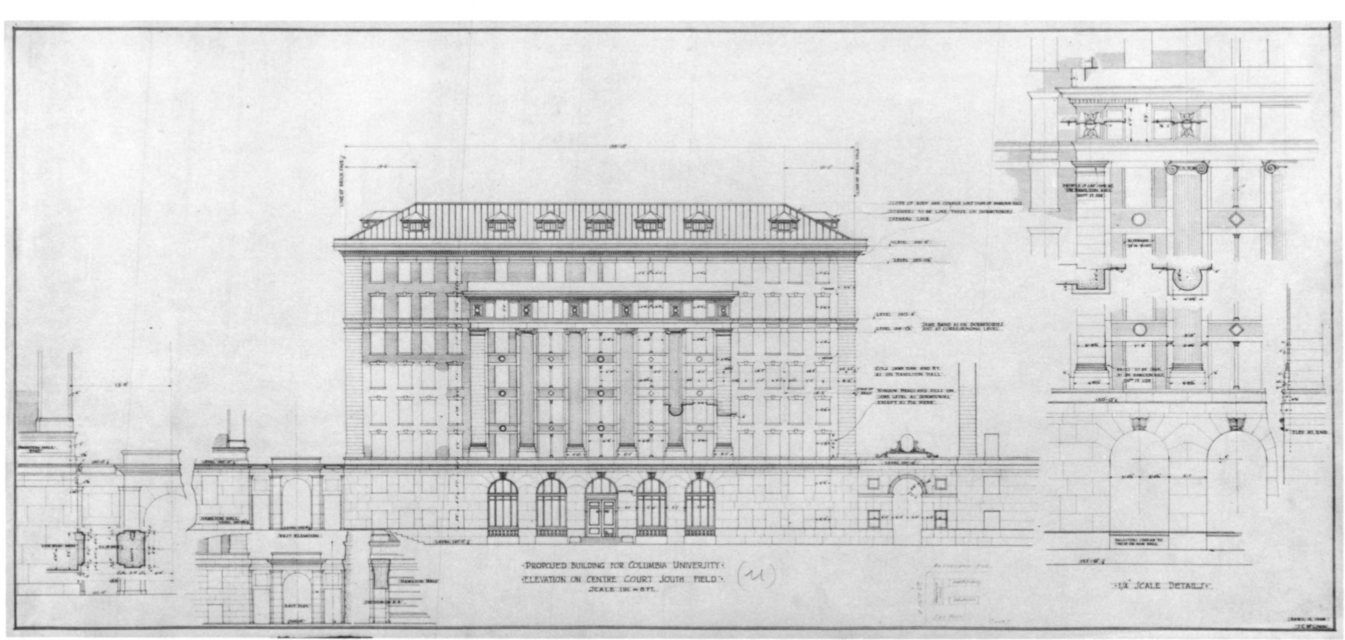

FIGURE 127

VIII. SOUTH HALL (BUTLER LIBRARY) AND CLOSING THE VISTA

56

McKIM, MEAD & WHITE

Proposal for Students Hall

1923

Photograph of a drawing, 8⅛ x 10 in.

The New-York Historical Society

Fig. 56

By the early 1920s, five buildings had been built on South Field but none along 114th Street. One early scheme for the central site was Students Hall, a multipurpose building with facilities for student clubs, athletics, and dining. It was to be entered on the second floor from an outdoor terrace. [JP]

57

JAMES GAMBLE ROGERS

Low Library extension: ground floor plan

ca. 1931

Pencil on tracing paper, 24 13/16 x 18 5/16 in.

Fig. 128

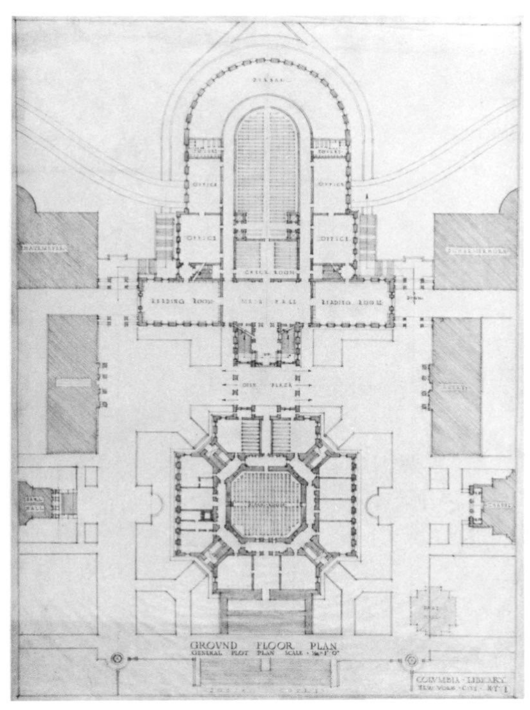

FIGURE 128

Had this project been built, it would have been the first major departure from the program of McKim's master plan. Not only would the dominance and isolation of Low Library have been compromised, but the entire circulation pattern of the upper campus would have been altered. The large plaza between Low and University Hall was narrowed to a single passage under an arcade of the new building connecting the two halls. The reading rooms and main hall would have eliminated the vista from Havemeyer to Schermerhorn. How much the building would encroach on existing structures is indicated by the loss of the grassy areas in front of Avery and the Chapel. Even the flagpoles were moved to accommodate the changes in layout. [JP]

58

JAMES GAMBLE ROGERS

Low Library extension: longitudinal section

ca. 1931

Pencil with red pencil on tracing paper, 18¼ x 25 in.

Fig. 129

In the course of a little more than fifty years, Columbia built three major libraries: Haight's library of 1889 at Forty-ninth Street, McKim's Low Library, and ultimately James Gamble Rogers's South Hall (Butler Library), finished in 1934. Throughout the trustees' minutes and chief librarian's reports are statements about the unprecedented growth and usage of the libraries and their collections.

By the 1920s, Low Library was no longer adequate and President Butler turned to Edward Harkness, an heir to Standard Oil and a benefactor to Yale, Harvard, and Columbia's College of Physicians and Surgeons, as a potential donor. Harkness's architect, James Gamble Rogers, was given the task of designing a structure to accommodate a 6-million-volume library, a capacity requested by the chief librarian, Charles Williamson. Rogers's first solution was to connect Low Library to a completed version of University Hall. The underground area below the plaza behind Low was to be excavated to provide stack space. The grandiosity of this solution, in

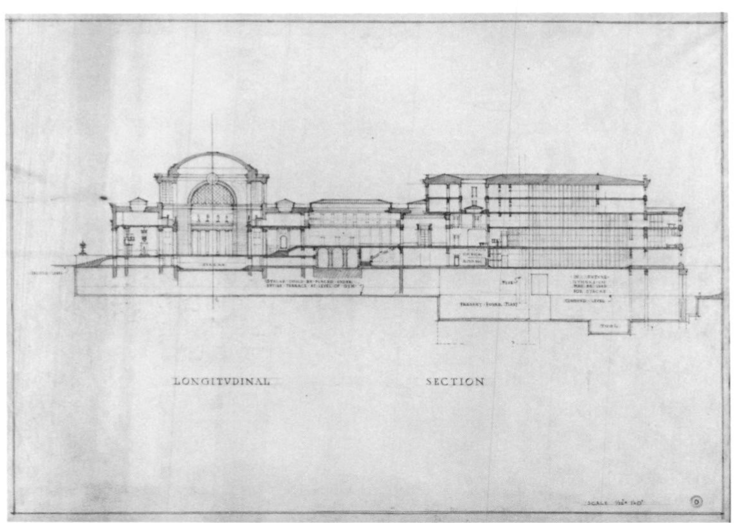

FIGURE 129

its effect as well as its costs—notably in spanning the space above the gymnasium and pool on the lower floors—led to the demise of this impractical scheme. [JP]

59

JAMES GAMBLE ROGERS

South Hall under construction

6 February 1933

Photograph, by A. Tennyson Beals, 7¼ x 9⁵⁄₁₆ in.

Columbiana Collection

Fig. 62

The new library on South Field had a capacity of 4 million volumes, one-third fewer than the head librarian Charles Williamson's ideal 6 million volumes. The new library had a central book stack constructed of steel, visible here at the top of the nearly completed building. The arrow on the snow-covered field in front of the library was the long-jump track, as South Field was still the location of many athletic events. [JP]

60

JAMES GAMBLE ROGERS

South Hall: first-floor plan

1931

Ink on paper, 18⅛ x 26⅛ in.

Fig. 130

James Gamble Rogers probably sighed with relief when the site for the new library was changed from University Hall to an open area on South Field. The general logic and arrangement of the building was an improvement over the problematic merger of Low Library and University Hall. The specialized reading and seminar rooms were features requested by the faculty. [JP]

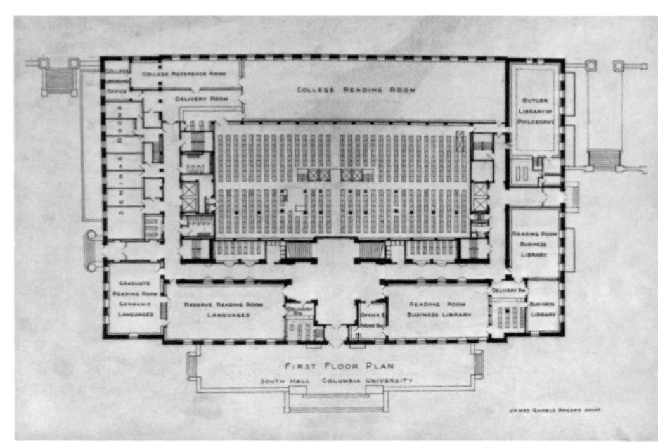

FIGURE 130

IX. FROM GROVE TO SKYSCRAPER: NORTH CAMPUS DENSIFIED

61

MᶜKIM, MEAD & WHITE

Proposal for University Hall: rear elevation as seen from the Grove

ca. 1896

Watercolor on paper, 28½ x 40½ in.

Plate 4

Ironically enough the building that McKim, Mead & White expended the greatest energy on designing, the largest building on the master plan, was the only one of the major buildings originally proposed never to be completed. University Hall was redesigned no fewer than three times between 1894, when it first appeared as a footprint on McKim's master plan approved by the trustees and by Seth Low, and 1901 when the first floor above the 150-foot grade of the campus pedestal was added to the foundations, which housed the gymnasium and the power plant built between 1895 and 1897.

The program for the building was itself complex, an extraordinary hybrid of fundamental services and great ceremonial spaces for the new campus. From the first both architects and administrators hoped to find a way to combine a gymnasium, academic theater, and dining hall into a single building. This sort of combination was inspired by recent monumental buildings on other campuses, most notably Harvard's Memorial Hall, which combined dining room and theater. That combination was already challenging to a designer, since a theater demands a facade with few windows while a dining hall should be flooded with light. At Columbia the stakes were raised higher not only by the decision to add a gymnasium, and eventually even the central power house, to the formula essayed by Ware & Van Brunt at Harvard, but also because the new building would be situated on a very difficult site. McKim's plan gave the building pride of place as the culmination of the principal north-south ceremonial axis of the campus plan, but it also situated it on the cusp of the artificial platform that he hoped to create for the new university buildings and the natural terrain at the northern edge of the site. The building would thus form an integral part of the great retaining wall running across the site. Its rear facade facing the Grove would be several stories taller than its campus facade.

This large-scale watercolor rendering of the northern facade of the building facing the Grove is probably the earliest image of what the future building might look like. Most striking is the absence of the great semicircular apse, recorded on most of McKim's plans and ultimately constructed to house the gymnasium and pool. This would seem to suggest a very early date, perhaps as early as 1894 but more likely early 1896, when a plan that would correspond to this facade was published in a pamphlet issued for the ceremonial dedication of Columbia's new site. By that time, however, McKim and his associates were at work on a very different treatment, the remains of which can still be glimpsed below the library of the School of Business. [BB]

62

McKIM, MEAD & WHITE

Dormitory proposal for the Grove

1899

Watercolor and pencil on paper, 15⅛ x 25¼ in.

Hughson Hawley, renderer

Plate 5

The question of living space for the students arose immediately after the move to Morningside Heights. This proposal for dormitories on the Grove was the earliest scheme. McKim had always envisioned that the northern perimeter of the campus would also have an entrance. In designing these living quarters, a friendlier, less formal tone was established by moving the buildings back from the street and enclosing the yard with a fence, instead of a high wall.

The renderer, Hughson Hawley, was an Englishman of prodigious skill and speed who worked for many architectural firms in New York. As in numerous other renderings, the reality of the site is distorted in favor of a more favorable presentation of the architecture. In 1898, Teachers College already stood along much of 120th Street between Broadway and Amsterdam, and had there ever been a house with a clothesline and goats on the site, it had long vanished by that time. This drawing is also interesting in that the border of the paper contains several notes by the renderer and holes used in marking the perspective lines for the drawing. [JP]

63

McKIM, MEAD & WHITE

University Hall: front view

27 May 1896

Ink on paper, 18½ x 31⅝ in.

The New-York Historical Society

Fig. 33

This perspective rendering of the campus facade of University Hall corresponds to the early views of the future campus published in *Harper's Weekly* and *King's New York Views* and reflects McKim, Mead & White's initial solution to the problem of housing both a theater and a dining hall in a single building. The dining hall would be developed as a generously dimensioned vaulted room, rising the full height of the structure above the 150-foot level of the campus platform. This vaulted hall would be set at the center of the building and wrapped by two stories of offices as well as corridors that would lead to the semicircular theater set at the back of the building, atop the gymnasium and pool in the lower stories. The dining hall would be entered directly from the large central door under the broad Corinthian portico, while smaller flanking entrances would lead to corridors connecting to the theater. In keeping with the hierarchy of materials and ornamentation that McKim defined for the campus, this building would be faced in a mixture of brick and limestone, deferring to Low but considerably richer in ornament and detail than the academic pavilions. [BB]

64

McKIM, MEAD & WHITE

University Hall: south elevation

11 June 1900

Ink with pencil on linen, 34$\frac{5}{16}$ x 36⅝ in.

William Mitchell Kendall, delineator

Fig. 131

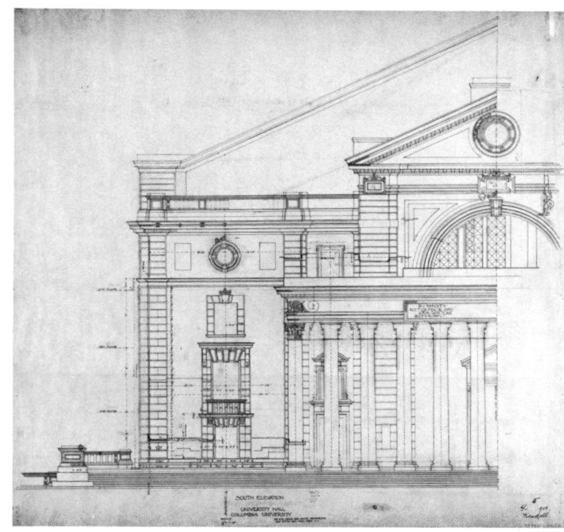

FIGURE 131

No building occasioned as much discussion and disagreement among the trustees, architectural faculty, and campus designers as University Hall. Models of the building were debated in several animated meetings of the trustees, and Professor Ware of the School of Architecture as well as John B. Pine, clerk of the trustees and passionately involved in the planning and building of the campus, both expressed skepticism over McKim's scheme of a partition between theater and dining hall that could be moved on important occasions to combine the two rooms into one vast space.

When it was decided to proceed with construction of the first story of the building above the 150-foot grade of the campus to provide dining facilities and administrative offices, McKim, Mead & White insisted that even this partial construction would necessitate developing a fully detailed project and usable working drawings. These drawings date from that moment and are thus interesting to compare with existing photographs of the first level of University Hall as constructed; it was demolished in 1962 to make way for Uris Hall. Also noteworthy is the great thermal window over the portico, which William Kendall of McKim, Mead & White added in this revised design. This not only gave a greater monumentality to the facade and provided greater illumination for

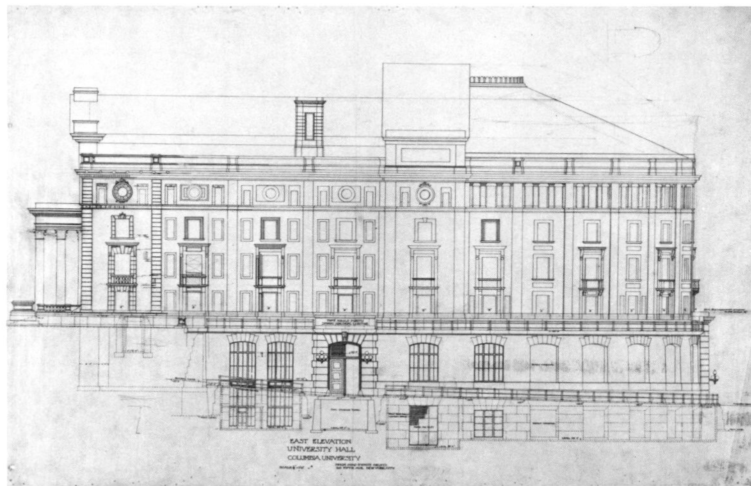

FIGURE 132

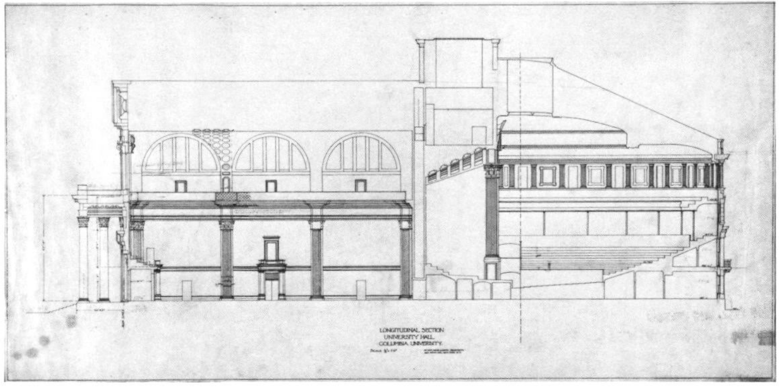

FIGURE 133

the dining hall within, but it related the new building to the great thermal windows in the drum of Low Library's dome. [BB]

65

McKIM, MEAD & WHITE

University Hall: east elevation

1900

Ink with pencil on linen, 27⅛ x 41⅞ in.

Fig. 132

66

McKIM, MEAD & WHITE

University Hall: longitudinal section

1900

Ink with pencil on linen, 23 9/16 x 44 3/16 in.

Fig. 133

67

University Hall: first story with view of Teachers College

ca. 1910–14

Photograph mounted on board, 11 x 13¾ in.

Columbiana Collection

Fig. 32

University Hall was planned to be the largest building on campus, and it also became the most expensive, surpassing even Low Library. Fund-raising sources were limited, although many schemes were floated. In 1900 it was decided to add only one story above grade.

In this photograph the strange result of this decision can be seen. Even for this abbreviated structure, construction costs had risen to more than $800,000, only slightly less than the $1 million plus consumed by a completed Low Library. The articulation of this part, truncated just at the first story, makes no sense without the system of the whole building. The smokestacks from the university's boiler plant prompted some observers to refer to the building as the "ocean liner." The bases of the columns intended for the portico can be seen in outline on the top of the steps.

In the eyes of McKim, Low, and Nicholas Murray Butler, University Hall was a symbol of the greatness of the university. It was an idea that did not die easily. Sprinkled throughout trustees' minutes and reports are the repeated pleas from Butler for the completion of the building. One particularly poignant note came as late as the 1930s, when Butler stated that the one-story beginning was a daily reminder to all who passed of the university's unfinished business. In the official guide to the university published in 1937, John Robson writes that it is doubtful the building will ever be finished. It was only in 1962, sixty years after University Hall was begun and more than fifteen years after Butler retired, that the university demolished the first floor to make way for Uris Hall. The steps of University Hall were used as the entrance to the new Uris Hall. [JP]

68

HOWARD E. BAHR

Skyscraper project for University Hall, McKim Fellowship

1932

Clipping from the *New York Times* mounted in scrapbook

Fig. 64

On the basis of Boring's suggestion (cat. 69) that McKim's master plan might accommodate a skyscraper, the program for the 1932 McKim scholarship-prize competition in the School of Architecture was "to design a building to provide Columbia with greatly expanded accommodation of its ever widening activities." Not surprisingly the first two prizes were awarded to skyscraper projects rising over University Hall. There is a certain irony in this situation, given McKim's lifelong disdain for the emerging American commercial skyscraper, but also a certain acknowledgment that McKim's cornice heights would have to give way to the increasing pressure for space in the city, even on a harmoniously planned campus.

The competition was judged in May 1932 by a jury consisting of Dean E. V. Meaks of Yale; Arthur Harmon of Shreve, Lamb and Harmon; Harvey Wiley Corbett; Ely Jacques Kahn; and William A. Delano. Most of these men, notably Harmon, whose firm was just completing the Empire State Building, and Corbett, who had been inventing visions of the skyscraper city for many years, were enthusiasts of high-rise buildings. First prize of $2,500 was awarded to Howard E. Bahr of Sayville, Long Island, whose project received considerable press attention; second prize of $500 to James Sasso of Brooklyn; and third prize of $500 to Joseph De Marco of Farmingdale, Long Island. This newspaper clipping is one of many concerning the activities of the School of Architecture that are contained in this album. [BB]

69

WILLIAM ALCIPHRON BORING

Project for a skyscraper completion to University Hall: perspective and site plan

1932
Autograph letter, 8½ x 13 in.
Columbia University Archives
Figs. 134 & 135

Although in 1932 America was in the throes of the depression, and the great expansion of the campus envisioned by Nicholas Murray Butler and McKim, Mead & White in the 1920s had ground to a halt, the dean of the Architecture School William Boring suggested that with a single skyscraper Columbia could nearly double in size. "It is proposed to build a tall structure on the Campus equal in capacity to all of the space now occupied for educational activities," he began the memorandum accompanying these two small sketches sent to the president and trustees of the university on 18 February 1932.

No doubt the design was to a certain extent offered in jest, and quite likely had a polemical thrust, for only two weeks earlier an exhibition called *Modern Architecture* had opened at the Museum of Modern Art. Boring had taken a critical position against the functionalism promoted by this show in his annual report on the activities of the school and had later been quoted in the *New York Sun*: "In architecture it is claimed that function is the most important expression," he said; "there is no doubt that this quality is evident in all good architecture, but the raw exterior statement of its purpose on the outside of a building in no way assures it to be beautiful."

High-rise buildings for universities were very much a trend in the 1920s, most famously in the thirty-six-story Cathedral of Learning designed in 1924 by Charles Klauder

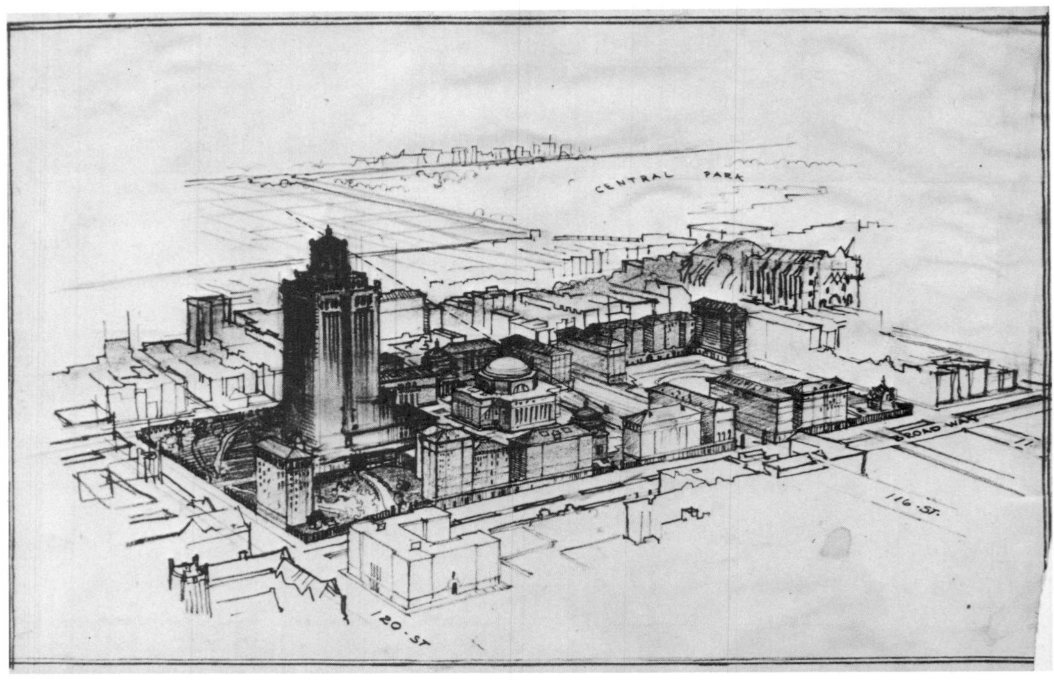

FIGURE 134

for the University of Pittsburgh. Boring also pointed to tall buildings under construction at Penn and NYU; he might also have pointed to the recently developed project by Ernest Cormier for the Université de Montréal.

Although McKim, Mead & White had looked increasingly to the construction techniques of commercial office buildings in their recent buildings for Columbia, they had avoided abandoning the controlling matrix of cornice lines and Italian Renaissance facade organization. Not only would Boring's tower dwarf even fourteen-story Pupin Hall, which a few years earlier many had worried was out of scale for the classical campus, but for the first time it offered an architectural image in which verticality was emphasized. In keeping with McKim's original conception of University Hall, however, Boring proposed that a single building house a great variety of functions. Just as such contemporary commercial buildings as Rockefeller Center were veritable microcosms of the city in the vast number of activities they housed, so Boring maintained that the new building might be a veritable university in a single building. "This building is to be flexible to accommodate every type of space required, with every facility for offices, class rooms, laboratories, auditoriums, etc."

Although it is hard to imagine McKim's accepting such a departure from his classical ideals, the new tower was presented as a logical culmination of McKim, Mead & White's master plan. Boring proposed the tower as a completion of University Hall, the head of McKim's processional axis still unfinished thirty-five years after classes had begun on Morningside Heights. "The base line of the building up to five stories would be in harmony with the present buildings, and like the original design of

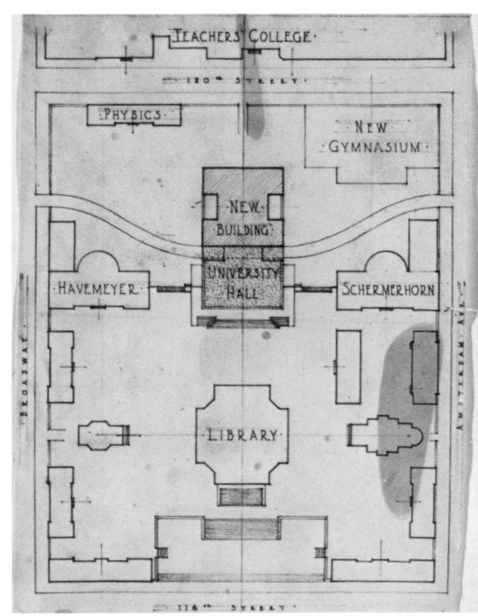

FIGURE 135

University Hall. In this building could be an auditorium, social rooms, perhaps a restaurant and organizations for the students." In his bird's-eye view Boring set out to demonstrate that the new high-rise scale of the tower would be in harmony with McKim's system of perspectival projections. He calculated the way the tower would fit into the overall picture when seen as a silhouette behind the dome of Low Library by a viewer standing on the site of the inscription to McKim on Low Plaza.

The accompanying floor plan reveals that the tower would actually rise behind University Hall from the Grove. Also visible on the plan is a new gymnasium projected for the southwest corner of 120th Street and Amsterdam Avenue, one of the earliest proposed to replace McKim's original gymnasium in the lower stories of University Hall. [BB]

70

MCKIM, MEAD & WHITE

North elevation of 120th Street

15 December 1924
Pencil on tracing paper, 15¾ x 63 in.
J.C.M. (John C. McGowan?), delineator
The New-York Historical Society
Fig. 50

Although the university commissioned new science buildings one by one as needed, President Butler reminded department heads, when asking them in the early 1920s to outline future requirements, that their new building would "not be designed as a thing itself, but as one element of a plan for the future development of academic buildings on the Green" (letter from Butler to George B. Pegram, 20 January 1922; CUA, Central Files). Between 1921 and 1927 the firm of McKim, Mead & White outlined several approaches to developing the Grove—protected as open land during Columbia's first two decades on Morningside Heights—in each of which they sought to balance the demands of rapid growth in scientific research with the harmony and order of the original master plan.

The major difficulty would be accommodating the radical change in the terrain, for the strip of greenery occupying one and a half city blocks at the north edge of the campus was nearly three stories below the 150-foot grade level that McKim had established for the campus. President Butler hoped that the buildings could be developed in such a way that they would "conform in water table level and in cornice line to Havemeyer Hall and the buildings to the south," but he admitted as early as 1922 that "it is quite possible . . . that the buildings on the south side of 120th Street, may be carried still higher. Personally I doubt this will be the case, but it is a possibility that must be reckoned with. I have no intention of proposing any structures of the tall office building type at any time, but it might at some future date be thought desirable to carry the buildings on the north side of 114th Street and those on the south side of 120th Street to a somewhat greater height than the present cornice and roof lines" (ibid.). [BB]

71

MCKIM, MEAD & WHITE

Broadway and 120th Street elevations

9 October 1924
Pencil on tracing paper, 15½ x 24 in.
John C. McGowan, delineator
The New-York Historical Society
Fig. 136

Between 1924 and 1929 the McKim, Mead & White firm, under partner William Kendall's supervision, studied numerous alternatives for the development of the northern end of the original campus for the rapidly expanding science departments. While the early schemes, dated autumn 1924, looked principally at continuing the cornice lines of McKim's original campus with the addition of two- or three-story belvederes at key points, later schemes looked to the incorporation of taller buildings, including slabs of up to fourteen stories and even towers at the Broadway and Amsterdam Avenue corners. All of the schemes were posited on the assumption that the future development should complete the densely built perimeter of McKim's original campus with buildings rising above a consistent granite base. [BB]

72

McKIM, MEAD & WHITE

120th Street elevation, Scheme B: two versions for building in center of block

31 December 1926
Colored pencil and pencil on paper mounted on board, 19 x 33¼ in.
Plate 10 (version 1); Fig. 137 (version 2)

The development of 120th Street, something left unstudied between the late 1890s when McKim and Mead looked briefly at the possibility of building a quadrangle of dormitories on the Grove (cat. 62) and the late 1920s, occasioned vibrant discussions. While new high-rise slab buildings could accommodate the explosion in laboratory research in Columbia's science and engineering departments—all in buildings thin enough to maximize natural light and ventilation—the firm seemed to have reservations about closing the vista of Low Library from the north. In this long elevation of the new street facade the architects offered two alternatives. In addition to the possibility of maximum development by building

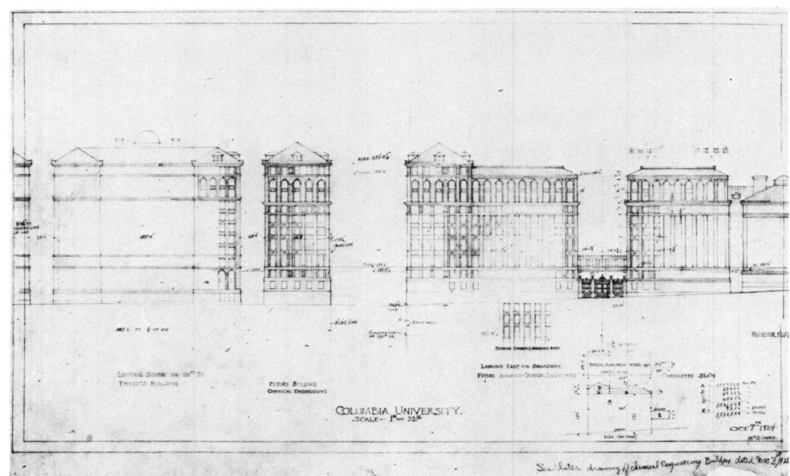

FIGURE 136

FIGURE 137

a series of large, nearly uniform slabs (of the type adopted for Pupin Hall), a flap over the center of this elevation allowed Columbia administrators and trustees to consider the possibility of substituting a two-story building at the center to house an art gallery. This would not only have provided space for Columbia's successful public lectures and University Extension (the forerunner of the School of General Studies) courses in fine arts, but would have preserved the buildup of volumes that McKim hoped for along the central axis of the campus in both directions. This drawing, like a contemporary tracing-paper sketch (cat. 70) now in the New-York Historical Society, is particularly concerned with the overlapping silhouettes of the rectangular art gallery with its low pitched roof, the great apsidal hemicycle of University Hall (never completed), and Low Library's dome as seen by a viewer standing in front of the main building of Teachers College. [BB]

73

MCKIM, MEAD & WHITE

Proposed art gallery on 120th Street

December 1928
Pencil on tracing paper, 20 x 10¼ in.
The New-York Historical Society
Fig. 63

The absence of the fine arts from the Columbia curriculum had been an episodic concern of the faculty and trustees since the 1890s. At the time of their discussions over the removal of the college from Forty-ninth Street some members of the board of trustees advocated locating the component schools of the emerging university in different parts of the city so as to take advantage of existing city institutions, an approach that would both reinforce the teaching collections and provide greater contact of the faculty with the public. Under such an arrangement, the School of Architecture (founded in 1881) would have been located near the Metropolitan Museum of Art since its collections, including important displays of plaster casts of architectural ornament and elements, would be a valuable adjunct to the book collections of the Avery Library, founded at Columbia in 1890. By the end of the century Columbia faculty were offering public lectures on the history of art and aesthetics at the museum, a reflection of Seth Low's idea that the university should reach a larger urban public.

The idea of a school of fine arts —combining architecture, music, classical archaeology, and the fine arts—was promoted by Nicholas Murray Butler from his first years in the president's office. "A liberal culture that offers no instruction upon art, except as art is represented by archaeology and by music, cannot be considered complete. The absence of such a chair in the University, therefore, creates a gap that ought to be filled at the first possible opportunity," he asserted in his 1901 annual report (p. 63). In 1902 Butler submitted the *Report on the Organization of Instruction in the Fine Arts* to the trustees' committee on education. He argued that the university should develop instruction in the philosophical and historical study of art, but that studio instruction was best left to existing art schools, a view endorsed by the architect Russell Sturgis, who served on the advisory board of the Avery Library. The first result was the decision in 1902 to remove the School of Architecture from the Faculty of Applied Science, with the view that it, like the Department of Music, would eventually form part of a school of fine arts.

By 1905 an elaborate scheme of cooperation and affiliation between Columbia, the National Academy of Design, which offered studio instruction in painting and sculpture, and the Metropolitan Museum had been drawn up and publicized. The National Academy had already acquired property at the corner of 110th Street and Amsterdam Avenue with a view to taking a place on New York's new cultural acropolis, but the trustees wondered if some sort of exchange might be possible whereby the academy would either build or have built for it a building on campus. Already in 1902 President Butler had suggested that McKim, Mead & White restudy their plans for University Hall to add exhibition and teaching space for the history of art on the top floor. After the addition of South Field, it was even suggested, in 1909, that a gallery building might find its place there. For want of students, and because of issues that could not be resolved among the three institutions, the cooperative agreement was canceled in 1914 without a single course ever having been offered; but in the same breath the trustees insisted that a course of study in the history of art should be introduced as soon as possible.

The Department of Fine Arts, the forerunner of today's Department of Art History and Archaeology, was organized in 1921 and given quarters first in Avery Hall and after 1926 in Fayerweather Hall, renovated after the removal of the Department of Physics to Pupin. Around the same time a new cooperative agreement with the Metropolitan Museum was forged. Courses in the history of art drew large audiences in the University Extension, and throughout the 1920s there was intermittent discussion of creating a building that could house both exhibition space and lecture rooms for the growing public audience for Columbia's art historians.

In the late 1920s as William Kendall and other members of the McKim, Mead & White firm were studying schemes for the development of 120th Street, they explored the possibility of reserving the central site for an art building. With its northern exposure on a wide crosstown street such a building would have excellent natural light for galleries. The site would also allow for a neoclassical limestone building to complete the main north-south axis that McKim had defined with Low Library and University Hall. Although never officially commissioned by the university, the proposal was put aside in 1930 when Butler recommended exploring the use of the structure on East Thirty-fourth Street, vacated by the School of Dental and Oral Surgery, as a fine arts building for the University Extension. [BB]

74

EGGERS & HIGGINS

Project for a gymnasium in the Grove: perspective of west elevation

March 1947

Photograph of a lost pencil rendering by O. R. Eggers, 9½ x 12⅞ in.

Peter A. Juley & Son, photographer

Fig. 65

Over the course of a quarter century the firm of Eggers & Higgins (and its successor the Eggers Partnership) studied six gymnasium designs on different sites for Columbia. This is the first, although ironically enough the final, built design of 1972 would be for nearly the same site. McKim's original gym and swimming pool in the lower level of University Hall, opened in 1897, seemed a quaint relic by the 1920s, totally inadequate to the growing number of students on Morningside Heights and to changing recreational tastes and trends. Butler and McKim, Mead & White studied the possibility of a new gym on South Field, notably on the site now occupied by Butler Library. After the war, as American campuses swelled with returning GIs, improved gymnasium facilities seemed imperative.

Eggers & Higgins's scheme is interesting in two respects. For the first time a building proposed for the Grove would not front on the street, thereby acknowledging that the verdant open space at the north end of the campus, whittled away over the years, was destined to disappear. This is also one of the first projects for the campus to grapple with the issue of departing, even if respectfully, from the literal classicism both of McKim's original buildings and of Eggers & Higgins's own master, John Russell Pope. [BB]

75

EGGERS & HIGGINS

Administration Building: perspective view of Scheme A

14 March 1956

Blueline print with colored pencil, 18 x 24⅛ in.

Fig. 138

Eggers & Higgins had first worked for Columbia in the 1940s, when they were selected to design the Branders Matthews Theater (cat. no. 85). Although trained as ardent

FIGURE 138

classicists in the office of John Russell Pope—most famous as the designer of the National Gallery of Art and the Jefferson Memorial in Washington, D.C.—they began to explore ways in which a classicizing modernism might be developed for the completion of McKim's grand scheme for Columbia.

In the mid-1950s they were one of a group of firms invited to develop schemes for a projected expansion of the university under the watchful eye of the university's consulting architect Fritz Woodbridge of Adams & Woodbridge. Part of this ambitious program called for the completion of University Hall as a modern office building to accommodate the central administration which had outgrown even Low Library in the two decades since the removal of the books to South Hall (Butler Library). The one-story, campus-level fragment of University Hall, built reluctantly by McKim, Mead & White in 1900 to house dining facilities and offices, had been given over completely to offices after the opening of the John Jay Hall dining room in the late 1920s. It housed principally the office of the bursar, the registrar, the admissions office, and, ironically enough, the Department of Buildings and Grounds.

Harrison & Abramovitz had recommended demolishing the building to extend the open space at the north of the campus, but in 1955 Adams & Woodbridge rejected this approach. They proposed completing University Hall as "an attractive central feature of the entire group," at the same time as they allowed "that a change in scale in any additions to University Hall would be permissible because it is a central, axial building and would not be considered against a matching building opposite to it" (Adams & Woodbridge, *A Report on the General Development of the Campus, Columbia University, 19 July 1955*; [CUA]).

Within this framework Eggers & Higgins studied alternatives for creating a five-story building—the maximum number of floors that could be constructed on the existing steel and masonry foundations of McKim's building without alterations—the last of which dates from March 1956 and is exhibited here. These studies are considerably scaled back from earlier versions proposed as Adams & Woodbridge objected to any new building significantly wider than McKim's original footprint because it would encroach "too much on valuable open space and damage the shape and character of the court between University Hall and Low Library."

Columbia's planning efforts were viewed skeptically by many outside observers, including the acerbic architectural critic Douglas Haskell, editor of *Architectural Forum* from 1949 to 1964. Among his papers, now in the Avery Library, is a memo to his staff containing "confidential information" from an unnamed informant who reported on a major meeting of the several architectural firms then working for Columbia: "CU seems to be taking the very first steps towards rectifying a remarkable way of running a building program. . . . A couple of days ago the meeting was called by Fritz Woodbridge . . . coordinator of the program. All the participating architects, with about a dozen or more

FIGURE 139

buildings in their separate charge, were asked to bring along drawings or models showing progress they are making. According to my informant, the confusion was simply immense. Eggers & Higgins brought an administration building which had the rest of the crowd simply floored. By a stroke of tact, Woodbridge declared that the site should be open campus, and thus gave time to improve this situation." Five years later construction began on Moore and Hutchins's Uris Hall. [BB]

76

ADAMS AND WOODBRIDGE

Section through main campus looking north, showing proposed new building on site of University Hall

6 March 1957

Blueline print with colored pencil, 14⅜ x 28¾ in.

Fig. 139

In his role as consulting architect to Columbia, Fritz Woodbridge advocated at once the preservation of McKim's axes and patterns of open and bounded spaces and the introduction of a tame brand of modernism that could harmonize with the materials and volumes of McKim's incomplete master plan. This project to complete University Hall as well as to construct new buildings on the site behind it on 120th Street at the center of the block reveals an interest in creating a monumental northern approach to the campus. The building facing 120th Street was to be treated as a propylaeum. Visitors would arrive on campus via a pair of open switchback stairs and then pass under the building, raised on piers above a plaza at the center, before entering the heart of the campus on McKim's 150-foot plinth.

The building planned for University Hall was kept deliberately low to respond to the maximum of five stories above campus level which the structural engineers had found possible, given the existing foundations, and to respect the roofline of Havemeyer and Schermerhorn Halls. Although modern in vocabulary, the new building would be axial, symmetrical, and clad in brick with limestone accents. [BB]

77

ADAMS AND WOODBRIDGE

Elevation on 120th Street

16 March 1957

Blueline print with colored pencil, 14 x 26 ⅞ in.

Plate 12

78

PETER GLUCK

Addition to Uris Hall

ca. 1985

Pencil on paper, 20 ⅝ x 27 in.

Courtesy the architect

Fig. 140

This perspectival drawing attests to the care with which Peter Gluck inserted his extension to Uris Hall into the stylistic collage of the north campus. While the lines of his building were determined by the existing lateral wings of Uris Hall, he was careful to study both scale and detailing in relation to the flanking McKim buildings, notably Havemeyer Hall of 1895 to 1897 seen to the left. The materials of his building, however, and the patterns of the masonry relate equally to the modernist vocabulary of Uris. [BB]

FIGURE 140

X. EAST CAMPUS: AN ALTERNATIVE MASTER PLAN?

FIGURE 141

79

McKIM, MEAD & WHITE

Scheme A for proposed East Campus project

ca. 1922–25

Pencil on tracing paper, 11 x 14½ in.

Fig. 141

The city block immediately east of the original campus, bounded by 116th and 117th Streets, Amsterdam Avenue and Morningside Drive, had been assembled beginning in 1910 with a view to creating a site for the medical school, the College of Physicians and Surgeons, which had remained at 59th Street in 1897 when the undergraduate college, the School of Mines, and young graduate divisions of Columbia had moved to Morningside Heights. Shortly thereafter a new president's house was built (1911–1912) facing away from campus, but the lion's share of the site was still available for a comprehensive scheme of development in the early 1920s. Only temporary buildings had been constructed on the central part of the site, including greenhouses (1911) and the Crocker Research Laboratories (1914).

The signing of an agreement in 1921 with Presbyterian Hospital to create a major medical school/hospital center at 168th Street on Washington Heights released this land for new projects. In 1922–1923 the Faculty House was added next to the President's House with its main entrance facing north onto 117th Street. But whereas these two buildings faced onto city streets, the tall dormitory building for women, at first known as Johnson Hall and now called Wien Hall (1923–1925), was set perpendicular to the block with its entrance on a courtyard, a fragment of a projected quadrangle to be defined within the block and isolated from the city by high-rise perimeter buildings.

Between 1922 and 1925 William Kendall and his associates at McKim, Mead & White studied a series of alternative layouts and massings for these buildings (these documents are today divided between the Drawings and Archives Collection of Avery Library, Columbia University Archives, and the New-York Historical Society). At its 28 June 1922 meeting the trustees approved a U-shaped scheme for the overall development as well as the project for Johnson Hall to include a dining hall commons seating three hundred women as well as rooms at the northern end to house the Women's Faculty Club. In the 1920s it was assumed that this area would be used for future expansion of graduate residence halls, while South Field would be reserved for undergraduate residence halls for the all-male Columbia College. The plans were put on hold in the late 1920s, motivated at first by the acquisition of sites on the north side of 117th Street, which might require a revision to the overall scheme—in December 1925 the architects were asked to make a study "of the future development of the north side of 117th Street, particularly as to the skyline"—and then after 1929 by the stock market crash and the uncertain economic situation. [BB]

80

McKIM, MEAD & WHITE

Scheme B for proposed East Campus project

ca. 1922–25

Pencil on tracing paper, 11 x 14⅞ in.

Fig. 142

81

McKIM, MEAD & WHITE

Elevation on 116th Street for East Campus

ca. 1922–25

Pencil on tracing paper, 8⅞ x 24¾ in.

82

McKIM, MEAD & WHITE

Elevation on 116th Street for East Campus

16 October 1922

Pencil on tracing paper, 9⅛ x 19⁵⁄₁₆ in.

83

McKIM, MEAD & WHITE

Plan for East Field: Scheme A (center block having two wings)

3 August–7 October 1926

Pencil on tracing paper, 30⅛ x 34 in.

The New-York Historical Society

Fig. 143

84

JAMES GAMBLE ROGERS

Project for a fine arts center: site plan

1935

Pencil on tracing paper, 9 x 12⅛ in.

Columbia University Archives

Fig. 144

From spring 1936 to spring 1937, Nicholas Murray Butler and James Gamble Rogers courted the financier and collector Chester Dale as a potential benefactor of the university. Having made his fortune in stocks and investment banking, Dale had retired in 1934 to devote himself full time to art collecting. His collection, then numbering some three hundred paintings, was first exhibited in 1928 and constituted one of the most important private collections of eighteenth- and nineteenth-century French art in America. Although he was active on the boards of several museums, Dale was at just that point reconsidering the provisions of his will, drawn up to relieve tax pressures. Rogers—always adept at acting as a middle-man between wealthy donors and institutions—pressed Columbia's president to act quickly, writing on 29 May 1936 that Dale "has taken care of the tax question by having willed his pictures to a number of institutions, but wishes to have a settled home for them in one place so he can rearrange his will. In other words he is anxious to get the building going" (Rogers to Butler, 29 May 1936; CUA). Butler responded that the pictures could be stored in Low Library, empty of its books since Rogers's South Hall had been completed a year earlier. At the same time he outlined his vision of the gallery as the centerpiece of the school of fine arts for which he had been campaigning for decades.

By July 1936 Rogers had drawn up sketches for a new building and begun to meet with Dale about the appropriate size and layout of the gallery and the style of its facades. At the same time he met with Butler and with Henry Lee Norris of the university's buildings department to study possible sites. By

FIGURE 142

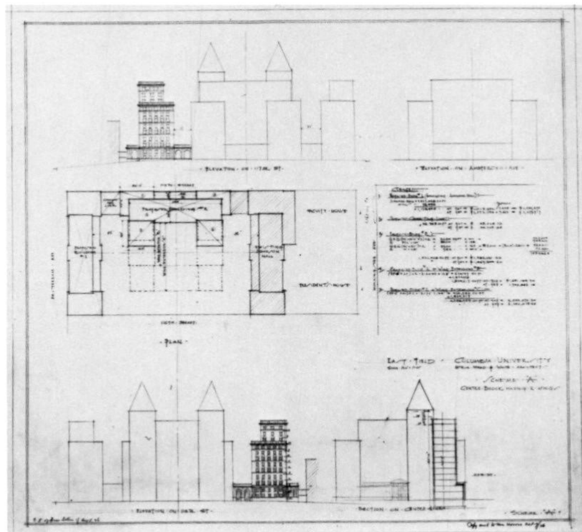

FIGURE 143

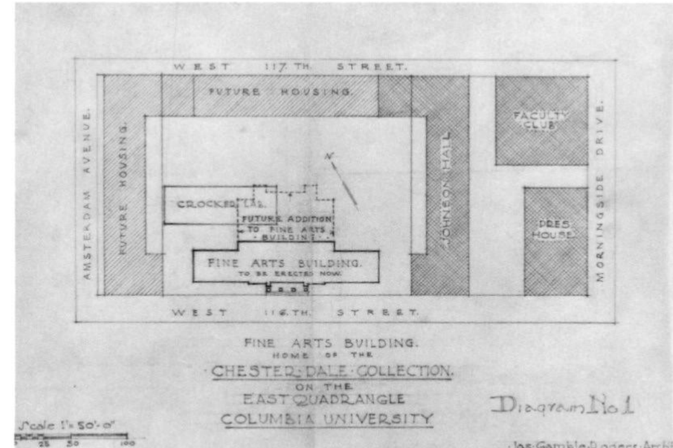

FIGURE 144

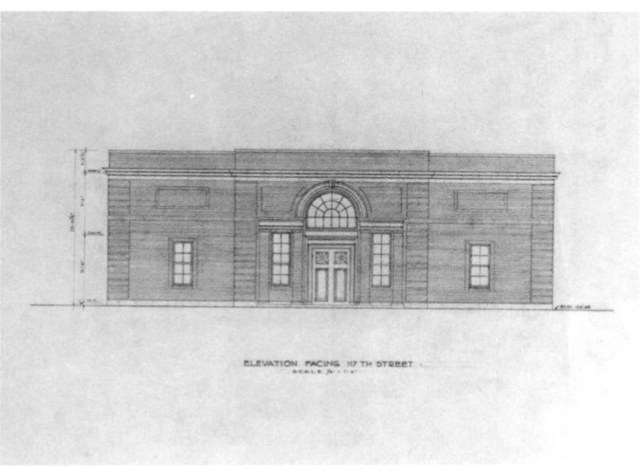

FIGURE 145

August it was decided that the fine arts building should form part of the projected development of the East Campus block to the west of Johnson Hall and that it should include classrooms and offices for the Department of Fine Arts and Archaeology, as the department had been renamed in 1934, as well as a library and slide collection. Butler raised the possibility of combining the Fine Arts Library with the Avery Architectural Library, a project not in fact realized until forty years later. Refinements to the design and discussions continued through the summer of 1937 but ultimately broke down. The paper trail in the University Archives peters out but suggests that Dale had serious reservations about the integration of his collection with classrooms. By 1941 he had begun lending major parts of his collection to the National Gallery of Art in Washington, where he served as a trustee after 1943 and museum president after 1954. Today the Chester Dale Collection is one of the most significant groups of paintings exhibited at the National Gallery. [BB]

85

EGGERS & HIGGINS

Elevation on 117th Street of Brander Matthews Hall

24 April 1940
Pencil with black ink on tracing paper, 24¼ x 34 in.
Fig. 145

Named for America's first professor of dramatic literature, Brander Matthews, who taught at Columbia from 1890 until his retirement in 1924, Brander Matthews Hall was designed as both an experimental theater and a lecture hall. Its 298-seat auditorium could be used during the day for instruction, while its deep stage—75 feet instead of the 20 feet usual at the time—allowed both for experiments in staging of plays and for use as a workshop for sets. The Flemish-bond brick walls and Palladian-arch entry motif of the modest two-story structure (total cost $75,000) were chosen by architects Eggers & Higgins to relate the building to the two most prominent campus buildings visible as playgoers approached the new building on the south side of West 117th Street: Philosophy Hall, with its large central round-arched window on the rear or Amsterdam elevation, and Johnson (now Wien) Hall with its American Federalist detailing. The interior was of the greatest simplicity, described at the time as "a factory for making a play and playing a play."

Designs were approved in April 1940, construction finished by early November, and the building dedicated by President Butler on 7 December 1940 with a performance of *Caesar and Anthony*, adapted from Shakespeare. The building survived only eighteen years; it was demolished in the summer of 1958 to clear the site for Harrison & Abramovitz's School of Law, the first piece of the much heralded East Campus superblock. [BB]

86

HARRISON & ABRAMOVITZ

School of Law

ca. 1961
Tempera on board, 25 x 38 in.
Robert Schwartz, delineator
Plate 13

In 1956 the university announced plans to develop East Campus—the block from 116th to 117th Street acquired in 1910 for the College of Physicians and Surgeons as well as the block to the north assembled over the course of the 1920s—as a superblock to be devoted largely to professional schools, faculty offices, and graduate student housing. As originally planned the complex would consist of three large buildings set above a raised pedestrian plaza at the same level as McKim's raised plinth and connected to it by a wide "bridge plaza" across Amsterdam Avenue. The base would contain common services and parking for about two hundred faculty and student cars. Seven apartment houses were to be demolished to clear the site. For a press conference at city hall three striking renderings were prepared by Robert E. Schwartz, a professional renderer and an alumnus of Columbia's School of Architecture (class of 1950).

The Law School, as built between 1959 and 1961, had a revised facade treatment but occupied essentially the site and volume projected in 1956. The concrete-frame building set perpendicular to it at the north end of the site, behind the Casa Italiana, was originally planned as a faculty office building. It would house offices displaced in clearing older buildings from the site as well as others moved from McKim's campus buildings to relieve overcrowding in many departments. That faculty offices and classrooms might be separated from one another, an idea prevalent in much modernist campus planning which emphasized efficient grouping of functions, would resurface in I. M. Pei's schemes for faculty and administrative office towers on South Field in 1970. In the mid-1960s the planned faculty office tower became a tower for the newly created School of International Affairs, built between 1967 and 1970. [BB]

87

HARRISON & ABRAMOVITZ

Dormitories for East Campus

ca. 1965
Tempera on board, 33 x 29⅞ in.
Robert Schwartz, delineator
Plate 11

The original superblock scheme called for the construction of a 742-room graduate men's dormitory at the corner of Morningside Drive and 118th Street to house students mostly from the Schools of Engineering, Law, and Business. In the mid-1960s, when the superblock scheme was substantially revised to create a building for the School of International Affairs, the original design of the dormitory as a high-rise, L-shaped slab was replaced by a scheme for two towers, both twenty-three stories tall and set above a common base. The base was to include dining and common facilities with balconies overlooking Morningside Drive meant to bring this gargantuan scheme down to a pedestrian level. In the late 1970s the site was finally developed as undergraduate housing by Gwathmey/Siegel Associates. [BB]

88

COLUMBIA UNIVERSITY DEPARTMENT OF BUILDINGS AND GROUNDS

Project for a boulevard leading up to South Hall (Butler Library): aerial view

1933

Ink on linen, $21\,^{13}/_{16}$ x $20\,^{1}/_{16}$ in.

Fig. 146

This bird's-eye view of a projected mid-block boulevard connecting Cathedral Parkway (110th Street) to the rear of South Hall (Butler Library) was produced by the university's Department of Buildings and Grounds in 1933 but has left no trace in the minutes of the board of trustees. Butler Library itself was under construction in 1933, so the drawing might be related to the lingering hesitation about closing the axial vista from Low Library. The proposed new vista is no doubt more satisfying in this view than it would have been in reality. Starting from the mid-way point of a cross-town street and creating a processional approach to the somewhat austere brick rear facade of James Gamble Rogers's new library, the drawing can be related to the new mid-block cuts in the contemporary projects for laying out Rockefeller Center on Columbia's valuable Midtown property. The drawing also reflects Butler's often-repeated regret that Columbia had not acquired all the property between 110th and 120th Streets when it had moved to Morningside Heights. [BB]

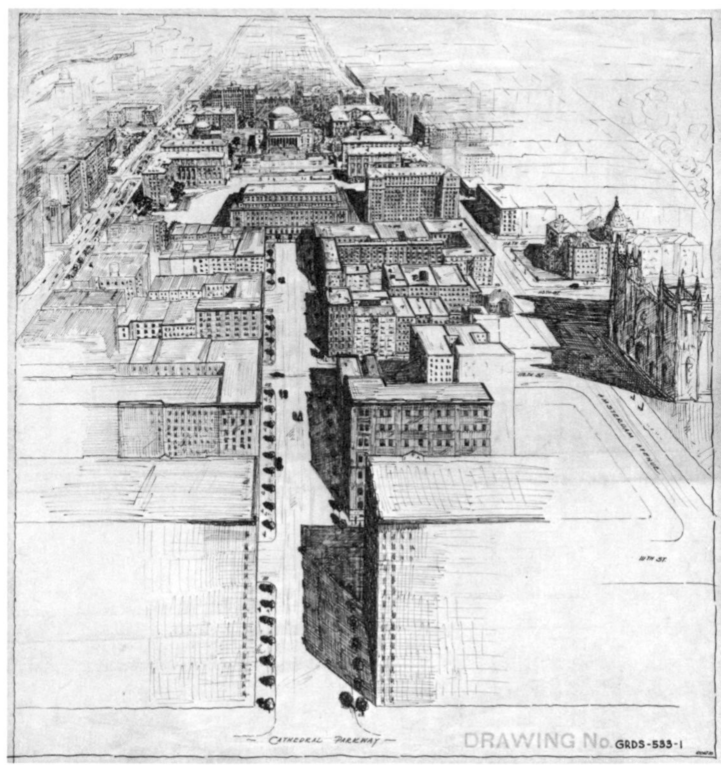

FIGURE 146

89

MAX ABRAMOVITZ

Design for stadium in Riverside Park

1931

Watercolor, colored pencil, ink, and charcoal on paper, 31½ x 20⅜ in.

Plate 9

A recent graduate of the University of Illinois, Max Abramovitz had come to Columbia to teach studio in the School of Architecture. This prize drawing continued the practice, still current today, of assigning university design problems to studios and competitions. The stadium in Riverside Park at the foot of 116th Street was located at the same site where Palmer and Hornbostel had proposed a more overtly classical facility in 1906. This project is another remnant of Columbia's long search for a suitable athletic field.

Abramovitz won a scholarship in 1933 to study in Paris, like so many architects trained in the Beaux-Arts tradition before him. Upon his return, he joined Wallace Harrison and André Fouilhoux's office and soon became a partner. In the 1950s and 1960s, Abramovitz was responsible for the design of the East Campus, building both the Law School and the School of International Affairs. [JP]

90

VOORHEES, WALKER, FOLEY & SMITH

Engineering Building at 125th Street and Riverside Drive

ca. 1951–54

Photograph of photocollage, 10 15/16 x 13 15/16 in.

Columbiana Collection

Fig. 147

As early as the 1920s the School of Engineering began studying the possibility of expanding its laboratory space at an off-campus location. In 1924, as Baker Field at the northern tip of Manhattan was being laid out to provide Columbia with long-desired athletic space, there was discussion of using an edge of the site for laboratories but the idea was quickly abandoned. A 1927 report *Development of Engineering Research and Engineering Research Laboratories at an Engineering Center* identified a number of potential sites in Upper Manhattan and the Bronx and even upstate, all of which combined the basic needs of "unlimited water, freight transportation by rail or by water, lack of restraint by neighbors as to noises, bad smells, dangerous operations, electrical and gas connections, waste disposal, and passenger transportation connections to the Morningside Heights campus." The same report recommended that the future building should be like contemporary factory structures, a shell that provided uninterrupted and highly flexible space that could accommodate both heavy machinery and frequent changes brought on by the rapid evolution of engineering research. By 1935 a two-pronged approach had been defined. Butler promised the school a site on the Grove at the northeast corner of campus for classroom and office expansion and committed the university to a fund-raising effort to create an off-site laboratory facility, probably along the Harlem River. The Great Depression and the Second World War shelved these plans for nearly twenty years.

A major campaign was opened in 1951 with the goal of raising more

FIGURE 147

than $20 million for new buildings in time for Columbia's bicentennial celebrations in 1954. The architectural firm of Voorhees, Walker, Foley & Smith studied a range of proposals for on- and off-campus sites, including various approaches to developing a difficult site at the western end of 125th Street, abutting the viaduct of Riverside Drive. Both tower and contour schemes were proposed, many of them using the technique of photocollage to show how a new building could be integrated into the northern edge of the Morningside Heights community precisely at the point where its residential fabric touched the manufacturing and warehousing facilities that had always been associated with the 125th Street piers on the Hudson River. By the late 1950s it was decided to concentrate efforts on campus, developing a major Engineering Center at the corner of 120th and Amsterdam, the first significant building on the McKim campus since Butler Library. The 125th Street and Riverside Drive site (560 Riverside Drive) was subsequently developed in the 1960s, as faculty and graduate student housing. [BB]

91

VOORHEES, WALKER, SMITH, SMITH & HAINES

Engineering Center: views of phase I (Mudd Building and Graduate School of Business) and phase II (Tower Building)

1962

Two photographs with ink mounted on board, 8 1/16 x 10 in. each; 20 1/16 x 18 in. (board)

Fig. 69

The Engineering Center was envisioned as a three-part project that would eventually transform the northeast corner of the campus. While the original Mudd Building (1959) was a modernist rendering of one of the slabs that the firm of McKim, Mead & White had projected for 120th Street in the late 1920s—as is apparent from comparing the profile of Mudd to Pupin Hall in these bird's-eye views—the other two buildings offered a departure in thinking about the campus. Engineering Terrace, labeled "Phase I" in this presentation although it was in fact the second component in the Engineering Center, would be built on the Grove and constructed in such a way that its roof would provide an extension of the great plinth of McKim's main campus level with the 150-foot datum line. Future construction, labeled here "Tower Building" or "Phase II", would complete the center by transforming Mudd from a simple slab to an asymmetrical L-shape. The tower building would be aligned with the western edge of Schermerhorn Hall to continue the axes and walkways of McKim's original campus. Engineering Terrace was built with steel members sufficiently strong to carry aloft this future high-rise building. [BB]

92

VOORHEES, WALKER, SMITH, SMITH & HAINES

Engineering Center: south elevation

1963

Photograph of rendering, mounted on board, 19 1/2 x 15 3/8 in.; 24 9/16 x 19 3/8 in. (board)

Fig. 148

FIGURE 148

In 1963 Voorhees, Walker, Smith, Smith & Haines, who had been working on designs for Columbia's School of Engineering for more than a decade, redesigned the third and final component of the Engineering Center that they had first projected in 1959. The tower building that was to rise perpendicular to the Seeley Witherspoon Mudd Building was now to be faced in limestone slabs in order to harmonize with the facade treatment of Moore and Hutchins's Uris Hall, built between 1962 and 1964. Although expansion on this site remained a goal of the university throughout the 1960s, the Engineering Center was still incomplete when the campus was rocked by political troubles in 1968 and 1969 and by fiscal difficulties in the early 1970s. In 1973 it was decided that the needs of the Department of Biological Sciences, overcrowded on the uppermost floors of Schermerhorn Hall, were so pressing that the site would be used for a long-promised new building, the Sherman Fairchild Center for the Life Sciences. [BB]

93

SHREVE, LAMB AND HARMON

Citizenship Center

1948

Photograph of a lost rendering by Schell Lewis, 8 x 9 15/16 in.

Columbiana Collection

Fig. 66

94

SHREVE, LAMB AND HARMON

Citizenship Center

1953

Photograph of a lost rendering by Ted Kautzky, 8 1/16 x 10 in.

Columbiana Collection

Fig. 67

After World War II Columbia College administration and alumni began discussing strategies for forging a sense of community among the undergraduates and creating a distinct identity for the college on the campus. Attention quickly focused on South Field, where numerous sites designated for future dormitories, particularly the inner line of buildings on McKim, Mead & White's 1903 expanded master plan, remained open. Alumni response to appeals for funds for a new student center to occupy one of these sites was tepid at first, but after the building was recast as a "citizenship center" fund-raising picked up, even as nationally the mentality of the Cold War was set in motion.

As president of Columbia University in 1949 Dwight D. Eisenhower had lent his support to a program at Teachers College, funded by the Carnegie Corporation, to develop programs in citizenship education for American public schools. In the early 1950s, after Eisenhower had left Morningside Heights for the White House, the Columbia College faculty began discussing ways in which this much publicized program might be adopted on the college level. The Citizenship Program was to consist of voluntary community service complemented by lectures, seminars, and other events intended to foster awareness of the responsibilities of citizens in a democracy. The idea sparked considerable interest on other campuses, fueled by debates in many states over lowering the voting age from twenty-one to eighteen.

In 1953, when Shreve, Lamb and Harmon made this drawing to be used by the Alumni Association of Columbia College in its fund-raising efforts, the project was much in the spotlight. At a press conference on 21 October 1953 Eisenhower, now president of the United States, made impassioned remarks on citizen responsibility in reacting to the announcement that several American veterans of the Korean War had decided "to espouse the Communist cause." As paraphrased later in the *Congressional Record* (5 April 1954), "It was the President's view that American soldiers were being asked to fight communism without an adequate education in the responsibilities of democratic citizenship." Eisenhower praised Columbia College's "model program" for "breaking new ground" and cited it as an exemplar for other colleges to follow. "Certain it is that there is no time to be lost in providing such training in our colleges, and in extending present programs in the public schools. The shadow of world communism is lengthening, and there is barely time to strengthen what . . . is our first line of defense: our citizen army."

In 1956 Mr. & Mrs. Willis H. Booth pledged $1 million toward the project, which was followed by donations from others, so that by January 1957 the college was able to announce its plans to build a citizenship center to be named Ferris Booth Hall in memory of the late son of the donors. In the interim the college had also devised ways of using federal funding for a new dormitory, and the two buildings were designed together by Shreve, Lamb and Harmon on a site at the southwest corner of the campus, at 114th Street and Broadway; the Van Am Quadrangle was left open on its western edge and remains so to this day. Its original function long forgotten, the citizenship center was demolished in June 1996 to make way for Alfred Lerner Hall, now under construction. [BB]

95

COLUMBIA UNIVERSITY OFFICE OF ARCHITECTURAL PLANNING

Map of building projects for the $200-million campaign

1966

Ink on Mylar with overlays, 42 x 72½ in.

Fig. 74

A model corresponding to this plan has recently been located.

96

EGGERS & HIGGINS

Aerial view of Morningside Heights showing gymnasium in Morningside Park

ca. 1968

Photograph of a lost drawing, 9⅞ x 9⅜ in.

Columbiana Collection

Fig. 71

97

EGGERS & HIGGINS

Construction site during excavation for gymnasium in Morningside Park

25 April 1968
Photograph, by Mac Wegweiser,
7¾ x 11 in.
Columbiana Collection
Fig. 76

Ever since the move to Morningside Heights, Columbia administration and alumni had been seeking sites near the campus to extend the athletic facilities. From the first the possibility that such facilities might be built on park land in a cooperative agreement with the city had been raised, most spectacularly in the projects studied from 1906 to 1910 by Henry Hornbostel for a stadium in the Hudson River adjacent to Riverside Park. Even after the acquisition of Baker Field in northern Manhattan in the 1920s, South Field continued to serve as an area for recreational team sports, particularly baseball and track and field events.

With the decision to landscape South Field in the mid-1950s, and thus remove the playing fields, the issue became urgent. Tennis courts and baseball diamonds were laid out in both Riverside and Morningside Parks, and by 1950s it was thought to extend this mixed use of park land by Columbia and the neighborhood to an indoor gymnasium. First negotiated under Mayor Robert Wagner and Parks Commissioner Robert Moses, the plan was called into question by students, faculty, and residents of Morningside Heights and West Harlem in the 1960s: the project came to be seen as symptomatic of the university's expansionism and lack of concern for the needs of the underprivileged families and children in the area. Much delayed by opposition and redesigned to incorporate larger facilities in a neighborhood gymnasium on the new building's lower level, work on the cliffside site began in late February 1968. On Tuesday, 23 April 1968, a group of some three hundred demonstrators, led by Students for a Democratic Society and the Society of Afro-American Students, tore down construction fences and returned to campus to occupy Hamilton Hall, taking the acting dean of the college, Henry Coleman, hostage. By the time this photograph was taken two days later a total of six campus buildings had been occupied. [BB]

XII. AFTER 1968: I. M. PEI TO ROMALDO GUIRGOLA

98

I. M. PEI & PARTNERS

Planning for Columbia University: an interim report

New York, 1970

121 pages, illustrated

Fig. 77, 79–83

99

I. M. PEI & PARTNERS

South Field project

[1970]

Robert Schwartz, renderer

Tempera on board, 24¾ x 32¾ in.

Courtesy Facilities Management

Plate 14

100–101

I. M. PEI & PARTNERS

Two views simulated from under tower on South Field

1970

Photographs of collages,

18 1/16 x 24¾ in.; 18 x 23⅞ in.

Figs. 149 & 150

FIGURE 149

FIGURE 150

102

I. M. PEI & PARTNERS

Aerial view of Morningside Heights with two proposed towers on South Field and chemistry lab behind Uris

1970

Ink on Mylar, 16 x 28 in.

Fig. 78

103

WARNER, BURNS, TOAN, LUNDE

Lunde Science Tower

November 1969

Blueline print, 36 1/16 x 27 in.

Bon Hui Uy, delineator

Fig. 84

104

ALEXANDER KOUZMANOFF

Avery Library extension

ca. 1974

Collage with ink on paper, 23 x 29 in.

Plate 15

The underground extension to the School of Architecture and Avery Library is housed primarily under the courtyard formed by Avery, Schermerhorn, and Fayerweather Halls and St. Paul's Chapel and connects the basements of the three academic buildings. In addition to reading rooms, offices, and stack space for the combined Fine Arts Library of the Department of Art History and Avery Architectural Library, founded by Samuel Putnam Avery in 1890, the extension provided lecture halls, classrooms, and exhibition space for the School of Architecture. The project is the only one in I. M. Pei's 1970 master plan for Columbia to have been carried out. Additional impetus to go underground came from the opposition of Avery's heirs who opposed earlier proposals to move the Avery Library to a newly planned arts center at a different location. The extension also involved the remodeling of the only one of McKim's courtyards actually completed. [BB]

105

ROMALDO GUIRGOLA

Two development sketches for Sherman Fairchild Biological Sciences Building

ca. 1972

Brown ink on yellow tracing paper,

17⅞ x 10⅜ in.; 18 x 10⅞ in.

Fig. 85

XIII. NEW APPROACHES TO THE MASTER PLAN SINCE 1980

106

JAMES STIRLING, MICHAEL WILFORD & ASSOCIATES/WANK ADAMS SLAVIN ASSOCIATES

Chandler North project: site plan

April 1982

Print with colored pencil on board, 15 x 20$\frac{7}{8}$ in.

Fig. 86

107

JAMES STIRLING, MICHAEL WILFORD & ASSOCIATES/WANK ADAMS SLAVIN ASSOCIATES

Chandler North project: perspective view from Broadway and 120th Street

April 1982

Print with colored pencil on board, 17$\frac{3}{8}$ x 16$\frac{7}{16}$ in.

Fig. 151

108

JAMES STIRLING, MICHAEL WILFORD & ASSOCIATES/WANK ADAMS SLAVIN ASSOCIATES

Chandler North project: perspective view from campus

April 1982

Print with colored pencil on board, 17$\frac{5}{16}$ x 16$\frac{7}{16}$ in.

Plate 16

109

JAMES STIRLING, MICHAEL WILFORD & ASSOCIATES/WANK ADAMS SLAVIN ASSOCIATES

Chandler North project: campus elevation

April 1982

Print with colored pencil on board, 15 x 20$\frac{7}{8}$ in.

Fig. 152

110

R. M. KLIMENT & FRANCES HALSBAND

Computer Science Building: axonometric projection

1983

Ink on Mylar, 32 x 32 in.

Fig. 153

This axonometric drawing of Kliment and Halsband's building for the Department of Computer Sciences reveals the complexity of the site and the number of diverse elements and differing contexts that needed to be juggled to create a building that brought order to a cacophonous landscape. [BB]

FIGURE 151

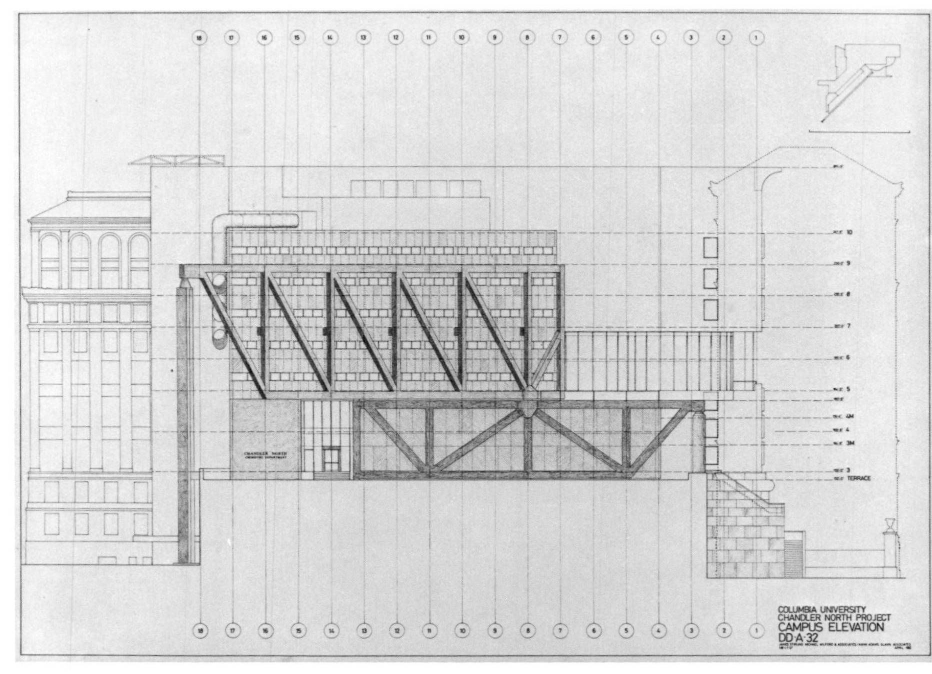

FIGURE 152

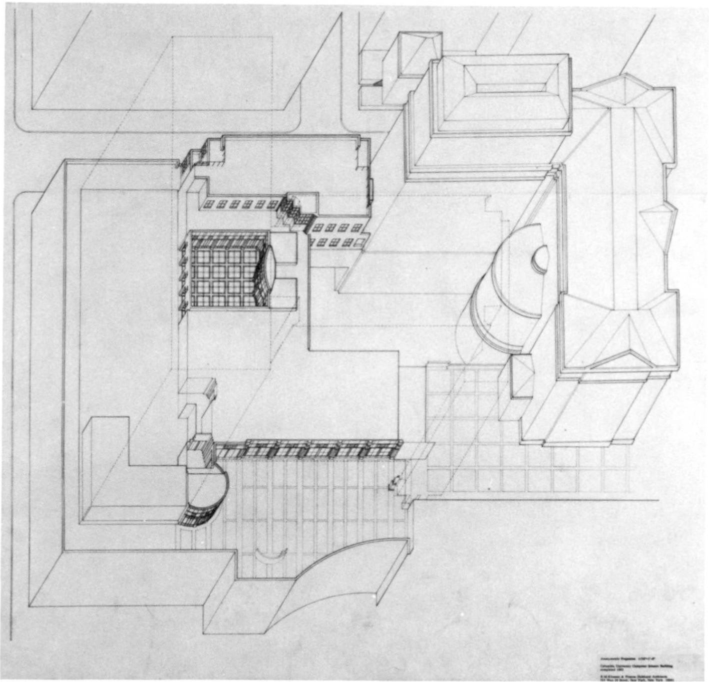

FIGURE 153

FIGURE 154

111

R. M. KLIMENT & FRANCES HALSBAND

Computer Science Building: model

1983

Composition board and paper, 28 x 31½ x 21 in.

Courtesy the architects

112

SKIDMORE, OWINGS & MERRILL

Columbia University: East Campus Development

March 1990

Bound report, illustrated, 11½ x 12 in.

Fig. 87

113

KOHN PEDERSEN FOX ASSOCIATES

Feasibility Study: Columbia University East Campus Redevelopment, Vol. 2, Design Study

12 March 1990

Bound report, illustrated, 11 x 17 in.

Fig. 88

114

BERNARD TSCHUMI

Alfred Lerner Hall

1996

Computer-generated rendering printed on paper, 11 x 14 in. (approx.)

Courtesy the architect

Plate 17

115

BERNARD TSCHUMI

Alfred Lerner Hall: developmental model

1996

Fome-Cor, Plexiglas, basswood, and aluminum, 60¼ x 22 7/16 x 29½ in.

Courtesy the architect

116

ROBERT A. M. STERN ARCHITECTS

Dormitory proposal for 113th Street and Broadway: perspective

8 April 1997

Hand-colored computer-generated print, 24 x 24 in.

Courtesy the architect

Fig. 154

117

ROBERT A. M. STERN ARCHITECTS

Dormitory proposal for 113th Street and Broadway: elevation of Broadway from 116th to 110th Street

1997

Hand-colored computer-generated print on paper, 24 x 70 in. (approx.)

Courtesy the architect

INDEX OF NAMES

King's College was founded in 1754 and was renamed Columbia College in 1787; the name Columbia University in the City of New York was adopted in 1896. A page reference in bold-face type indicates an illustration of the building or other work named.

PHOTOGRAPH CREDITS

Photographs of the works reproduced in this volume were provided by their custodians or owners. References are to figure numbers.

Bard College 47

University of Chicago Library 16

Avery Architectural and Fine Arts Library, Columbia University 3, 4, 7, 8, 12, 13, 14 (courtesy Francesco Passanti), 15, 17, 18, 22, 23, 24, 26, 27, 37, 38, 41, 42, 61, 64, 65, 69, 73, 74, 75, 77, 78, 79, 80, 81, 82, 83, 84, 85, 86, 87, 88, 89, 95, 96, 97, 98, 99, 100, 101, 102, 104, 114, 115, 116, 117, 119, 121, 122, 123, 124, 125, 127, 128, 129, 130, 131, 132, 133, 134, 135, 137, 138, 139, 140, 141, 142, 144, 145, 146, 148, 149, 150, 151, 152, 153

Columbia University Archives 59, 72

Columbiana Collection, Columbia University 1, 5, 9, 10, 11, 19, 25, 28, 31, 32, 34, 35, 36, 39, 40, 45, 49, 51, 58, 62, 66, 67, 68, 70, 71, 76, 90, 91, 92, 94, 107, 108, 109, 110, 111, 112, 113, 126, 147

Mathematics Library, Columbia University 2

Office of Art Properties, Columbia University 6

Courtesy the New-York Historical Society 21, 29, 30, 33, 43, 44, 46, 48, 50, 52, 53, 54, 55, 56, 57, 60, 63, 93, 103, 105, 106, 118, 120, 136, 143

The photograph of the painting in Urbino (20) was supplied by Alinari/Art Resource, NY.

COLOPHON

This book has been typeset in Adobe Garamond and Bauer Text Initials, and printed by fine-line offset lithography on Monadnock Dulcet paper at The Stinehour Press.
Design by Jerry Kelly.

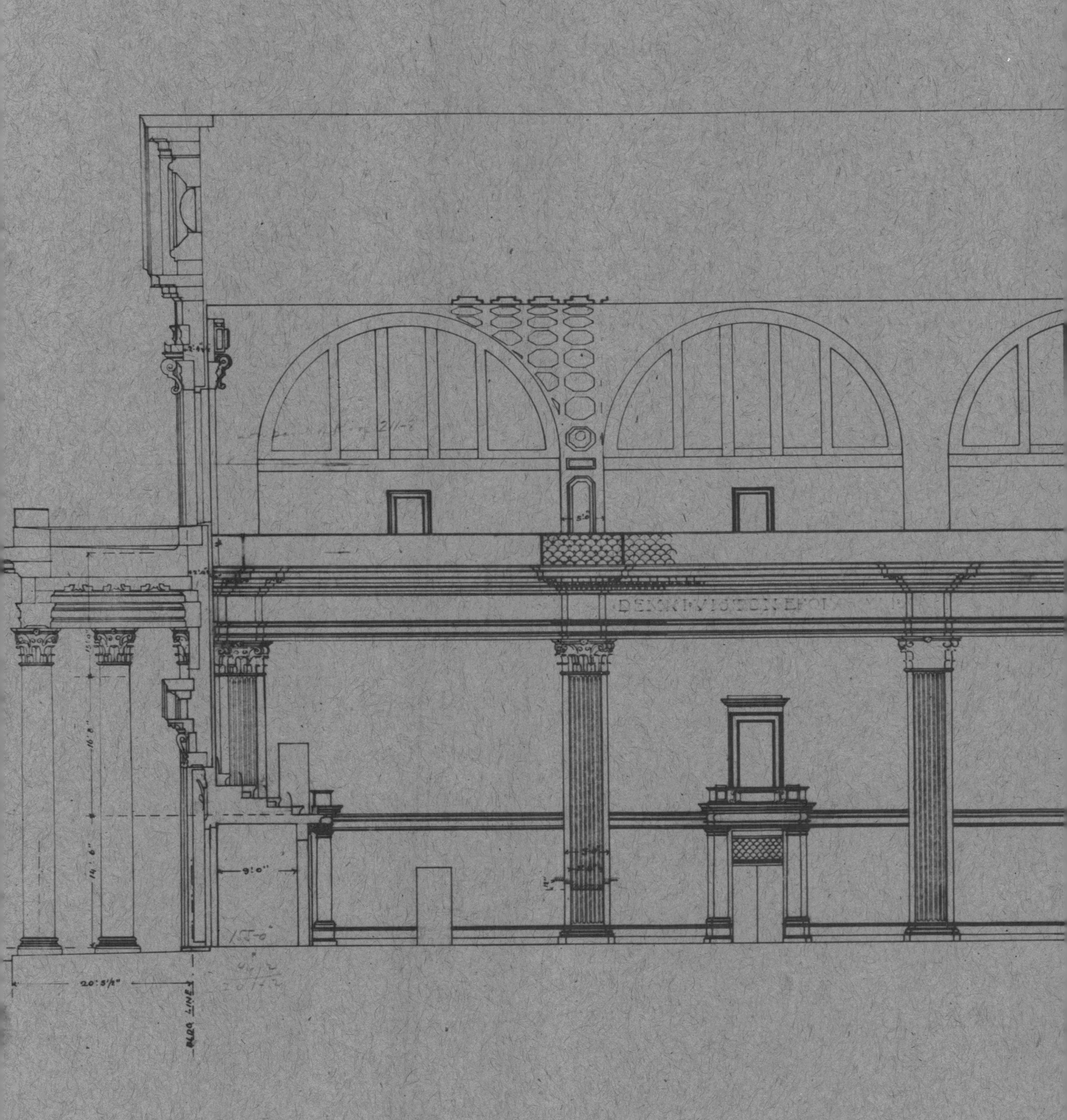
9' 0"
14' 6"
20' 5 1/2"
BLDG LINE

> only the higher echelons of society were allowed to view it from special windows; its death was treated on a par with the death of pharaoh; and the remains were mummified. Images of calves or bulls were associated with the strength and power of the deity, and the idols as well as certain live animals came to be regarded as embodiments of the god.[3]

Once again it was proving to be more difficult to get Egypt out of the Israelites than it was to get the Israelites out of Egypt. At the first sign of trouble, God's people always wanted to run back to Pharaoh. This time it was Pharaoh's gods they were after. So as soon as Aaron made their unholy cow, they started to worship it, and by the next day the camp had degenerated into pagan debauchery.

Sin Is Disobedience

This whole sordid episode was written down for our spiritual benefit. The New Testament says, "These things took place as examples for us, that we might not desire evil as they did. Do not be idolaters as some of them were; as it is written, 'The people sat down to eat and drink and rose up to play.' . . . Now these things happened to them as an example, but they were written down for our instruction, on whom the end of the ages has come" (1 Corinthians 10:6, 7, 11). Here the Bible refers specifically to what the Israelites did when Aaron made the golden calf. What they did ought to serve as a warning to us because we are tempted to commit the same sins.

As we study Exodus, we see how the story of Israel's salvation gets retraced in the geography of our own souls. Like the Israelites, we are living in the wilderness between baptism (remember the Red Sea!) and the Promised Land. When things get difficult, we often try to return to the Egypt of our sin. So the story of the golden calf tells us more than what happened; it tells us what *happens*. It exposes the anatomy of our own idolatry. By looking carefully at how the Israelites fell into sin, we can see the pattern of sin in our lives, with the goal of learning how to obey God.

The lessons we learn from Israel's unholy cow can be summarized by completing the following sentence: "We fall into sin when . . ." To start with what is most obvious, *We fall into sin when we do what God tells us not to do*. Sin is disobedience to God's revealed will.

Here it is important to remember that the Israelites already knew the Ten Commandments. First God revealed his law to Moses (20:1–17), then "Moses came and told the people all the words of the LORD and all the rules" (24:3a). And this all happened *before* Moses went back up the mountain to get the instructions for the tabernacle. So the Israelites knew God's law. They knew the first commandment, which told them not to have any other gods. And they knew the second commandment, which prohibited them from making idols.

Scholars sometimes debate which of these two commandments they broke